VAULT GUIDE TO THE TOP
MEDIA &
ENTERTAINMENT
EMPLOYERS

EDITED BY LAURIE PASIUK
AND THE STAFF OF VAULT

For information about permission to reproduce selections from this book, contact Vault Inc., 150 W. 22nd St., 5th Floor, New York, NY 10011, (212) 366-4212.

Library of Congress CIP Data is available.

ISBN 1-58131-337-3

Printed in the United States of America

ACKNOWLEDGMENTS

Thanks to everyone who had a hand in making this book possible, especially Laurie Pasiuk and Mary Conlon. We are also extremely grateful to Vault's entire staff for all their help in the editorial, production and marketing processes. Vault also would like to acknowledge the support of our investors, clients, employees, family and friends. Thank you!

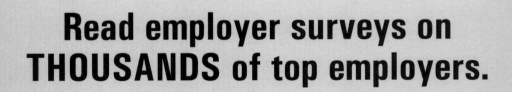

Table of Contents

THE INDUSTRY   1

EMPLOYER PROFILES   9

Visit Vault at **www.vault.com** for insider company profiles, expert advice,
career message boards, expert resume reviews, the Vault Job Board and more.

VAULT CAREER LIBRARY   vii

ABOUT THE EDITOR   309

The Industry

The media universe is dotted with veritable galaxies of companies – from multi-billion dollar diversified conglomerates to small, independent movie studios and production facilities. High school dropouts and PhDs in philosophy, MBAs and computer programmers, septuagenarians and twentysomethings, all work cheek by jowl to bring to life creative endeavors, to grow sustainable billion-dollar franchises like *Batman* and *Harry Potter*, and to create new ways to keep the American public entertained and spending money on leisure.

There are two broad subcategories within media and entertainment: creative and business. The creative side actually makes the products or content and has four major areas: motion pictures, television, publishing and music. The business side sells the content, ensures that everything is legal and helps the business grow. The business encompasses the corporate high-level strategy groups, the divisions (a.k.a. business units) that work in the trenches of a specific operation and the standard overarching business functions evident in every company (e.g. accounting, legal, human resources, IT).

First and foremost, entertainment and media industries start with creative content. Everything else stems from this. (See the chart on Media Companies for a graphic overview at the end of this chapter.)

Motion Pictures

Movies are by far the biggest segment of the media and entertainment industry, not only because of their prominence within the American cultural landscape, but also because of a successful motion picture's ability to sell products in other enormously profitable places as well (also known as ancillary revenue streams) – home video, international distribution, TV rights and so on. Each of the eight major film studios releases about 20 to 30 films each year, with the average studio release costing about $30 million. Studios are typically broken down into two functional components, the business side and the creative side.

The creative side is the where the movies are actually made. There are a few key divisions on the creative side of the movie business:

- **Development:** The key players in the development stage are producers, screenwriters, agents and studio executives. Production companies, the "homes" of producers, start with a script. Every year, these companies are

Visit Vault at **www.vault.com** for insider company profiles, expert advice, career message boards, expert resume reviews, the Vault Job Board and more.

VAULT CAREER LIBRARY

1

delivered hundreds of scripts (mostly unsolicited) from famous, semi-famous and unknown writers. The executives at each of the production companies then sort through the scripts (written by both new and established screenwriters), negotiate with agents to purchase interesting ones, and then bring together key players (e.g. a director, lead actors, other producers) who will commit to starring in or making the film if a studio finances it. A studio is then "pitched" the idea and if the film is approved, the film then gets a "green light" to go into production. The latter stage of development is also often called pre-production.

- **Pre-production:** This is everything that happens to get a movie rolling just before filming starts – location scouting, and the casting and hiring of the crew, for instance.

- **Production:** Once a movie is "green lit," production starts. To use an analogy, if the screenplay is the blueprint, production is when the movie is built by the cast and crew. Filming sometimes happens on a soundstage on a film studio's property, but often it occurs "on location," at an out-of-studio venue.

Top Studios

- Disney
- Dreamworks SKG
- MGM/UA
- Paramount
- Sony/Columbia
- Universal
- Warner Brothers
- 20th Century Fox

Top "Indy" Studios

- Artisan
- Fine Line/New Line
- Fox Searchlight
- Miramax
- Sony Pictures Classics
- USA Films

- **Post-Production:** After all the raw footage has been filmed, it is taken to an editing studio, where professional film editors and the director work together with sound effects artists and special effects wizards (if necessary) to pull a movie together. This is also the stage when music, titles and credits are added and when the film preview (called a "trailer" in industry-speak) is created and sent to movie theaters.

Vital in the movie business is the relationship that studios have with movie theaters, or exhibitors, as they are called in the industry. Exhibitors decide which movies they will show and often split marketing costs with theaters. Because of the 1948 antitrust ruling that divorced theaters from studios, the power of studios weakened. Multiplexes (cinema theaters with multiple screens) then came into the picture, taking advantage of the separation from studios to release many different types of movies, contributing to the proliferation of movie niches and independent films produced on small budgets.

The other side of filmmaking is the business side, which deals with ancillary revenue streams and creative vehicles (e.g., theme parks, licensed products, home video) that come after the filmmaking process. These are often completely separate businesses that employ different media for dissemination (e.g., stores, third party distributors like McDonald's, the Internet). Because many of the most successful movies of all time are franchises (*Star Wars*, *Indiana Jones*, *Lord of the Rings*), the business side works to exploit the enormous revenue opportunities that come with leveraging those properties. As the business side has come to generate billions of dollars in recent years, movie studios have grown into diversified conglomerates with many different business arms. The main divisions are:

- **Home video:** Tapes and DVDs are the second phase of a movie's life cycle, bringing films into the homes of consumers after its life in the box office has run its course.

- **Consumer products:** All filmed properties and characters with commercial appeal are further exploited by other companies that pay licensing fees for the rights to use images and names.

- **Retail:** Virtually all major film studios sell customized items directly to customers either through stores, catalogs or direct mail, some in larger endeavors than others (e.g. The Disney Stores, Warner Brothers Studio Stores).

- **Theme parks:** Large destination parks (e.g. Disneyland, Universal Studios) provide the opportunity to further leverage a film's appeal to consumers in an exciting, live-action setting.

Television

With televisions in the homes of over 99% of the U.S. population, TV is arguably the most powerful media vehicle in the entertainment industry. Deregulation of cable companies and increased bandwidth in distribution (with digital cable) has further increased the options of television networks. This has resulted in a glut of channels targeting ever-narrower niches (e.g. golf, cooking, independent movies).

Visit Vault at **www.vault.com** for insider company profiles, expert advice, career message boards, expert resume reviews, the Vault Job Board and more.

VAULT CAREER LIBRARY

3

This growth, however, has resulted in the popularity of several successful cable channels eroding the once dominant share of the networks (ABC, CBS, NBC). Success stories include ESPN, E!, Lifetime, USA and MTV. One result of all this change is the growth in career opportunities for people considering television careers.

The TV industry is structured somewhat differently from film. One of the key difference is that TV is full of sales and marketing positions, since most networks make money on advertising. (If a show is particularly successful, it can make even more money by being sold into syndication (e.g., *Law & Order*), by being made into a movie (e.g., *The X-Files*) or by launching spin-offs

Top TV Networks	
ABC	USA
NBC	ESPN
CBS	A&E
Fox	CNN
PBS	TNT
TBS	Nickelodeon
Discovery	Lifetime

(e.g., *Cheers* launching *Frasier*). Typically, the network does not make much money from these types of deals; the winners are usually the creators of the show and the production company that originally produced the show. Advertising, therefore, is all the more critical for networks.

Here are some key divisions of television networks:

- **Development:** The television industry parallels the film industry in that scripts for new television shows are constantly sought out and studied in the hopes of creating the next *Friends* or *ER*. Job positions within TV development are typically divided into the different types of programming that appears on TV – sitcoms, dramas, miniseries, specials and daytime. Network executives are "pitched" ideas by production companies and writers. If the executive likes an idea, a "green light" is given for the show's pilot, the introductory episode. If the pilot is successful, it then becomes a series.

- **Production:** Because television typically calls for shorter production cycles, television studios are often fully equipped soundstages where TV shows are filmed and edited and where final cuts are put into post-production.

- **Programming:** Once a show is on the air, it is watched carefully to see how it performs. Programming executives closely monitor Nielsen ratings, provide comments on scripts to develop shows with the most promising audience appeal, reconfigure schedules to improve performances and cut shows when they fail to build a loyal audience. Shows may be kept when their ratings are low but they attract the desirable 18- to 34-year-old audience.

- **Network affiliates:** While the bulk of ad revenues come in at the national level, the major networks have bodies of network affiliates throughout the country that have individual sales forces that sell local advertising, which comprises most of the remaining portion of overall company revenues. In addition to ad sales, affiliates also manage some content creation, primarily local news production.

Publishing

While the overall revenue from publishing is dwarfed by film and television, books and magazines occupy a place of cultural significance in America that is unparalleled. The trade book industry (that is, all the mass market fiction and non-fiction books that you see in the bookstore, as opposed to academic textbooks and journals) is one of the most important sources of story ideas; in the film world books are constantly being brought to life as movies. Likewise, magazines are also important because they illustrate cultural trends and societal shifts, raise intriguing questions that become hot topics-du-jour, and are able to market businesses more effectively than most forms of advertising.

Top Trade Publishers
• Bantam Doubleday Dell
• Harcourt Brace
• HarperCollins
• Hyperion
• Little
• Brown
• W.W. Norton
• William Morrow
• Putnam Berkley
• Penguin
• Random House
• Simon & Schuster
• St. Martin's Press
• Warner Books

Trade and magazine publishing is similar to both film and TV in that the former makes money from direct sales while the latter makes money based on advertising and overall circulation.

The key divisions of trade publishing houses are:

- **Editorial:** Editors receive raw manuscripts from literary agents, decide what gets published in their annual roster and work to shape the text into a commercially viable form.

- **Publicity:** Since book sales are largely dependent on word of mouth, publicity becomes an extremely important part of a book's success. Book

Visit Vault at **www.vault.com** for insider company profiles, expert advice, career message boards, expert resume reviews, the Vault Job Board and more.

VAULT CAREER LIBRARY

5

publicists orchestrate book tours, bookstore signings, live readings by the author, appearances on television programs, press releases and press kits, and place reviews in publications.

- **Marketing:** Book marketers work with graphic designers and artists to create book jackets and ads, and work with programs like book-of-the-month clubs in order to promote sales. They also create in-store shelf displays for bookstores to help sell books.

- **Operations:** Many major book publishers have their own printing presses and warehouses, where they can ship directly to key bookstores (like Barnes & Noble and Borders) and distributors (like Ingram).

- **Distribution:** A crucial component of a book's sale process is getting the book distributed to both chain and independent bookstores. Publishers have representatives at headquarters who work with the largest chains to place books, signage and displays, as well as regional representatives who pitch, promote and sell books to smaller independent bookstores. Distribution's key objective is to ensure placement and instant availability of books in the retail channels where consumers seek product.

The key divisions of a magazine publisher are:

- **Editorial:** Magazine editors are often given credit for determining a publication's "voice." Magazine editors determine what goes on the cover and manage writers (both full-time staff writers as well as freelancers), photographers, artists and graphic designers. The editorial team has responsibility for the overall editorial calendar, which is the list of upcoming stories that is provided to advertisers who may wish to run ads in a particular issue to target a particular sub-segment of an audience.

- **Advertising sales:** Magazine salespeople work with major advertising agencies and their clients. Much schmoozing is involved in the sale of ads.

Top Magazine Publishers

- Time Inc.
- The Washington Post Co.
- Forbes
- Hearst
- Hachette Filipacci
- Gruner & Jahr
- Martha Stewart
- Conde Nast
- Wenner Media
- Primedia
- Weider
- American Express Publishing
- Ziff Davis

- **Distribution/Circulation/Marketing:** A magazine is able to command ad rates depending on how broad its circulation is, who subscribes to the magazine and who ultimately sees each issue (the "pass-through rate"). This department is primarily involved with maintaining subscriptions, attracting subscriptions through direct mail and other marketing, distributing free copies to appropriate channels and increasing the number of 'eyeballs' that view each issue.

Because most publishing headquarters are in New York, a career in the industry almost certainly means living in New York City.

Music

The music industry has several components – there are divisions that discover new artists, there are those that develop and produce music with mass appeal, and there are the promoters and marketers. And now, in the age of the Internet, there are lots of people hired to make sure that the record labels do not get fleeced by music freeloaders who find ways to acquire and disseminate the product for free, or to figure out how to create profitable businesses distributing or marketing music through the Internet.

> **Big 5 Record Labels**
> - BMG (Arista, Jive Records, RCA)
> - EMI-Capitol (Virgin)
> - Sony (Columbia, Epic)
> - Universal (MCA, Polygram)
> - Warner (Warner Brothers, Elektra, Atlantic)

While the music industry is enormous, and one of the most globally-significant parts of the entertainment industry because music is so universal and ubiquitous, the threat of its erosion due to Internet piracy concerns poses a serious threat to the growth of new artists and revenue opportunities.

That said, for job seekers, the most promising opportunities continue to be in A&R, distribution and marketing.

- **A&R:** These are the talent scouts that listen to demo tapes, attend shows, travel and keep their ear to the ground to understand new trends and to uncover fresh voices that best bring those trends to life.

- **Production:** Once an act has been signed onto a record label, the producers perfect the music to make it commercially palatable for radio stations, critics and consumers. The packaging of the CD and creation of the artist image is also finalized in this stage.

Visit Vault at **www.vault.com** for insider company profiles, expert advice, career message boards, expert resume reviews, the Vault Job Board and more.

VAULT CAREER LIBRARY

7

- **PR/Marketing:** This is the group that toils to get airplay on radio stations, gets the music video shot and hopefully aired, leverages television and press coverage and puts the artist in the public eye. Arbitron ratings, essentially Nielsen ratings for radio, let both radio stations and record labels know what consumers are listening to, what is working and what is most popular.

- **Distribution:** This group specifically deals with getting the CDs into record stores and venues where consumers can purchase them.

- **Concerts:** Concerts and live performances that are able to attract large numbers of consumers are increasingly underwritten by large corporate sponsors to defray expenses (e.g., Pepsi sponsoring a Britney Spears concert tour).

The biggest media companies (i.e. AOL Time Warner, Viacom, The Walt Disney Company, Viacom) span across all of these industries (and then some). The chart below shows roughly how these large organizations are structured.

Media Conglomerate Relationships

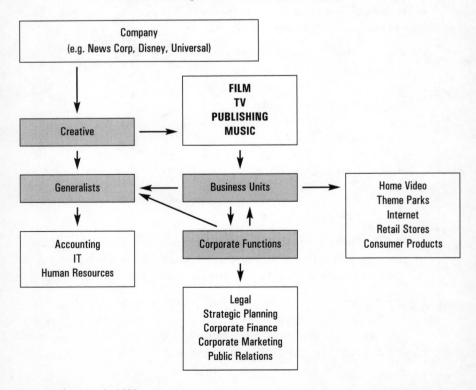

EMPLOYER PROFILES

ABC, Inc.

77 W. 66th Street
New York, NY 10023-6298
Phone: (212) 456-7777
Fax: (212) 456-1424
www.abc.go.com

LOCATIONS

New York, NY (HQ)
Century City, CA

THE STATS

Employer Type:
Subsidiary of Walt Disney Co.
President, Disney-ABC Television:
Anne M. Sweeney
2004 Revenue ($mil.): $11,778.0

KEY COMPETITORS

Fox Entertainment
NBC Universal
Time Warner
Viacom

EMPLOYMENT CONTACT

corporate.disney.go.com/careers/
  index.html

THE SCOOP

At first there were two

The merger between Walt Disney and Capital Cities/ABC in 1995 may have been one of the most talked about of the time – at $19 billion, it was the second-highest price that had ever been paid for a U.S. company. For quite some time after the deal, it seemed that none of that Disney magic was filtering down to the network, as its ratings went on a perpetual slide. Trailing behind CBS and NBC, in 2003, ABC found itself vying with FOX for an unimpressive fourth-place slot. But network officials kept plugging away, optimistic that ABC would develop a roster of solid programming. Nay-sayers became speechless when ABC introduced *Desperate Housewives*, one of the biggest hits to premier on any network in years, and *Lost*, which has been moderately successful in the ratings and a critical success in the fall of 2004.

When the radio era was ushered in, CBS and NBC were the two sole existing networks. The American Broadcasting Company, ABC, got its opportunity to break onto the scene when the Federal Communications Commission forced NBC to give up one of its two radio networks, NBC-Blue and NBC-Red. In 1943, when candy magnate Edward J. Noble (the man behind Lifesavers) bought NBC-Blue and changed the name, ABC made its debut. The ABC radio network lagged behind NBC and CBS. (Today, the ABC Radio Group reaches 147 million people weekly with 4,500 radio stations and broadcasts. News service networks include ABC News Radio, Paul Harvey News and Comment, Radio Disney and ESPN Radio.) It was during the 1940s, as television loomed on the horizon, that ABC got its chance to shine when United Paramount Theaters and Leonard Goldenson purchased it for $25 million in 1951. The network remained under their leadership until 1986 when ABC was bought by Capital Cities for $3.5 billion. The deal started a trend – the other major networks were soon snatched up for purchase in the 1980s.

Disney begins to court ABC

The 1995 merger was not the first connection between ABC and its current parent; Disney's association with ABC can be traced back to 1954 when Walt and Roy Disney approached Goldenson for funding assistance to build their famed California theme park. Goldenson agreed in exchange for a percentage of the park as well as some programming options. Disney Studios began producing *The Wonderful World of Disney*, which became the network's first Nielsen top-10 hit. Ten years later, in

1964, ABC won the ratings war for the first time. Fast forward a few decades and Disney buys ABC, shocking the industry with a new paradigm for the global media business.

What's on the screen?

In 1970, ABC celebrated the birth of its first No.-1 show, *Marcus Welby, M.D.* The network went on to embrace a slew of popular series from *Happy Days* to *Laverne & Shirley* to *Three's Company* to *Mork & Mindy*. Its 12-hour miniseries *Roots* scored the largest Nielsen ratings in broadcast history in 1977. During the 1980s, the network launched successful comedies such as *Roseanne* and *The Wonder Years*.

In 1989, ABC successfully debuted a Friday night line-up of comedies, marketed under the tagline TGIF, Thank God It's Funny. The line-up, which included *Full House* and *Family Matters,* introduced the Olsen twins to the limelight and provided memorable characters like Steve Urkel. This block of family-oriented entertainment was also a hit with the much-in-demand 18-49 demographic.

But in later years, ABC had problems attracting this audience. In an effort to gain more ratings, ABC revamped its TGIF lineup for the fall of 2003 with trendier programming on Friday nights like *Hope & Faith* and *Life with Bonnie*. (*Bonnie* has since been cancelled, but *Hope & Faith*, starring America's newest sweetheart, Kelly Ripa, remains a Friday night stronghold.) The new schedule was a breath of fresh air for the network, which just a year earlier may have gotten a little too wrapped up in the reality television frenzy of *The Bachelor* and *Are You Hot? The Search for America's Sexiest People*. But then again, ABC has experienced a history of programming gaffes, from turning down *All in the Family* in the 1970s, to perhaps going a little overboard with almost-nightly episodes of *Who Wants to be a Millionaire*.

The problems were only complicated by the fact that there have been other troubled spots as well. For instance, the ABC Family channel hasn't caught on the way executives had hoped when the company purchased it from Fox in 2001 for an eye-popping $5.2 billion. ABC Family, which is being marketed to teens and the 18-34 demographic, has yet to develop any break-out hits like its Disney Channel cousin has had with teen stars Hillary Duff of *Lizzie Maguire* (who will film another movie based on the show for Disney, but has opted to not renew her contract with the studio) and Raven of *That's So Raven*.

A media pioneer

Programming blips aside, it can't be denied that ABC has been a pioneer. In 1976, it was the first network to hire a woman – Barbara Walters – as an evening news anchor. During the 1978-1979 season, ABC was the first network to break the $1 billion-dollar revenue mark. The network must have had a little ESP when it purchased sports cable station ESPN in 1984, before the small cable channel had a chance to grow and bring in huge profits via new magazine and restaurant ventures. During the fall for many seasons, Monday nights on ABC were dedicated to *Monday Night Football*, the highest rated sports program on television. In April 2005, the news came that *Monday Night Football* would end its run on ABC and move to the network's sibling, ESPN, starting in 2006.

The aforementioned Walters is now synonymous with two highly watched ABC shows, newsmagazine *20/20* (from which she departed in 2004) and female-gab-fest *The View*. (Walters also popped up on *Good Morning America* in 2005, conducting an exclusive interview with actor Robert Blake who had just been acquitted of the murder of his wife. Blake publicly thanked Walters for his freedom, crediting a previous interview they'd done with giving him a chance to plead his case.) The network often lands exclusive interviews with people in the headlines. In December 2002, ABC aired *Primetime Live* anchor Diane Sawyer's revealing and much-talked-about interview with pop singer Whitney Houston, during which the star admitted having used drugs. In November 2003, ABC secured the first interview with POW Jessica Lynch when she sat down with Sawyer.

People will talk

Like any major media organization, ABC has received its share of criticism. ABC raised eyebrows from skeptics with its decision to continue producing *8 Simple Rules for Dating My Teenage Daughter* after the sudden death of the show's star, John Ritter, in September 2003. The idea to incorporate his death into the storyline was viewed by some skeptics as a desperate attempt to boost ratings and a concept that was unlikely to work in the show, a light-hearted family comedy. But again, nay-sayers were quieted: The show is currently in its third season (its second without Ritter) and has tried to balance the laughs with staying true to the storyline of a family recovering from a sudden loss.

Of course, criticism is nothing new for ABC. In 1997, the network was forced to pay for having reporters lie on job applications and pose as employees as part of an exposé for *Primetime Live* about unsanitary practices at the Food Lion supermarket

Visit Vault at **www.vault.com** for insider company profiles, expert advice, career message boards, expert resume reviews, the Vault Job Board and more.

VAULT CAREER LIBRARY   13

chain. (The good news is that a federal judge reduced the network's payout in punitive damages to the supermarket from $5.5 million to just $315,000.)

Ratings boon

Under massive pressure to increase viewership, ABC unveiled some edgy new shows and has become the ratings darling of the 2004-2005 season. The addition of *Desperate Housewives* and *Lost*, two hour-long dramas about the trials and tribulations of four suburban housewives and a group of plane-crash survivors, have performed well. A November "sweeps" episode of *Housewives,* in which a recurring character was murdered, scored young-adult ratings of 16.1 million, numbers that surpassed such other recent ratings favorites as Fox's *American Idol 3* season finale (15.4 million) and Game 7 of the storied Yankees-Red Sox American League championship series (15.3 million).

ABC's reality offerings include *Wife Swap*, in which two mothers with disparate lives switch places for two weeks, and *Extreme Makeover: Home Edition*, a tear-jerker in which a team of carpenters and design experts fix up homes for families overcoming hardship in a breakneck seven days, have also been critical and commercial successes.

Continuously in the news

Even without the success of its prime time slate, ABC repeatedly made headlines throughout the second half of 2004. Barbara Walters signed off as co-anchor of *20/20* in September after a 25-year run at the age of 73, declaring, "If indeed, over the years, my work has opened doors and made things easier for other women, I am very grateful." Ken Jennings, a fresh-faced software engineer from Salt Lake City, Utah, became an overnight celebrity after posting the longest winning streak in game show history with his 74-episode *Jeopardy!* run, which earned Jennings a total of $2,522,700, and boosted the game show's ratings by 22 percent as millions of "KenJen" fans tuned nightly to watch their quiz king correctly answer more than 2,700 questions correctly. (Although syndicated, *Jeopardy!* and other ratings favorites, *Oprah* and *Wheel of Fortune*, air primarily on local ABC stations. The network's 10 owned-and-operated stations alone reach 24 percent of American households, according to a July 2004 *Broadcasting & Cable* article.)

FCC scandal

On the flipside, the FCC received thousands of complaints in November 2004 from viewers upset with ABC's decision to run *Saving Private Ryan*, an award-winning film that graphically depicts the horrors of World War II, on Veteran's Day. While more than half (159 out of 225) of ABC's affiliated stations broadcast the film, 66 stations, including those in Dallas and Atlanta, declined to air the Steven Spielberg-directed production. ABC said in a statement that showing the film on Veteran's Day was "a timely tribute to the sacrifices and valor of all Americans engaged in service to their country."

The same month, the network took a few lumps when it ran a racy *Monday Night Football* promo featuring Nicollette Sheridan, a sultry *Desperate Housewives* star, dropping her towel and leaping into the arms of Philadelphia Eagles' wide receiver Terrell Owens. While a large number of viewers may have wondered what all the hoopla was about (only Sheridan's bare back was visible), the American Families Association and a number of outraged individuals vigorously complained that the segment crossed the lines of decency for a show that is viewed by families; Michael Powell, then-chairman of the FCC intoned, "I wonder if Walt Disney would be proud."

Investigative journalism - going too far?

On a more serious note, a November 2004 *20/20* report that re-examined the 1998 murder of Matthew Shepard, a 21-year-old gay college student found beaten to death outside Laramie, Wyo., ignited outrage from gay rights advocates, upset at the report's suggestion that the murder was not a hate crime. In prison interviews with Shepard's confessed killers, the incident was portrayed as a mere robbery gone wrong, devoid of any homophobic intentions. (The killers said the killing came about because of their drug-induced state.) The Gay and Lesbian Alliance Against Defamation believed the report did not produce a "sound argument" for the robbery-gone-wrong defense and suggested the program relied on speculation and the killers' decision to change their stories. A lawyer for the Shepard family slammed the segment as "just bad journalism" that overlooked "a mountain of evidence that anti-gay bias was a trigger for the beating that left Matthew dead." Jeffrey Schneider, ABC News' vice president, said the report, the culmination of a six-month long intensive investigation, was "both fair and accurate."

GETTING HIRED

By visiting www.disney.com, interested applicants can browse all current job listings for ABC Inc., ABC Radio Group, ABC Family Channel and ABC Cable Networks Group. Applicants can submit an online resume. On www.abc.com, direct links can be found to over 200 ABC local affiliates and their job postings. Disney also maintains a jobs hotline at (818) 558-2222 and (407) 828-1000 with current ABC job opportunities.

AMC Entertainment Inc.

920 Main Street
Kansas City, MO 64105
Phone: (816) 221-4000
Fax: (816) 480-4617
www.amctheatres.com

LOCATIONS

Kansas City, MO (HQ)

THE STATS

Employer Type: Private Company
Chairman and CEO: Peter C. Brown
2004 Employees: 17,200
2004 Revenue ($mil.): $1,782.8

KEY COMPETITORS

Carmike Cinemas
Loews Cineplex
Regal Entertainment

EMPLOYMENT CONTACT

www.amctheatres.com/careeropps/
index.html

THE SCOOP

The definitive movie experience

For more than 85 years, AMC Entertainment has provided moviegoers around the globe the chance to catch their favorite flicks on the big screen. As one of the world's largest movie exhibition companies, AMC was the first to incorporate innovations such as stadium-style seating, loveseat-style seating, cup-holder armrests and digital surround sound into its theaters, affirming its quest to bring "the best possible movie-going experience" to its customers. The company has operations throughout the U.S., Canada, France, Portugal, Spain, the U.K., Hong Kong and Japan. In 2003, 26 of the top theaters, ranked by admissions revenue, were owned by AMC. The company also operates the top-grossing theater in the world, New York City's AMC Empire 25, located in Times Square. AMC's average number of screens per theater – 15 – is the highest among major theater companies in North America.

Creating the "American" cinema

The first AMC theater was a far cry from the huge multiplexes associated with the brand today. Edward Durwood established the first Durwood Theatre in Kansas City, Mo., in 1920, slowly expanding to create a small chain of Midwestern movie houses and drive-in theaters in the surrounding area. Edward's son, Stanley, became president of Durwood Theatres in 1960. Building on his father's vision with the concept of a multiple-screen theater, Stanley created the first-ever mall-based multiplex in 1963, and followed that feat with the world's first four-screen and six-screen theaters in 1969. Stanley carried the Durwood brand into Arizona, California, Nebraska and Texas, and by the end of the 1960s, had amassed 68 screens under the Durwood name. In honor of the multiplex, by then a Durwood specialty, the company changed its name to American Multi-Cinema Inc. in 1969. Expansion and innovation continued across the U.S., with cup-holder armrests and computerized box offices revolutionizing the movie theaters in the 1980s. AMC jumped across the pond in 1985, establishing its first AMC multiplex theater abroad in the United Kingdom in 1985.

Reaching out to movie buffs

As a reward for loyal customers, AMC established the MovieWatcher program in 1990, the theater industry's first and largest loyalty program, through which members can earn points for every ticket bought at an AMC theater, and cash in the points for free concessions and movie tickets. The same year, the company installed the first-ever ATM-style ticketing system, providing the opportunity for guests to purchase tickets with credit cards. A year later, AMC launched TeleTicket, an automated system for ordering tickets by phone.

Birth of the mega-plex

Despite the continuing modernization of the movie-going experience, AMC really hit its stride in 1995, with the creation of the first mega-plex concept. The Grand 24, located in Dallas, featured the standard stadium-seating AMC would become associated with in later years. A year later, the first international mega-plex theater opened in Fukuoka, Japan. Today, AMC operates over 2,400 mega-plexes worldwide.

Expanding the brand

After Stanley Durwood's death in 1999, Peter C. Brown became chairman and CEO of AMC, building mega-plexes in new locations, shuttering nearly 548 poorly performing screens (nearly 20 percent of the company's whole), and co-founding MovieTickets.com, an online ticketing service, in 2000. The innovation was much needed. For the quarter that ended in December 1999, AMC lost $8.9 million, despite posting record revenue of $285 million; the margin of loss widened to $29.1 million the following quarter. In 2002, the company acquired General Cinema and Gulf States' theater operations, adding 689 screens in the Upper Midwest and Northeast, and picked up MegaStar Cinemas the following year, expanding the brand into Atlanta the and Minneapolis-St. Paul area. AMC signed a partnership with Walgreens to sell Entertainment "stored value" cards at more than 3,000 Walgreens locations nationwide in February 2003, becoming the first company in the exhibition industry to offer stored-value technology to moviegoers.

Going private

As part of ongoing streamlining efforts in 2003, AMC eliminated 145 jobs from its National Cinema Network Inc. subsidiary, saving $5.5 million a year. AMC and Loews Cineplex hinted in November 2003 about a possible merger, but, in the end, no final plan materialized. If the merger had gone through, the resulting company would have been of relative size to the industry's No.-1 chain, Regal Entertainment. Instead, AMC began working on a plan to go private. In July 2004, the buyout unit of J.P. Morgan Chase & Company announced it would acquire a majority stake in AMC in a $2 billion agreement to take the movie theater chain private. J.P. Morgan took 50.1 percent of the shares, while Apollo Management, another buyout firm, held on to 49.9 percent. In a December 2004 announcement following the shareholders' overwhelming vote to privatize the company , CEO Brown said he doubted AMC would ever become public again. The company reported a $59.9 million loss during its third-quarter, due in part to spending $57 million on the bid to go private.

Friendly rivalry

AMC and rival Regal Entertainment announced the creation of National CineMedia LLC, a joint advertising venture, in March 2005. The new company, a combination of Regal's CineMedia unit for media and new business development and AMC's National Cinema Network advertising unit, will represent 11,200 movie screens across North America and reach 450 million customers. The creation of National CineMedia reduced the headcount at AMC's National Cinema Network by about 70, but roughly half of the affected employees were offered an opportunity to work for the new business venture.

Reorganization

In March 2005, the company laid off some employees and said it would move its film booking office from Los Angeles to Kansas City. A company spokesperson told the *Kansas City Star* that this step was part of a reorganization plan designed to make the company more efficient. The laid-off employees were provided with severance packages.

GETTING HIRED

Hiring overview

AMC offers the longest-running professional management training program in the motion picture exhibition industry, combining classroom-style training and hands-on experience for all facets of theater operations. To apply, job seekers can complete an online employment application, found on the company's corporate web site, fax a resume to (816) 480-4725 or mail it to the following address:

AMC Theatres
Attn: Human Resources
P.O. Box 219615
Kansas City, MO 64121-9615

Candidates can also apply for staff positions, including concessionist, usher and cashier. Applicants should download the online employment application form, and specify all theater location(s) of interest.

Visit Vault at **www.vault.com** for insider company profiles, expert advice, career message boards, expert resume reviews, the Vault Job Board and more.

V/\ULT CAREER LIBRARY   21

Bertelsmann AG

Carl-Bertelsmann-Strasse 270
D-33311 Gütersloh, Germany
Phone: +49-5241-80-0
Fax: +49-5241-80-9662
www.bertelsmann.com

LOCATIONS

Gütersloh, Germany (HQ)
Offices in 63 countries worldwide

THE STATS

Employer Type: Private Company
Chairman and CEO: Gunter Thielen
2004 Employees: 76,266
2003 Revenue ($mil.): $23,20.8

KEY COMPETITORS

Axel Springer
Disney
Time Warner

EMPLOYMENT CONTACT

www.myfuture.bertelsmann.com

THE SCOOP

The big picture

German media conglomerate Bertelsmann has its hands in everything – from books to magazines, and television to music, the billion dollar business houses works from a diverse array of big names, including Bill Clinton, pop star Britney Spears, and Dan Brown, the scribe behind runaway bestseller *The DaVinci Code*. The company today is the largest media corporation in Germany, and one of the world's major players in the industry, ranked the No. 4 media company in worldwide sales. For the fiscal year 2004, revenue topped $23 billion. Bertelsmann generates two-thirds of total revenue outside Germany, mostly in other European countries, the U.S., and Asia.

Bertelsmann family circle

Carl Bertelsmann, a German printer, founded the company that would bear his name in 1835, publishing religious books and hymnals from his own book-printing plant in Gütersloh, Germany, moving onto non-fiction and fiction in 1849 (among Bertelsmann's early classics were works from the Brothers Grimm and Lord Byron). In 1944, the Nazi Party temporarily shut Bertelsmann's business down after it was deemed "non-essential to the war effort." A British air raid on Gütersloh in 1945 destroyed a large chunk of Bertelsmann's facilities, leaving only printing machines intact. Following the end of the war, Reinhard Mohn, Bertelsmann's great grandson, took control, charged with the task of building the company back up to its former glory. Mohn's family still controls Bertelsmann today in conjunction with a family-controlled nonprofit foundation. During the late 1990s and early 2000s, the Mohns held fierce against former CEO Thomas Middelhoff, who tried unsuccessfully to take the company public, and was ultimately booted by the Bertelsmann board in July 2002. Gunter Thielen, a longtime executive at Arvato, was named CEO the following month.

Middelhoff did, though, leave Bertelsmann with at least one success: the 1998, $1.4 billion acquisition of U.S. publisher Random House, today the world's largest commercial book publisher with over 100 imprints. Bertelsmann is chock full of other media powerhouses as well, including the BMG music publishing unit; Arvato, a media service provider; Gruner + Jahr, a publisher of newspapers and magazines; RTL Group, Europe's largest broadcasting and production company; and Direct Group, a source of media and entertainment products.

Visit Vault at **www.vault.com** for insider company profiles, expert advice, career message boards, expert resume reviews, the Vault Job Board and more.

VAULT CAREER LIBRARY   **23**

Musical mayhem

After a 2003 lawsuit from Universal Music Group and EMI Recorded Music accused Bertelsmann of "willful participation" of copyright infringement stemming from its support of the infamous file-sharing software service Napster, CEO Thielen moved quickly to repair the company's name in the music industry by engineering a major merger between BMG and Japan's Sony. The joint venture, finalized December 2003, involved a 50-50 valuation of the two assets instead of cash payment, and passed approval from both the European Union and the Federal Trade Commission in July 2004. The deal joined BMG and Sony's recorded music businesses, but did not include music publishing, distribution or manufacturing. Thielen vowed that the merger would prove Bertelsmann had a lasting commitment to the music industry.

Not so thrilled with the merger, though, was Impala, a trade association representing 2,400 independent European labels. In November 2004, Impala filed an appeal with the European Court of First Instance in November 2004, claiming the Sony-BMG firm would decrease competition in the music industry. In March 2005, Impala gained headway after the Court announced it would expedite procedure to rule on the case within three to six months. An overall outcome has yet to be decided.

The company teamed up with Intel, the world's largest chipmaker, in March 2005 to announce a plan to develop technology for legally downloading and sharing films, music, and games from the Internet for PCs, notebooks and mobile phones. Additionally, Arvato will develop a new online media file-sharing platform, which will be compatible with the Intel chips. The joint venture surprised many industry insiders, who thought Bertelsmann's days in dabbling with file sharing were long gone after the Napster fiasco.

Pulling through

Bertelsmann saw good news in the first nine months of 2004, when net profit more than quadrupled to $647 million, spurred by a slow-but-sure turnaround in the company's struggling BMG business and record-breaking sales of former President Bill Clinton's personal memoir *My Life* and increased success of RTL, which, overall in 2004, was Bertelmann's profitable division.

Earnings before interest for the fiscal year 2004 registered at $2.3 billion, an increase of 39 percent from the year prior. Thielen has used his money shrewdly, choosing to grow Bertelsmann organically through smaller purchases, such as the April 2005 acquisitions of Privat, France's largest independent bookstore chain, for $64 million. Bertelsmann hopes the purchase of Privat will revive its DirectGroup book club division, the smallest of the six Bertelsmann units. The following month, Bertelsmann joined the gravure printing operations of Arvato and Gruner + Jahr with those of longtime rival Axel Springer AG to combat increasing competition in the European illustration printing market. Bertelsmann will have control of the new company, which will be Europe's biggest printer of magazines, catalogs and brochures once it's up and running. Additionally, Gruner + Jahr added international Motorpresse Stuttgart publishing group to its portfolio in the spring of 2005.

Big deal

In May 2005, Bertelsmann broke its string of low-cost acquisitions with a $400 million deal for Columbia House, the membership-based seller of DVDs and music, which will be integrated with BMG Direct, Bertelsmann's U.S. music-club business. Once the sale is complete, BMG Direct will boast some 16 million members and $1.5 billion in annual revenue. The buy was Bertelsmann's biggest since Random House, and further proof of the commitment Thielen made in 2002 upon taking the CEO position to turn around Bertelsmann's membership clubs. The move also made BMG Direct more apt to compete with growing competition from Internet retailers and mass merchants.

Staying focused

With plans underway for a printing plant in Britain and a growing interest in Eastern European and Asian acquisitions – not to mention the 2004 sale of its trophy office tower in New York City's Times Square – Bertelsmann is slowly but surely evolving into a more European-centered company. Case-in-point: in spring 2005, Bertelsmann's Gruner + Jahr division divested popular American magazines *Family Circle*, *Parents*, *Child*, and *Fitness Magazine*, as well as *Inc.* and *Fast Company*.

One thing the organization will not be doing, though, is splitting up its assets. Thielen shrugged off rumors in March 2005 that Bertelsmann would break apart the way rivals like Viacom and AOL Time Warner have. Instead, his restructuring measures and minor investments have increased earnings by more than 50 percent in the past two years. Throughout its history, it's been clear Bertelsmann isn't afraid to march to its own drum – which, as the company continues to gain speed and earnings, might be the best thing.

Visit Vault at **www.vault.com** for insider company profiles, expert advice, career message boards, expert resume reviews, the Vault Job Board and more.

VAULT CAREER LIBRARY   25

GETTING HIRED

Hiring overview

Bertelsmann's career web site, www.myfuture.bertelsmann.com, offers job seekers the chance to search jobs by four categories: intern, entry-level, professional and experienced professional. Since the company is home to so many different media outposts, jobs at Bertelsmann range anywhere from receptionist to production associate to database marketing manager to senior editor. Internships are available in some divisions during the school year for undergraduates, and during the summer for students entering their senior year of undergraduate study. In addition, the My Future web site offers information on Bertelsmann's main groups: Arvato, Direct Group, Gruner + Jahr, Random House, RTL Group and Sony BMG.

Black Entertainment Television

One BET Plaza
1235 W. Street, NE
Washington, DC 20018
Phone: (202) 608-2000
Fax: (202) 608-2589
www.bet.com

LOCATIONS

Washington, DC (HQ)

Visit Vault at **www.vault.com** for insider company profiles, expert advice,
career message boards, expert resume reviews, the Vault Job Board and more.

VAULT CAREER LIBRARY   27

THE SCOOP

Black America's brand of choice

BET founder Robert Johnson's mission was to do more than just entertain Black America – he also wanted BET to be "Black America's brand of choice." Starting in 1979, Johnson began cultivating a company that "eats black, thinks black and sleeps black." BET employees certainly meet his standards as most of the employees – from administrative positions to managers – are black. (The company does not discriminate in hiring, however, and employs workers of a variety of races.) BET reaches more than 78 million homes and more than 90 percent of all black households with cable. While broadcast networks have drawn fire for excluding minorities, BET has provided an outlet for black artists and executives alike. The company's success has not been limited to TV, either: BET.com is among the most highly trafficked African-American sites on the Internet.

The network became part of Sumner Redstone's Viacom family in 2000. In addition to the original BET channel and BET.com, the company also has a strong footing in other entertainment markets, including a digital cable channel (BET Digital Networks), a book publisher (BET Books), a film production company (BET Pictures) and a national radio service available through XM Satellite Radio (BET Uptown).

History

A former lobbyist for the cable industry, Johnson founded BET in 1979 with seed money from cable mogul John Malone (head of the former TCI). Malone remains a significant minority owner and a member of the board. Legend has it Johnson's business plan was copied (with permission) from a fellow entrepreneur's proposal for a cable channel aimed at senior citizens. In an interview with the *Chicago Tribune* in 1989, Johnson explained that "wherever he had the world 'elderly,' I wrote in 'Black,' and it worked!" Johnson's cable industry contacts helped him to locate additional investors – including HBO and Taft Broadcasting. Those contacts added to the seed money provided by Malone. His investors also provided Johnson with more than just money – they gave him expert advice and access to the channel lineups of the two largest cable service providers in America: TCI and Time Warner.

Smashing debut

The BET television network debuted in 1980 with a weekly two-hour music video show. By 1991, BET offered programming 24 hours a day and had broadened its line-up to include not just music videos, but also gospel programs, public affairs shows and Black college sports. The company also created a publishing division, with the purchase of now-defunct teen magazine *YSB* (*Young Sisters & Brothers*) and a majority stake in the also-defunct *Emerge*, known as "Black America's News Magazine." That same year, BET went public, becoming the first African-American-owned company to trade on the New York Stock Exchange. Much of the money raised in the public offering was used to reduce the company's debt and to buy back stock held by Great American Broadcasting (which had acquired Taft Broadcasting in the interim).

BET joined the World Wide Web in February 2000, creating a web portal backed by Microsoft, Liberty Digital Media, News Corp. and USA Networks that's geared toward African-Americans and offers everything from message boards to political news to home buying and career advice. Johnson cited a widening gap in Internet usage between blacks and whites, in addition to his desire to integrate technology with the "economic and social enrichment of the African-American community" as the impetus behind the creation of the site. The $35 million investment provided by BET Holdings represented the largest investment ever in a site targeted to blacks. The site is currently one of the top Internet portals for African Americans and was named the "Best African-American Community Site" in 2001 by *Yahoo! Internet Life* magazine.

Entering the world of Viacom

In September 1999, Johnson publicly announced he was interested in purchasing a large stake in UPN television to create a larger network that would focus on the growing urban entertainment market. However, media giant Viacom Inc. beat BET to the punch, swallowing up a 50 percent stake in the struggling UPN from Chris-Craft Industries. Then, in November 2000, media giant Viacom Inc. purchased BET itself for $2.3 billion in stock. Johnson called the sale "a historic day ... an opportunity for BET to align its brand with the premium brand in the world of Viacom." The sale made Johnson the world's first African-American billionaire.

Social responsibility

Through its web site and television broadcasts, BET provides its audience not only with music and entertainment news, but also relevant current events, like impending changes to Social Security, the war in Iraq and presidential election coverage, in addition to annual programs celebrating Black History Month. Recently, *The Higher Ed Hook-Up*, a five-part series aired in November 2004, offered helpful tips to high school students for getting ready for college, covering the areas of financial aid, prep courses, admissions, entrance exams, scholarships, choosing a major, researching and visiting prospective campuses, and the importance of historically black colleges and universities.

The company is often criticized, however, by members of the black community for giving too much air time to music videos (especially as videos have become more and more risqué over the years) and reruns of comedies that were originally aired on network television and not focusing enough on producing its own dramatic and public affairs series. Additional criticism was leveled at the company following the April 2005 announcement that the network was cancelling *BET Nightly News,* which was broadcast weeknights and focused on "the latest news affecting the Black community." Instead, the company said it would broadcast news briefs throughout the day, as well as periodic news specials and a quarterly public affairs program.

Changes in store

Johnson's contract with Viacom expires in January 2006. The man credited with pioneering the nation's first channel geared solely to an African-American audience has publicly announced he will leave the company he founded, choosing instead to focus on other projects, including his NBA expansion team, the Charlotte Bobcats. Debra Lee, Johnson's wingman and an 18-year BET veteran, is set to replace him. Lee says she has a lot in store for the network.

Twenty-five years after first hitting the airwaves, BET is searching for new business ventures, now that rivals such as Comcast's TV One, pioneered by African-American broadcaster Cathy Hughes, are entering the realm once dominated by BET. As of February 2005 TV One, established in January 2004, reached 18 million homes. This can be considered a paltry figure at best, compared to BET's audience of 80 million, but TV One has plans to capitalize on its partnership with Comcast to gain ground in the future. TV One insists it is not looking to displace BET, and says its shows are aimed at black viewers underserved by all major network, broadcast and cable channels, with a focus on mature programming covering everything from cooking to makeovers to financial advice.

Big plans

Viacom has big plans for BET and hopes to establish the name as a lucrative brand in multiple media properties, similar to MTV and Comedy Central. Viacom execs have said the cable channel's "over-reliance on music videos and infomercials" will change as the network is transformed into the "first choice for African-Americans." Media analysts agree that BET has just scratched the surface of what it can offer its target audience, statistically proven to be both avid television watchers and strong consumers. Additionally, analysts consider African-Americans "a giant segment of the population clearly underserved" by the television market today, and in need of a "break-out hit" to secure its market position.

Johnson, however, disagrees. "We couldn't program everything that everyone wanted us to be," he said in a February 2005 *Newsweek* article. "People wanted us to be the black kids' channel. Others were asking, 'Why can't I see black dramas?' The economics were impossible for cable networks." However, with Viacom's strong backing, BET released several new shows in the winter of 2005, including a second season of *College Hill*, a *Real World*-ish show starring black college students; *The Cousin Jeff Chronicles*, a quarterly series hosted by social activist Jeff Johnson; and *Rip the Runway*, described as a "red-hot catwalk collision ... of hip-hop music and high fashion." In addition, BET will air the BET Awards and made-for-TV movies co-produced by the company, throughout the 2005 programming season.

GETTING HIRED

Hiring overview

BET hires new employees into each of its six national offices, though most begin their careers at the Washington, D.C., headquarters. BET's affiliate sales, finance, network operations and computer information services are the most active areas of recruitement for entry-level positions. Applicants should consult the company's job hotline for a list of current job openings. BET forwards submitted resumes to the appropriate department, where they are kept on file for 90 days. However, BET discards those resumes that are not directed to a specific opening within 30 days.

Visit Vault at **www.vault.com** for insider company profiles, expert advice, career message boards, expert resume reviews, the Vault Job Board and more.

VAULT CAREER LIBRARY   **31**

Bloomberg L.P.

499 Park Avenue
New York, NY 10022
Phone: (212) 318-2000
Fax: (917) 369-5000
www.bloomberg.com

LOCATIONS

New York, NY (HQ)

THE SCOOP

Bloomberg blossoms

Bloomberg L.P., a news and media company headquartered in New York, has customers in 126 countries and employs more than 8,200 people in 110 offices. The company publishes books and magazines, runs a news service and also offers its information services across television and radio programs and the Internet.

Bloomberg creates Bloomberg

In 1981 Michael Bloomberg, the company's founder, used a portion of his $10 million severance package from Salomon Brothers to found his own company, then called Innovative Market Systems. Over the course of the next year, he developed the Bloomberg terminal, a financial information system that allowed users to analyze bond data. Merrill Lynch was so impressed with the product that in 1982 it ordered 20 terminals and invested $30 million in the company. Today, Michael Bloomberg owns 72 percent of the company; Merrill Lynch controls 20 percent, and a number of long-time Bloomberg executives hold the remaining stake.

Riding the 1980s boom

Bloomberg's eponymous company prospered during the boom of the 1980s. It expanded internationally, opening offices in Europe, Asia and Australia. In 1990, the Bloomberg News Service was launched and it now provides information to approximately 350 newspapers and magazines worldwide, including *The Economist*, *The New York Times* and *USA Today*. Bloomberg launched its 24-hour radio and television news services in 1992 and 1993, respectively. Since then the company has introduced *Bloomberg Personal Finance*, a magazine; Tradebook, an electronic platform for trading securities; and the Bloomberg Press line of investment books. Bloomberg employs more than 1,600 reporters in its 94 news bureaus worldwide who churn out about 4,000 stories a day and offer financial analysis, mutual fund information, breaking news and global market summaries.

News never stops

As a specialized service, Bloomberg currently has more than 170,000 of its "Bloomberg Professional" terminals in operation for clients around the world. The terminal combines two flat computer screens and a keyboard that is connected to the

Visit Vault at **www.vault.com** for insider company profiles, expert advice, career message boards, expert resume reviews, the Vault Job Board and more.

VAULT CAREER LIBRARY   33

Bloomberg network. The Professional service runs subscribers around $1,285 per month, which covers the terminal, the company's proprietary financial analysis software and real-time reporting on worldwide capital markets. While it may not come cheap, the 24-hour service makes it convenient for financial analysts to research breaking financial news by location, keyword, industry and language.

In addition to several international (local language) news channels, the company runs an executive interview series called *The Bloomberg Forum*, which features the most talked-about businesspeople of the moment. The interviews are broadcast across Bloomberg's radio and television properties. The company also launched two new multimedia ventures in Malaysia in 1999 as part of its efforts to extend its coverage. With the aid of LendingTree.com, Bloomberg developed Bloomberg.com, a site that carries select data, news and fee-based research reports. Since its emergence on the Internet scene in 1995, Bloomberg.com consistently ranks as one of the top five financial sites in terms of traffic.

The small screen

Bloomberg Television, launched in 1993, is a 24-hour global network that broadcasts across 10 networks in seven languages, reaching more than 200 million homes worldwide. *Bloomberg Business News* premiered in January 1994, and following its successful launch, switched from a 15-minute to 30-minute format a year later. *Bloomberg Information Television*, which debuted in 1995, covers news, weather, sports and financial information seven days a week. By the summer of 2001, Bloomberg Television was logging an astounding one million subscribers per month, with plans to reach over 40 million households by the end of 2002. The network's distribution increased by 151.2 percent from the spring of 2000 to the spring of 2001. The company attributed the success of the channel to the increasing abundance of direct broadcast services packages.

In October 2003, Bloomberg was nominated for an Emmy Award in the First Annual News and Documentary Emmy Awards For Business and Financial Reporting. The nominated series, *Showdown on Secrecy*, explored conflicts around disclosure issues in the mutual-funds industry. The show didn't win, but it's an honor just to be nominated, isn't it? In December 2003, Bloomberg Television anchor Catherine Yang won the title of Best News Presenter for the third year in a row at the Asian Television Awards, held in Singapore. Yang hosts *Moneycast Asia*, one of Bloomberg Television's major financial news programs, broadcast live each weekday from Tokyo around the globe. The program was also nominated for Best Business News Programme, a recent addition to the categories in the Asian Television Awards.

Moneycast Asia delivers early-morning financial news from across the region that includes market analysis, interviews and live reports from the Tokyo Stock Exchange, the Singapore Stock Exchange and Bloomberg's bureaus in Hong Kong and Sydney.

Bloomberg Television can also be seen in more than 200 banks and financial institutions worldwide, and has become the No.-1 business television network in the U.S. from 5 a.m. to 8 a.m. Its average audience was up 31 percent in 2003, according to Nielsen ratings. The company also struck a deal with the E! Entertainment channel to air Bloomberg's programs Monday through Friday 5 a.m. to 8 a.m. and Saturdays 5:30 a.m. to 7 a.m. Bloomberg Radio, launched in 1992, currently boasts about 16 million listeners in the United States. In 2004, Bloomberg News was awarded the Gerald Loeb Award for Best News Services/Online Content.

In print

The company puts out several publications in the U.S. for both consumers and financial professionals. *Bloomberg Wealth Manager* is published for money managers and advisers; *Bloomberg Markets* is a business magazine for and about people who move markets and complements the Bloomberg Professional service; and *On Investing* is a personal investment magazine produced exclusively for Charles Schwab's top-tier clients. Bloomberg also publishes, in conjunction with local partners, *Bloomberg Money* in the U.K. and *Bloomberg Investment* in Italy.

But wait, there's more: Bloomberg also has its own book publishing interest: Bloomberg Press (thought it'd be called something else?), publishes titles on money management, investing and other financial topics. The imprint also has a deal with *The Economist* magazine to publish a series of books called (what else?) *The Economist Series* and has published several books of *New Yorker* cartoons.

Legal disputes

Bloomberg found itself on the wrong side of the law in September 2000, after a Boston law firm filed a class-action lawsuit against the news service provider on behalf of Emulex shareholders, accusing Bloomberg of reporting a fake press release of "materially false and misleading information" that sent stocks in Emulex, a Costa Mesa, Calif.-based electronics company, plummeting.

Two years later, Bloomberg paid $340,039 to the Singapore Prime Minister Goh Chok Tong and two other government leaders for damages stemming from a

Visit Vault at **www.vault.com** for insider company profiles, expert advice, career message boards, expert resume reviews, the Vault Job Board and more.

VAULT CAREER LIBRARY   35

defamation lawsuit. The Singapore government claimed Bloomberg defamed the three in an August 2002 article implying that Goh's appointment of Lee Hsien Loong's wife Ho Ching was an act of nepotism. Lawyers for the Singapore officials called the accusation "grave and malicious" and the article "offensive." In addition to the cash payment, Bloomberg also posted an apology on its web site, admitting the allegations were "false and completely without foundation."

Mayor Mike

With the November 2001 election of Mike Bloomberg as New York City mayor, the company lost its most visible executive. Lex Fenwick, who had run the company's European sales operations, took over the CEO post upon Bloomberg's switch to the public sector.

Bloomberg overcame tremendous odds to become the first Republican ever to succeed another Republican as mayor of the nation's largest city. He certainly had his work cut out for him, winning the election just weeks after the September 11, 2001, attacks occurred. Bloomberg's massive campaign advertising blitz – funded with an estimated $50 million of his own money – focused on his background as a businessman. He contended that his experience building the billion-dollar financial information empire that bears his name would serve him well as a mayor charged with rebuilding the city's economy.

Billion-dollar bust

Reports surfaced at the start of 2002 that Thomson Corp., a Canadian publishing giant, was prepared to make a $10 billion bid for Bloomberg. Spokespeople for both companies refused to discuss the rumored deal. Turned out that the rumor was just that – a rumor.

Give 'em space

In May 2002, the company opened its own art gallery, called Bloomberg SPACE, in its European headquarters in London. Dedicated to commissioning and exhibiting contemporary art, Bloomberg SPACE is open to employees, clients and the community at large. Bloomberg SPACE goes a long way to complement Bloomberg's already existing program of arts sponsorship and extends the company's support of a wide range of arts and charities projects throughout the world.

Bye bye, Bloomberg?

Mike Bloomberg announced in January 2005 that he would not return to the company he helped found, and that he planned to sell the firm to finance a "post-public-office charitable binge" according to an article in the *New York Post*. Reports estimate that Bloomberg L.P. could fetch up to $10 billion based on its current financial standing. Potential suitors include Microsoft and former potential buyer Thomson, which has recently said it plans to expand in the electronic media and information services market.

GETTING HIRED

Let your career blossom at Bloomberg

For employment information, head to the careers section of the company's web site, www.bloomberg.com. In addition to a listing of current job openings, the web site offers a pretty comprehensive introduction to life at the company, and features videos on working at Bloomberg. There is also a comprehensive job search tool on the site that enables applicants to fill out an online application and attach their resume for consideration for a specific position.

The site also lists recruiting events the company participates in, mostly at its offices, around the world. The company also offers what it calls Bloomberg University, a place where employees can go to search for instructor-led training, self-study courses and other special training events. The University offers skill-building courses in employee development and job-specific courses in financial markets, sales, news and PC/technical training. Bloomberg University's services and seminars are free-of-charge, accessible online, on-site and even through conference calls for Bloomberg.com registered members.

Visit Vault at **www.vault.com** for insider company profiles, expert advice, career message boards, expert resume reviews, the Vault Job Board and more.

VAULT CAREER LIBRARY

37

CBS, Inc.

51 W. 52nd Street
New York, NY 10019
Phone: (212) 975-4321
Fax: (212) 975-4516
www.cbs.com

LOCATIONS

New York, NY (HQ)
Los Angeles, CA

THE STATS

Employer Type: Subsidiary of Viacom
Chairman, President and CEO: Leslie
(Les) Moonves
2004 Revenue ($mil.): $8,504.6

KEY COMPETITORS

Fox Entertainment
NBC Universal
Walt Disney

EMPLOYMENT CONTACTS

CBS Television Network
Internship Coordinator
51 West 52nd Street
New York, NY 10019
Attn: Internship Program

CBS News
Internship Program
524 West 57th Street
New York, New York 10019
Attn: Eldra Rodriguez-Gillman

THE SCOOP

Everybody loves CBS

The CBS network, part of the giant media conglomerate Viacom, celebrated its 75th anniversary in 2003. After struggling through most of the mid-1990s, CBS, under current president Les Moonves, has been on a roll the last few seasons – winning the overall ratings competition for the 2002-2003 television season. It's also home to some of the most popular shows on television, including the top-rated *CSI: Crime Scene Investigation*. Though its audience tends to be a bit older than the other networks' (supposedly a negative when it comes to selling advertising), CBS has stood by its strategy of appealing to the broadest possible audience. Aside from *CSI*, the network's other ratings champs include *CSI: Miami, Survivor, Without a Trace* and *Everybody Loves Raymond* (which took its final bow at the end of the 2004-2005 season and brought in more than 32 million viewers for its finale). Each of these programs has attracted close to 20 million viewers each week.

Radio days

CBS started out in 1927 as United Independent Broadcasters, a radio network founded by a talent agent named Arthur Judson. Less than a year into its existence, however, the fledgling organization was acquired by the Columbia Phonograph Company and renamed the Columbia Phonograph Broadcasting System. The network struggled financially at first and passed through the hands of several owners before finally falling under the control of William Paley. After purchasing the company in 1929 for $400,000, Paley changed its name once again – this time to the shortened Columbia Broadcasting System (CBS). Under Paley, CBS' stature would grow from upstart underdog to the "Tiffany Network." At first though, the network's prestige lagged far behind that of its rival, NBC. Paley was responsible for launching the careers of many stars such as singers Bing Crosby and Kate Smith, only to see them defect to NBC after rising to prominence. To compensate for the continual loss of its biggest attractions, CBS focused on building a world-class news gathering organization. The first broadcast news "star," Edward R. Murrow, made his name covering World War II for CBS from Europe. It was Murrow who was responsible for convincing another revered broadcaster to sign on with the network. After previously turning down an offer to join the network, Walter Cronkite joined CBS' Washington, D.C., affiliate in 1950. In April 1962, he became the anchor of the *Evening News*, a post he held until retiring in 1981. In 1967, the Cronkite-hosted

Visit Vault at **www.vault.com** for insider company profiles, expert advice, career message boards, expert resume reviews, the Vault Job Board and more.

VAULT CAREER LIBRARY   **39**

Evening News was named the top-rated evening broadcast and retained that lead for many years.

Channel one

The network truly came into its own with the advent of television. CBS began TV broadcasting in 1948, and soon was home to the new medium's most popular shows. Programs like *I Love Lucy*, *The Ed Sullivan Show* and *Gunsmoke* earned CBS its "Tiffany Network" nickname and helped the network consistently top NBC in the ratings wars. CBS remained on top in the 1960s with hit shows like *The Beverly Hillbillies* and *Green Acres*, though not without some grumbling from network insiders that its programming was being "dumbed-down" and tarnishing its classy image. The 1970s saw the network return to its former glory, however, as fresh hits like *All in the Family*, *The Mary Tyler Moore Show* and *M*A*S*H* proved to be popular with both audiences and critics alike. The 1970s were also a period of rapid expansion for CBS as it added new ventures such as a publishing house (Holt, Reinhart and Winston), a record label (Columbia Records), a magazine (*Woman's Day*) and briefly, a sports franchise (the New York Yankees). In recognition of the expanded scope of its business holdings, the company officially changed its name from the Columbia Broadcasting System to CBS Inc.

Paley passes the reins

As CEO William Paley neared (and later surpassed – it's good to be the boss) the network's mandatory retirement age, there was a great deal of speculation over who would eventually succeed him. Throughout the early 1980s, Paley hired – and then fired – a series of right-hand men, seemingly not ready to let go of the reins. Ultimately, though, a rumored takeover bid by cable kingpin Ted Turner compelled Paley to anoint Lawrence Tisch as his heir apparent. Tisch, who was president of Loews Cinemas at the time, acquired a 25 percent stake in the company and assumed the position of president and CEO in 1986. After Paley's death in 1990, Tisch became chairman of the board as well. Under Tisch, CBS began cutting costs and selling off its recording and publishing businesses. As budgets and payroll declined, however, so too did ratings and employee morale. The network's evening news broadcast, which had been the top-rated nightly news program since the Walter Cronkite era, had slipped to third place by the early 1990s. A further blow to the network's prestige came in 1994 when it lost the rights to broadcast NFL games to the Fox network. By 1995, Tisch had had enough and sold the network to the Westinghouse Corporation for $5.4 billion.

From W to V

Westinghouse breathed new life into the floundering CBS by acquiring several new media assets. It purchased the Infinity Broadcasting radio network in 1996 and later added the cable networks Country Music Television (CMT) and The Nashville Network (TNN) as well. These moves made CBS a powerful player in radio broadcasting, provided its first foray into cable television and, most importantly, allowed it to compete with the other media conglomerates, which were also rapidly growing in size during this period. In fact, Westinghouse became so enamored of the media business that it decided to sell its electronics manufacturing operation (the traditional core of the company) in 1997 in order to concentrate fully on its media holdings. Following the sale, Westinghouse changed its name to the CBS Corporation; in the space of two short years, the acquired had swallowed its parent.

And CBS was not done yet. In 1999, Mel Karmazin, former Infinity Broadcasting CEO, rose to the top spot at the network. In a frenzied first year on the job, Karmazin engineered the acquisitions of several smaller Internet companies including switchboard.com, medscape.com, rx.com and hollywood.com. Even bigger was his purchase of King World productions for $2.5 billion in April 1999. King World is one of the leading content syndication companies in the industry and is the distributor for programs such as *Wheel of Fortune*, *Jeopardy!* and the *Oprah Winfrey Show*. But Karmazin's crowning achievement came in 2000, when he played a key role in arranging the $45 billion mega-merger between CBS and Sumner Redstone's Viacom. Following the transaction, Karmazin assumed the role of president and COO of Viacom, while current CBS boss Leslie Moonves took over as CEO of the CBS subsidiary. In order to streamline the structure of the newly created conglomerate, Viacom shifted some of CBS' holdings to other parts of the company. It put the network's cable TV and web holdings under the control of its MTV Networks subsidiary and split off the Infinity Broadcasting unit to form its own business unit within Viacom. In return, CBS was given Viacom's other broadcast TV network, the United Paramount Network (UPN), to manage in 2002.

It's all here

Though just one piece of the larger Viacom media group, CBS retains its own CEO and management team to oversee its diverse holdings. The core of the company, obviously, is the CBS television network. With more than 200 affiliates nationwide, CBS reaches just about every television set in the U.S. Of these affiliate stations, 20 are owned by Viacom. CBS Entertainment is the division responsible for developing and scheduling the majority of the programming shown on the network. Among the

Visit Vault at **www.vault.com** for insider company profiles, expert advice, career message boards, expert resume reviews, the Vault Job Board and more.

VAULT CAREER LIBRARY   41

popular CBS Entertainment programs are *CSI*, *Survivor*, *The Late Show with David Letterman* and the two top-rated daytime TV shows: *The Young & the Restless* and *The Price Is Right*. The entertainment division also includes CBS Productions, the network's in-house production studio. CBS News maintains its headquarters in New York in addition to 14 other news bureaus around the world. The division is best known for producing the network's TV news programming, including *60 Minutes*, *48 Hours*, *The Early Show* and *Face the Nation*. In addition to its TV programming, the news division also airs radio programs on more than 2,000 affiliated radio stations and creates original documentaries, CD-ROMs and audio books through its CBS News Productions group. CBS Sports, meanwhile, covers many major sporting events, including Sunday NFL football games, the NCAA men's basketball tournament, the Master's and PGA Championship golf tournaments, the U.S. Open tennis championships and NCAA football. The sports division also handles the coverage of boxing matches for fellow Viacom network Showtime. Finally, the CBS Enterprises division, which includes King World Productions, distributes syndicated shows in the U.S. and to 120 countries overseas.

Moonves on up

CBS has performed well in recent years thanks largely to its CEO, Leslie Moonves. Moonves arrived at the network in 1995 as president of the CBS Entertainment division. At the time, the network was trying to adjust to new ownership and posting low viewer ratings. But within just three years, CBS had experienced a major turnaround, vaulting to first place in both number of viewers and households during the 1998-1999 season. Moonves is credited with playing an instrumental role in engineering this comeback. Shows like *Everybody Loves Raymond* (which debuted during Moonves' first year on the job), *Survivor* and *CSI* (both of which were developed under Moonves' watch) were the cornerstones for the CBS renaissance. *Survivor*, in particular, was an instant sensation when it debuted in 2000; the final episode of the show's first season attracted an astounding 58 million viewers. By 2003, CBS was comfortably settling into its role as "America's most watched network." After barely losing to NBC in 2002 (thanks mainly to NBC's broadcast of the Winter Olympic Games in Utah), CBS regained the top spot in 2003. *CSI*, the top-rated show on television, averaged 26.2 million viewers per week. And at the Emmy Awards in October 2003, the network again showed its strength, taking home 16 trophies, the most of any broadcast network and trailing overall leader HBO by just two.

Winning the annual ratings battle is great for prestige, but it doesn't always translate into dollars. Despite capturing the top spot in 2003, CBS still came in last in advertising revenue. That year, the network earned $3 billion in ad sales, $1.1 billion less than NBC and $400 million behind ABC. The reason for this disparity between ratings and revenue is that advertisers value viewers between the ages of 18 and 49 over all others. In this target demographic, CBS' ratings have generally not been as high as its rival NBC. But there are now signs that this, too, may be changing. CBS has been able to beat NBC's once untouchable "Must-See TV" Thursday night lineup on the strength of three shows that perform well among younger viewers: *Survivor* at 8 p.m., *CSI* at 9 p.m. and *Without a Trace* at 10 p.m. *CSI: Miami* on Monday nights has also posted solid ratings in the 18-49 category, as did *Everybody Loves Raymond*, which ended its run in 2005.

A new crop

Two and a Half Men, the network's only new sitcom for the 2003-2004 season, was the most watched new show during premiere week in September 2003. The show stars Charlie Sheen and attracted more than 18 million viewers for its first episode. Meanwhile, new dramas like *Joan of Arcadia* and *Cold Case* also turned in solid performances in their debuts. More than 13 million viewers tuned in to see the premiere of *Joan of Arcadia*, and 16 million watched *Cold Case*. In fact, the only one of CBS' six new series in 2003 to make a poor showing was the David E. Kelley drama *The Brotherhood of Poland, New Hampshire*. The show attracted just eight million viewers to its premiere and lasted a mere five weeks before being placed on hiatus, and later cancelled. In fairness to *The Brotherhood*, however, it should be mentioned that it faced the unenviable task of competing against ratings powerhouse *Law & Order* in the 10 p.m. Wednesday time slot.

In 2004, CBS further extended its *CSI* franchise with the debut of *CSI: New York*. That show, like its siblings has performed well for the network. But other shows that debuted in 2004 didn't fare as well, despite having recognizable stars leading them. *Dr. Vegas* (starring Rob Lowe), *Center of the Universe* (with John Goodman) and *Clubhouse* (featuring Dean Cain) all lasted just a few episodes. *Listen Up* (with Jason Alexander) fared somewheat better, but ended up being cancelled at the end of its first season.

For the 2005-2006 season, CBS is expected to add "at least five new dramas and three comedies to its schedule," according to a May 2005 article in *The New York Times*. The new series will feature a number of familiar faces, including Henry Winkler, Stockard Channing and Jenna Elfman.

Visit Vault at **www.vault.com** for insider company profiles, expert advice, career message boards, expert resume reviews, the Vault Job Board and more.

VAULT CAREER LIBRARY

43

Everybody loves money

Throughout its run, *Everybody Loves Raymond* was the quiet anchor on CBS's schedule. While never as flashy or high profile as hits like *Survivor*, it nevertheless retained a sizable and loyal following. And for a brief period, the amiable comedy was even the subject of industry gossip. In August 2003, right before filming on the 2003-2004 season was set to begin, the cast became embroiled in a noisy and public contract dispute. The impasse started when Brad Garrett, who played Raymond's brother Robert on the show, refused to show up for work, demanding a raise. Network executives responded by writing him out of the first episode. In a show of solidarity, however, the rest of the supporting cast also decided to demand more money and proceeded to call in sick. Hollywood insiders speculated that the cast revolt was prompted by the contract that star Ray Romano had signed over the summer – worth $40 million for one year – that made him the highest paid actor on television (edging out *Frasier*'s Kelsey Grammer). Garrett, meanwhile, was making "only" $150,000 per episode, while Patricia Heaton (who plays Raymond's wife) was taking home just $450,000 per show.

The real issue, though, was not the per-show pay, but rather the lucrative pot of riches for the show in syndication. Romano's contract entitled him to receive a cut of the syndication revenues, while the contracts of the supporting cast members did not. The dispute was ultimately settled when Garrett received a raise to $250,000 per episode and all of the cast members were offered a percentage of the show's syndication earnings. The desire to stake a claim to *Raymond*'s syndication revenue took on added urgency as both Ray Romano and executive producer Phil Rosenthal hinted that the show may have been entering its final season. In the end though, the series continued for an additional season and ended its run in 2005.

Ratings wars heat up

"Sweeps weeks" – the times when advertising rates are determined for the upcoming months – usually prompt the networks to roll out flashy and heavily promoted specials in the hopes of scoring the highest ratings possible. During the November 2003 sweeps, two of CBS's features generated especially heavy buzz. The first, a miniseries on the life of former President Ronald Reagan, eventually proved so controversial that it was pulled from the schedule. Conservative activist groups accused *The Reagans* of being historically inaccurate and distorting the former president's legacy. Even the Republican National Committee (RNC) got involved – lobbying CBS President Leslie Moonves to air a disclaimer during the film that reminded viewers that it was not historically accurate. The uproar revolved around a single scene, published in *The New York Times* in October 2003, that portrayed Reagan as unsympathetic toward AIDS victims. Ultimately, the network decided to pull the show from its lineup just two weeks before it was supposed to air and shift it to the cable network Showtime.

Without *The Reagans* on the schedule, CBS was forced to rely more heavily upon its other big ratings draw for sweeps week, *The Elizabeth Smart Story*. Earlier in 2003, CBS had gained exclusive rights to develop a movie based on the 2002 kidnapping of Utah teenager Elizabeth Smart. Smart's parents, meanwhile, signed a book deal with publisher Doubleday. CBS and Doubleday were reportedly in negotiations to come up with a plan to coordinate the Smart media blitz when the publisher opted to give an exclusive interview with the Smarts to NBC's Katie Couric. Doubleday claimed that Couric could bring in more viewers than any CBS personality. Afraid of having their film "scooped" by the NBC interview, CBS producers quickly aired a making-of special about the filming of the Elizabeth Smart movie in October 2003. The special featured interview clips with the Smarts that had been filmed for the movie's electronic press kit. NBC responded by scheduling its own sensationalistic TV movie, *Saving Jessica Lynch*, directly opposite CBS' Smart broadcast. CBS ended up with the last laugh, however, as Smart bested Lynch by a count of 15.7 million to 14.9 million viewers.

Dan Rather departs, sort of

After the validity of sources used for a *60 Minutes Wednesday* piece that presented President George W. Bush's military record in a negative light were called into question, the network itself became headline news. The ensuing fallout over the piece, which aired in September 2004 – just prior to the presidential election in November – cost four members of the news team their jobs. The incident also served as a source of embarrassment to Dan Rather, who reported the piece, in his last months at the network's lead anchor. Rather stepped down from his post at *The CBS Evening News* in March 2005. Veteran news correspondent Bob Schieffer took over as interim anchor and has drawn favorable reviews for his "conversational style and his habit of quizzing correspondents during unscripted, on-air exchanges," according to an April 2005 *Boston Globe* article.

Fans of Rather weren't left disappointed for very long by his departure from the news desk, however. While Rather did give up his anchor duties, he is far from retired. He continued reporting for *60 Minutes Wednesday*; in fact he appeared on the news magazine in an interview with former GE executive Jack Welch and his wife just a few days after giving up the anchor position. But *60 Minutes Wednesday* had been

Visit Vault at **www.vault.com** for insider company profiles, expert advice, career message boards, expert resume reviews, the Vault Job Board and more.

VAULT CAREER LIBRARY

45

plagued by low ratings and was cancelled in May 2005. The network announced that Rather would remain at CBS as a contributor to the Sunday edition of *60 Minutes*.

Good sports

CBS (and parent Viacom) became a lightening rod in the debate surrounding the media and standards of decency Janet Jackson's breasts was briefly exposed during the 2004 Superbowl halftime show. Citizens and the media jumped on the story, criticizing CBS for broadcasting the incident. In its defense, CBS pointed out that the show was live and it had no reason to suspect that Jackson and partner-in-crime Justin Timberlake would pull such a stunt. Still, the Federal Communications Commission considered the network culpable enough to levy a fine of $550,000 against Viacom (which the company has continued to fight).

Despite the unwanted events that emerged from Superbowl XXXVIII, CBS is committed to broadcasting NFL games. The network locked up a six-year, $3.7 billion agreement with the NFL in November 2004 that will enable it to continue showing Sunday afternoon games, and didn't shy away from airing the 2005 Superbowl. The choice of halftime performer this time around, however, was a decidely less risque Paul McCartney.

GETTING HIRED

An inside job

As a subsidiary of Viacom, all hiring for CBS is done through the parent company, and interested job seekers should go to the Viacom web site for information on the recruiting process. Positions at the network tend to be difficult to come by, so it helps to know an "insider" who can provide a heads-up regarding potential openings. For those determined to break into the broadcast business, two good ways to get a foot in the door are Viacom's internship program and CBS's Diversity Institute training program.

Entry-level programs

Internships at Viacom are offered in the legal, tax, treasury, corporate relations, investor relations, human resources and finance departments. These positions are offered during the fall, spring and summer and are open to both undergraduates and graduate students. Viacom offers special luncheons and mixers for its interns where students will get an opportunity to make contacts with current employees, managers and executives. It is important to note that since these positions are offered through Viacom, internships specifically with CBS may or may not be available. All open positions are posted on the company's web site.

An initiative to recruit and develop minority talent offers another path to break in at CBS. For a number of years, civil rights organizations have been critical of the lack of diversity in broadcaster's programming and staffs. In response, CBS announced in August 2003 that it was starting a new organization called the CBS Diversity Institute. The Institute combines the network's prior minority talent program (founded in 2002) with two newer initiatives to identify "ethnic" writers and directors. The programs will help connect young writers and directors with more experienced writers, directors, producers, executives and agents who will serve as their mentors. Details and applications for both the writing and directing programs, as well as the Institute's other programs, are available at www.cbsdiversity.com.

Visit Vault at **www.vault.com** for insider company profiles, expert advice, career message boards, expert resume reviews, the Vault Job Board and more.

VAULT CAREER LIBRARY

47

Clear Channel Communications

200 E. Basse Road
San Antonio, TX 78209
Phone: (210) 822-2828
Fax: (210) 822-2299
www.clearchannel.com

LOCATIONS

San Antonio, TX (HQ)
With operating units based in:
Denver, CO
Houston, TX
Phoenix, AZ
London
Operations in 63 countries

THE STATS

Employer Type: Public Company
Stock Symbol: CCU
Stock Exchange: NYSE
President and CEO: Mark Mays
2004 Employees: 60,000
2004 Revenue ($mil.): $9,418.5

KEY COMPETITORS

Citadel Broadcasting
Cumulus Media
Infinity Broadcasting

EMPLOYMENT CONTACT

www.clearcareers.com

THE SCOOP

A diverse giant

Founded in 1972 by investment banker Lowry Mays and local car dealer Red McCombs, Clear Channel Communications has grown from a single San Antonio radio station into a diversified media giant. With three business segments (radio broadcasting, outdoor advertising and live entertainment), Clear Channel owns more than 1,200 domestic radio stations and a national radio network. In addition, the company has equity interests in about 250 international radio broadcasting companies. Clear Channel also owns some 775,000 outdoor advertising displays worldwide, more than 120 live entertainment venues (operated by subsidiary Clear Channel Entertainment) and some 40 television stations.

The company's national radio network, which has a total audience of over 180 million weekly listeners, includes talk radio personalities such as Rush Limbaugh, Glen Beck and Jim Rome and well-known disc jockeys including Rick Dees and Casey Kasem. Clear Channel also operates news and agricultural radio networks in Georgia, Ohio, Oklahoma, Texas, Iowa, Kentucky, Virginia, Alabama, Tennessee, Florida and Pennsylvania. Most of its radio broadcasting revenue is generated from the sale of local and national advertising. Clear Channel's television stations are affiliated with a range of networks including ABC, CBS, NBC and FOX. Clear Channel struck a five-year deal late in 2004 with Fox News Radio to air Fox's programming on its stations.

Additionally, Clear Channel operates a sports representation business with clients such as basketball giants Michael Jordan and Tracy McGrady, New York Yankees pitcher Mike Mussina, tennis ace Andre Agassi and football legend Jerry Rice.

From humble beginnings to the No.-1 spot

Armed with only one radio station in 1972, Mays and McCombs quickly grew its business to include 12 AM and FM stations by 1984. That same year, the two decided to take the company public. Clear Channel's simple formula for success consisted of buying cheap, underperforming radio stations and turning them into moneymakers. In 1988, the company entered the television industry when it purchased a local station in Mobile, Ala., thus forming Clear Channel Television.

When the Federal Communications Commission (FCC) passed duopoly rules for allowing ownership of two AM and FM radio stations in the same market, Clear

Visit Vault at **www.vault.com** for insider company profiles, expert advice, career message boards, expert resume reviews, the Vault Job Board and more.

VAULT CAREER LIBRARY   **49**

Channel continued its takeover spree. By 1995, the company had set foot on international soil (owning half of an Australian radio network) and owned 35 radio stations and nine television stations. As a testament to its success, *The Wall Street Journal* named Clear Channel the eighth best performing stock over the last 10 years. In addition, *Selling Power* magazine named Clear Channel one of the best companies to sell for in its annual ranking in 2004. The company was also named to *Fortune*'s Most Admired Companies list in 2004.

With the Telecommunications Act of 1996 passed by Congress, lifting ownership restrictions of radio stations, and a string of major acquisitions in 1999 and 2000 (including the purchases of radio bigwigs Jacor Communications, from which it inherited Rush Limbaugh and Dr. Laura, and AMFM). The $2.4 billion AMFM deal in 2000 lifted Clear Channel to the top radio spot in the U.S., adding 443 stations in 100 markets to the growing company's list of assets. That same year, the company purchased SFXEntertainment, giving the company a foothold in the market for live entertainment.

Investigations and legal issues

Often accused for trying to monopolize the U.S. entertainment market, Clear Channel was the subject on an investigation by the Department of Justice in 2003. The case, which suggested Clear Channel radio stations have refrained from playing artists unaffiliated with the company's entertainment division, seems to still be pending, but little has been reported in the media about it as of late.

In 2004, in a much publicized row, Clear Channel cut its ties to several radio talk shows, most prominently "*The Howard Stern Show*," deemed indecent by the FCC. In April 2004, the FCC levied a $495,000 fine against Clear Channel because of potty-mouthed content aired on Stern's show. Stern, along with Clear Channel competitor Infinity Broadcasting, sued the company for some $10 million for dropping the notorious talk radio celebrity. Clear Channel agreed to pay almost $2 million in settlements relating to indecency complaints. Stern and Clear Channel agreed to drop their lawsuits in February 2005.

Competing with satellite radio

Considered the future of radio broadcasting, digital satellite radio (spearheaded by rivals Sirius and XM Satellite) is increasingly becoming Clear Channel's largest threat. Many broadcasters, including the aforementioned Stern, have been lured to satellite radio because it's a non-FCC regulated landscape. Clear Channel is combating the competition by upgrading thousands of its stations, equipping them to provide digital quality sound.

(A new) Mays in charge

Late in 2004, longtime CEO Lowry Mays officially handed over the company reins to his son Mark Mays when Mark was permanently named CEO by the company's board of directors. Mark, who has worked for the company since 1989, had been serving as acting CEO. Lowry Mays remains chairman of Clear Channel. Another family member, Randall Mays, is the company's CFO.

Mark Mays will face many challenges as he assumes the top spot. In addition to the aforementioned threat by satellite radio, Clear Channel must also deal with the issue of how it will continue its phenomenal growth. While there aren't any limitations regarding the number of stations a company can own nationwide, there is an FCC mandate that allows an individual company to own no more than eight stations in the top 10 markets (for a total of 80 in the top 10), and Clear Channel already had 69 as of October 2004. A likely source of continued growth is the company's live entertainment segment. According to an October 2004 article in *Forbes*, this segment has realized a 45 percent increase in profits over two years, but contributes just 7 percent of Clear Channel's operating income. Clearly (no pun intended), there's room for growth in that segment.

Pushing the envelope

Clear Channel prides itself on being the country's largest station owner and on bringing innovations to the radio industry. The company has pioneered the creation of the so-called "studio envelope," a concept that places all the stations in a particular market at one location. The concept is designed to reduce costs because the various stations can share overhead. So far, the company has set up an envelope in Los Angeles and plans to roll out the concept to other markets.

In another bold move, Clear Channel announced in July 2004 that beginning January 1, 2005, it would sell fewer ads and provide more music and talk content on its stations. The decision is designed to be a win-win-win: Listeners will hear more of the music and talk shows they tune in for; advertisers, who used to pay roughly the same price for short ads as for long ones, will now pay about 25 percent less for a 30-second ad; and Clear Channel will be able to claim more revenue if, for example, it sells two 30-second ads in the place a full-minute ad it used to sell.

Visit Vault at **www.vault.com** for insider company profiles, expert advice, career message boards, expert resume reviews, the Vault Job Board and more.

VAULT CAREER LIBRARY   51

Balancing the books

After losing a whopping $16 billion in 2002, Clear Channel streamlined its operations and shed about 5,000 employees in 2003. These measures allowed the company to return to profitability after posting sales of $8.9 billion and $1.15 billion in net profit in the fiscal year 2003. For that year, the radio broadcasting segment represented 41 percent of total revenue. The outdoor advertising segment represented 24 percent of sales and the live entertainment segment represented and additional 30 percent.

Clear Channel reported revenue of $2.65 billion in the third quarter of 2004, a 4 percent increase over the $2.5 billion reported for the third quarter of 2003, according a wire report from Knight Ridder Tribune Business News. Clear Channel's net income was $261 million for the third quarter of 2004. The company's third quarter 2003 net income included approximately $685.6 million of pre-tax gains, $0.66 per diluted share after tax, related to the company's investment in Univision. But in the next quarter, Clear Channel posted a loss of more than $4 billion after writing down the vaule of some of its radio licenses.

Clear Channel times three

In an unexpected turn of events, Clear Channel announced in April 2005 that it would spin off its entertainment division and sell 10 percent of its stake in its outdoor advertising business in an initial public offering. Revenue in the company's radio and live entertainment segments had declined in the first quarter of 2005, however revenue for outdoor ad sales for the same period had jumped by 11 percent. According to a report in the *Boston Globe*, the IPO will occur sometime in the spring of 2005.

GETTING HIRED

Clear Channel lists all job openings on the careers section (www.clearcareers.com) of the company's web site. Once registered, jobs are searchable by division, country, state, city and keyword. The company also allows a similar search of its Career Fairs. Clear Channel also lists all of its openings on Hirediversity.com, a web site promoting career development for minorities.

CNN News Group

1 CNN Center
Atlanta, GA 30303
Phone: (404) 827-1500
Fax: (404) 827-2437
www.cnn.com

LOCATIONS

New York, NY (HQ)

THE STATS

Employer Type: Business segment of Turner Broadcasting
President, CNN News Group: Jim Walton
2003 Employees: 4,000
2004 Revenue ($mil.): $887.0

KEY COMPETITORS

CBS
FOX News
MSNBC TV

EMPLOYMENT CONTACT

about.bloomberg.com/careers/
index.html

THE SCOOP

All the news that's fit to air

The founding of the Cable News Network (CNN) in 1980 marked a milestone in the history of both journalism and cable television. The company, started by media mogul Ted Turner, was the first all-news network. Though deemed little more than a curiosity at first, CNN ushered in the age of the "24-hour news cycle." Over the years, the network's credibility and influence grew – by the 1990s, opinion polls consistently named CNN the most reputable news source. The network's success has spawned imitators such as MSNBC and Fox News, the latter of which has since overtaken CNN in the ratings.

Today, the company is a part of the Time Warner media empire. Though CNN remains in many ways the marquee name in cable news, the network's leadership is concerned about the substantial ratings lead that Fox has opened up. In an effort to wrest the ratings crown back from Fox, sweeping changes to the network's management and organizational structure were enacted in 2003.

Network architecture

CNN is a part of the complex multi-tiered Time Warner corporate hierarchy. At the lowest level, the CNN News Group is a family of 16 cable networks, eight web sites, two private networks and two radio networks. In addition the flagship CNN network, the company's other television properties include: *Headline News*, the CNN Airport Network, CNN International (English-language news for non-U.S. audiences), CNN en Espanol and several other foreign-language broadcasting outlets. On the Web, the company offers CNN.com and CNNMoney.com, as well as foreign-language news sites such as: CNN.de (German), CNNenEspanol.com and CNN.com.mx (Spanish), CNN.co.jp (Japanese) and CNNArabic.com. All of these news outlets are served by CNN's global newsgathering operation made up of 38 bureaus and 900 affiliates.

The company's flagship network reaches more than 86 million households in the United States; worldwide, CNN and its sibling stations reach an audience of more than 1 billion people in 212 countries. The CNN News Group is owned by the Turner Broadcasting System, which also includes other cable networks such as the TBS Superstation, Turner Network Television (TNT), the Cartoon Network and Turner Classic Movies, as well as the Atlanta Braves, Atlanta Hawks and Atlanta Thrashers professional sports franchises. Turner Broadcasting is in turn owned by the media conglomerate Time Warner, which owns other properties in various media industries. A small sampling of Time Warner's other businesses includes: Internet service provider America Online, Warner Brothers Studios, Time Inc. magazine publishing, Time Warner Cable and the Home Box Office (HBO) network.

Cable pioneer

CNN broadcast its first news report on June 1, 1980, and has been reporting continuously ever since. Though the concept of around-the-clock news seems commonplace now, it was a radical idea at the time of the network's founding. CNN struggled early on, losing an estimated $2 million per month. Ted Turner was fully committed to seeing CNN succeed, however, and was willing to bankroll the network's growing pains with the profits from his other cable network, the TBS Superstation. With its studio headquarters located in Atlanta, CNN opened its first foreign news bureaus in London and Rome. The broadcast networks were unwilling to cede the cable news business to Turner, however, and soon announced plans for a competing service. In response, Turner founded CNN2, the predecessor of today's Headline News, in January 1982. The networks' offering, called the Satellite News Channel (SNC), was a joint venture between ABC and Westinghouse (then the owner CBS). Launched in June 1982, SNC failed to attract much interest or advertising revenue. In October 1983, Turner bought out his rival for $25 million and promptly killed SNC.

The spoils of war

Having eliminated its competition, CNN's future was secure. The network's reach expanded and by 1985 was available in more than 30 million homes in the United States. That same year, CNN recorded its first annual profit. In the late 1980s, it added additional foreign news bureaus in Bonn, Moscow, Cairo and Tel Aviv, but it was not until after the 1991 Gulf War that CNN's popularity really took off. Millions of viewers tuned in as CNN broadcast live from Baghdad as it came under attack by U.S. warplanes. The war turned CNN correspondents like Bernard Shaw and Peter Arnett into household names and elevated the network's reputation in the eyes of the American viewing audience. Drawing nearly 10 times as may viewers as it normally did, CNN's 24-hour coverage of the war proved irresistible. By the mid-1990s, opinion polls named CNN as the "most fair" and "most trusted" news source, topping the Big 3 broadcast networks.

Visit Vault at **www.vault.com** for insider company profiles, expert advice, career message boards, expert resume reviews, the Vault Job Board and more.

VAULT CAREER LIBRARY   **55**

Overtaken by Fox

In 1995, CNN launched its companion web site, CNN.com, touted by the company as the first news site on the Internet. That same year, with the network's annual revenue approaching $1 billion, Turner decided to sell the entirety of his Turner Broadcasting System to Time Warner. In 1996, CNN faced competition for the first time since the early 1980s when both Fox News (owned by News Corp.) and MSNBC (a joint venture between General Electric and Microsoft) went on the air. In February 1999, CNN invested an undisclosed amount in WebMD, a provider of services for the health care industry, as part of an agreement to exchange news and advertising with the company. That June, Lou Dobbs, executive vice president of CNN and president of CNNfn (the company's financial news network that went off the air in November 2004) left the company to start a new web site, space.com. Dobbs had been with CNN since its inception as anchor of *Moneyline*.

Despite the 1995 change in ownership, the Turner networks largely maintained their operational independence up until the 2001 merger of America Online and Time Warner. Following the deal, AOLTimeWarner's (now known simply as Time Warner) corporate "streamlining" resulted in the layoffs of more than 400 CNN staffers – nearly 10 percent of its workforce. Around the same time, CNN began losing ground to Fox News in the ratings competition, and morale at the network sunk. Chairman and CEO Tom Johnson announced his retirement in June 2001, after a 10-year run with the company. By January 2002, Fox News had scored its first ratings win ever over CNN.

Leadership change

Fox never looked back after pulling ahead. For the full year of 2002, Fox's lead over CNN ranged from 536,000 to 667,000 viewers daily. In January 2003, the network tapped Jim Walton to turn its fortunes around. He replaced Walter Isaacson as the chairman of the CNN News Group. Isaacson's tenure with the company was brief – just 18 months – after which he left to become president and CEO of the Aspen Institute, a Washington D.C.-based leadership and research organization. Isaacson's announcement came one day after Steve Case announced he would resign as chairman of Time Warner.

Walton, a CNN lifer, joined the network as a video journalist soon after its launch in 1980. He oversaw the network's failed attempt to start up a sports network (CNN/SI) in the 1990s, but evidently impressed the right people anyway. Since 2001, he had served as chief operating officer (COO) of the company, the network's No.-2 executive position. Soon after his promotion, Walton noted that the channel's ongoing uphill battle against Fox News was the last thing on his mind. "Across the news group the direction of our different businesses are headed in the right way," Walton said in January 2003. He faces a formidable set of challenges. Fox News now consistently places among the top 10 cable networks. With less flashy and personality-driven programming than Fox, CNN has struggled to entice viewers to tune in for extended periods of time. Still, CNN does have higher advertising revenue and subscription fees than Fox does, thanks to its longer history and premium brand. Even this advantage will soon erode however, unless the network is successful in reversing its recent ratings decline.

Back to the Gulf

One of Walton's first major moves was to cancel Connie Chung's evening show. Chung had been one of Isaacson's highest-profile acquisitions, but ended up lasting less than a year at the network. She departed with one year left on her $2 million/year contract. The show she hosted, *Connie Chung Tonight*, attracted fairly solid ratings numbers, but was unloved by many CNN staffers. Focusing on tawdry, tabloid-style news stories, many at the network felt that the show was tarnishing CNN's image. In a clear indication of his commitment to "serious" news, Walton filled Chung's slot in the schedule with a new show hosted by Paula Zahn. Around the same time, he also axed the call-in show *Talk Back Live* and downgraded the high-volume "debate" show *Crossfire* from an hour-long prime-time show to a half-hour afternoon program. The spring 2003 U.S.-Iraq War provided a predictable boost in ratings, but unlike the first Gulf War, this time CNN had competition. Despite having twice as many correspondents on the scene as Fox News had, CNN still lagged behind its rival. CNN tried to boost ratings with new shows, such as an hour-long daily television show called *Dolans Unscripted*, hosted by popular national radio show hosts and financial experts Ken and Daria Dolan. However, for the whole of 2003, CNN averaged 665,000 daily viewers (up a healthy 24 percent), but Fox turned in an even more impressive performance with 1.02 million daily viewers (up 53 percent).

The Prince of Atlanta

More changes came to the network in September 2003 when Walton named Princell Hair as his new general manager of CNN/U.S., succeeding Teya Ryan. Previously, Hair had been vice-president of news for the Viacom television stations group. In that position, he managed local news coverage at the 39 Viacom-owned stations in the United States. Having never worked for a national news organization before,

Visit Vault at www.vault.com for insider company profiles, expert advice, career message boards, expert resume reviews, the Vault Job Board and more.

VAULT CAREER LIBRARY

57

Hair's appointment to the high-profile CNN post raised a few eyebrows among industry insiders. Walton, however, expressed confidence in Hair's ability, praising his "extensive and impressive" credentials and his "demonstrated ability to lead a news organization." At the same time, the network announced that its 11 U.S. bureaus would be consolidated under the management of four regional bureau chiefs. In Washington, David Bohrman – who had been producing the New York-based prime-time program *NewsNight* with Aaron Brown – was appointed the new D.C. bureau chief, replacing Kathryn Kross. The D.C. position is one of the network's top news jobs. In addition to regular newsgathering responsibilities, Bohrman will also oversee the production CNN's D.C.-based shows: *Crossfire*, *Wolf Blitzer Reports*, *Inside Politics* and *The Capital Gang*. Despite the dramatic off-camera changes, both Hair and Walton insist that the network's programming will be largely unaffected. CNN execs are reportedly pleased at the performance of its primetime lineup as well as its weekday breakfast show *American Morning*. After experimenting with a number of different formulas for their evening schedule over the summer in 2003, CNN has settled on two one-hour programs at the start of their prime-time block: *Anderson Cooper 360* at 7 p.m. and *Paula Zahn Now* at 8 p.m. Both programs have their work cut out for them, though. Cooper draws 457,000 viewers each evening and Zahn attracts 610,000, while their Fox News counterparts, Shepard Smith and Bill O'Reilly, draw 1.3 million and 2 million viewers respectively.

In and out

Former CBS news executive Jonathan Klein joined CNN as president of CNN/U.S. in November 2004, overseeing CNN's domestic news network. Klein replaced Princell Hair, who was promoted to senior vice president of program and talent development for the entire CNN News Group portfolio. Before the CNN gig, Klein had been a founder and CEO of The FeedRoom Inc., a builder of broadband web sites for Fortune 1000 companies that oversees the world's largest broadband news network and is one of the top video streamers. Klein said his focus for CNN in the future would be to "address how we tell stories" and to create a "product that engages the audience in primetime." He said his inspiration will come not only from competitors like Fox News, but also from channels like the History Channel and Court TV, which "take events of the real world and turn them into compelling stories."

The news network suffered a public blow in February 2005, when Eason Jordan, the chief news executive, resigned amid a fiery debate over controversial remarks regarding journalists killed in the Middle East that he made at the World Economic

Forum in Davos, Switzerland, in January 2005. Though a definitive transcript from the forum was unavailable to the public, U.S. Democrats Rep. Barney Frank and Sen. Christopher Dodd criticized Jordan's remarks, which apparently suggested coalition trips "targeted" overseas journalists, citing such incidents as the U.S. bombing of Baghdad's Palestine Hotel, a refuge for foreign journalists, and the fatal shooting of a cameraman outside Abu Gharib prison. Defenders of Jordan, a 23-year CNN veteran, claimed the story had been blown out of proportion by bloggers, eager to take down a network seen as "too liberal."

GETTING HIRED

The world according to CNN

The majority of jobs with CNN are based at the company's corporate headquarters in Atlanta, though workers may also be based at one of the network's 38 worldwide news bureaus. CNN maintains 11 news bureaus in the United States and an additional 27 overseas. Domestic bureaus (aside from the Atlanta headquarters) are located in Boston, Chicago, Dallas, Denver, Los Angeles, Miami, New York, San Francisco, Seattle and Washington, D.C. International bureaus are located in Baghdad, Bangkok, Beijing, Beirut, Berlin, Buenos Aires, Cairo, Dubai, Frankfurt, Havana, Hong Kong, Islamabad, Istanbul, Jakarta, Jerusalem, Johannesburg, Lagos, London, Madrid, Mexico City, Moscow, New Delhi, Paris, Rome, Seoul, Sydney and Tokyo. The Turner Broadcasting web site contains more information on working and interning at CNN. For a list of open positions and to apply online, applicants should visit parent company Time Warner's web site.

Visit Vault at **www.vault.com** for insider company profiles, expert advice, career message boards, expert resume reviews, the Vault Job Board and more.

VAULT CAREER LIBRARY   59

Comcast Corporation

1500 Market Street
Philadelphia, PA 19102-2148
Phone: (215) 665-1700
Fax: (215) 981-7790
www.comcast.com

LOCATIONS

Philadelphia, PA (HQ)

THE STATS

Employer Type: Public Company
Stock Symbol: CMCSA
Stock Exchange: NASDAQ
Chairman and CEO: Brian L. Roberts
2004 Employees: 74,000
2004 Revenue ($mil.): $20,307

KEY COMPETITORS

DIRECTV
EchoStar Communications
Time Warner Cable

EMPLOYMENT CONTACT

careers.comcast.com

THE SCOOP

Family business gets big

A family-owned business, Comcast began with a single cable television franchise in 1963. Today it is the largest cable company in the United States, serving more than 21 million subscribers. The company sports impressive numbers across the board, with more than 7.6 million digital video customers, 5.2 million high-speed data customers and 1.2 million cable telephone customers. The company is also a leader in eight of the top 10 U.S. markets and boasts about 70 percent of the subscribers in the top 20 U.S. markets. "Diversification" is the latest buzzword in the cable industry, but Comcast has long focused on expanding its business lines. In the late 1980s, Comcast acquired the American Cellular Network and is now a major player in the cellular service market. Comcast also purchased a controlling stake in QVC, the cable shopping channel and provides some telephone services. It even owns a controlling interest in the NBA's Philadelphia 76ers and the NHL's Philadelphia Flyers. The company also has investments in content providers such as Comcast Spectacor, Comcast SportsNet, Cable Sports Southeast, E! Entertainment Television, G4 and others.

Cable ready

During the 1990s, Comcast began to devote more attention to investing in and developing cable content. In 1995, the company formed its C3 division (Comcast Content and Communication) to create new cable programming and plan ventures related to software and cyberspace. Together with Disney, Comcast owns a majority stake in the E! Television network. Comcast is also betting that cable will be the wave of the future for the Internet and that its diverse product line will enable it to sell product bundles, multiple telephone lines and Internet service packages to customers.

The return of the bartering system

In March 1999, Comcast jumped on the cable consolidation bandwagon and announced a plan to merge with rival MediaOne Group Inc., in an all-stock deal worth $48.6 billion. But two months later, MediaOne received a more lucrative offer from AT&T Corp. and terminated its deal with Comcast, which entered into a trade of some of its cable systems with those of AT&T instead. Comcast gained control of Lenfest, Philadelphia's major cable system, and all Washington, D.C.-area based cable systems except Fairfax County's. In November 1999, Comcast bought Lenfest outright for $5.2 billion in stock. Through the trades and acquisitions, Comcast gained one million cable subscribers, the ability to provide multiple services (Internet, cable, and local and long-distance telephone) to households and cachet as the nation's third-largest cable company. The trade of cable systems further allowed Comcast to cluster its systems while broadening its range of service. Comcast continued to swap cable systems throughout 1999 in order to strengthen its presence in the Mid-Atlantic area. Through an agreement with Adelphia Communications, Comcast gained approximately four million customers in a broad geographic swath that covered New Jersey to Washington, D.C.

Technology leaders

Comcast is constantly trying to improve its broadband technology. In coalition with WorldGate Communications Inc., Comcast launched a service offering Internet access, e-mail and channel hyperlinking to television-related web sites in the Philadelphia area in the fall of 1999. Hyperlinking allows television viewers to link to related web sites of television programs while actually viewing a particular program. Comcast is also among the first North American cable companies to deliver interactive television services, using Liberate TV Navigator, a software program developed by Liberate Technologies.

Patient suitor

A tumultuous series of events was set into motion once AT&T rejected Comcast's bid for its broadband operations in 2001, capped by AT&T's agreement to merge its cable and broadband operations with Comcast. AT&T's board championed Comcast's bid-sweetened with offers to assume more of AT&T's debt and liabilities – only after striking down proposals from AOL Time Warner and Cox Communications. After lengthy negotiations the deal was finally struck in November 2002 when AT&T spun off the broadband unit and merged it with Comcast in a $29 billion deal. This move created the nation's largest cable company with 21 million subscribers across 41 states, and is valued at around $60 billion.

The merger made Comcast, which formerly counted about 8.5 million cable subscribers as customers, a market leader in every digital technology category in the cable industry: digital cable services, video-on-demand and voice over IP telephony services. Under terms of the deal, AT&T shareholders still own about 56 percent of the merged company, and the Roberts family, which founded Comcast, holds about a

66 percent voting interest in the new company. And the deal looks to have had a positive effect on Comcast's bottom line. For the full year 2003, revenue rose from $8.10 billion to $18.35 billion.

Comings and goings

In September 2003, Comcast sold its interest in QVC home shopping network to Liberty Media Corporation for $7.9 billion in cash and stock. Liberty now owns 98 percent of QVC. At the time of the deal, Comcast said it will not use the cash to fund any acquisitions in the near-term. For now, the company's main priority is to upgrade the former AT&T systems so that Comcast's entire network will have state-of-the-art digital technology. The upgrade will also enable Comcast to offer high-speed Internet access and other services in markets where such services aren't currently available.

But the company did add to its holdings in March 2004 when it bought the TechTV cable network from Microsoft billionaire Paul Allen's Vulcan Programming Inc. for $300 million. Comcast intends to merge TechTV with its G4 network, which is devoted to the world of video games. EchoStar Communications Corp., which runs the Dish Network satellite television service, is also taking a stake of about 12 percent in the upstart network. The deal more than doubled the reach of G4, boosting its reach from about 15 million homes to about 44 million TechTV was originally launched in 1998 as Ziff-Davis TV.

Close, but not quite yet

In February 2004, Comcast launched a surprising, ambitious and unsolicited bid to acquire media giant Walt Disney Co. The $54 billion offer was firmly rejected by Disney's shareholders immediately, but that hasn't quashed speculation that Comcast may try again.

If the deal were to eventually go through, Comcast would own the ABC broadcast network as well as the Disney film studio, ESPN and other Disney assets. The proposed deal also put some unwanted added pressure on embattled Disney Chairman Michael Eisner, who at the time was facing a campaign by former Disney directors Roy Disney and Stanley Gold to oust him. In March, Eisner survived the coup attempt, but had to resign as chairman of the board of Disney. Since Eisner was unwilling to discuss the merger, Comcast made an end run around him and sent a letter to Disney's board making its offer public. As of April 2004, no deal was on the horizon, but don't count Comcast out.

Visit Vault at **www.vault.com** for insider company profiles, expert advice, career message boards, expert resume reviews, the Vault Job Board and more.

VAULT CAREER LIBRARY

63

GETTING HIRED

Comcast's employment web page, located at careers.comcast.com, provides links to each of the company's divisions and a listing of the available positions within each department as well as job descriptions. Comcast asks that those applying for a position within its Comcast Corporation or Comcast Interactive Communications division complete an online resume rather than sending one via snail mail. Following an electronic resume submission, the company may ask qualified applicants to send an actual resume as well.

Condé Nast Publications Inc.

4 Times Square, 17th Floor
New York, NY 10036
Phone: (212) 286-2860
Fax: (212) 286-5960
www.condenast.com

LOCATIONS

New York, NY (HQ)

THE STATS

Employer Type: Subsidiary of
Advance Publications
Chairman: Samuel I. (Si) Newhouse, Jr.
CEO: Charles H. (Chuck) Townsend

KEY COMPETITORS

Hachette-Filipacchi
Hearst
Time Warner

Visit Vault at **www.vault.com** for insider company profiles, expert advice,
career message boards, expert resume reviews, the Vault Job Board and more.

V/\ULT CAREER LIBRARY   65

THE SCOOP

Glamour and so much more

Boasting some of the world's trendiest magazines and led by some of New York's hottest writers and editors, Condé Nast is the epitome of the rarefied New York world of fashion publishing. In addition to its flagship magazine *Vogue*, Condé Nast also publishes *Vanity Fair*, *Glamour*, *Self*, *Allure*, *Condé Nast Traveler*, *Bride's* and *Architectural Digest*. Owned by S.I. Newhouse's Advance Publications – the publishing conglomerate that also owns the largest privately held empire newspaper chain – Condé Nast's presence is not limited to New York. As leaders of the world's foremost fashion magazines, the company's globetrotting editors have established outposts in London, Paris, Milan and other fashionable locales.

Glamour is the publisher's real cash cow. The beauty/fashion/career/sex/lifestyle publication has reached a paid circulation of 2.3 million, with profits reportedly in the millions. Despite today's high profits and high circulation figures, Condé Nast hasn't always been profitable. After former CEO Steve Florio took the helm at Condé Nast in 1994, the extravagant salaries and too-good-to-be-true perks the company was known for were drastically cut back. These moves proved to be a boon for Condé Nast's bottom line: By 1996, the magazine empire had produced its first profit in years – an estimated $100 million.

That's the way the ball bounces

Since that time, Condé Nast has continued to thrive. And while the fashion mags has been its bread and butter, the company has also sought to move outside of the fashion world – with mixed results. In 1997 the company launched two new magazines – *Sports for Women* and *House & Garden*. In January 1998, Condé Nast spent a reported $5 million to buy out a competitor to *Sports for Women*, a magazine started by tennis legend Billie Jean King called *Women's Sport + Fitness*, to protect its high-profile women's sports launch. But the aggressive move didn't pan out for CN; *Sports for Women* was itself later discontinued.

In February 1998, highbrow magazine *The New Yorker*, owned by S.I. Newhouse, was became a member of the Condé Nast fold. Condé Nast also ventured into the Information Age, agreeing to buy high-tech mag *Wired* for a reported $85 million.

A publishing giant to contend with

The company became even stronger, thanks to Advance Publications' acquisition of Fairchild Publishing (*Jane*, *W*, *Women's Wear Daily*) from Walt Disney in 1999. The only two top fashion magazines in the country not run by Condé Nast are *Harper's Bazaar* and *Elle*.

To augment its position as one of the country's leading publishers, Condé Nast has worked hard to establish a presence online. CondéNet.com consolidates its magazines into different categories in order to attract a broader audience. Epicurious.com draws from *Bon Appetit* and *Gourmet*, while Style.com supplements the company's fashion coverage and Concierge.com attracts readers interested in the travel magazines Condé Nast publishes. In 2001, Condé Nast also launched Swoon.com, an interactive site offering advice on love and horoscopes.

In 2001, Condé Nast's publications moved to a brand-spanking-new 48-story skyscraper (the first in New York since 1992) at 4 Times Square, complete with a cafeteria designed by the famed Frank Gehry, no less. What more would can one expect from the fashionable publishing empire?

A good idea

Condé Nast strengthened its commitment to bilingual publishing in March 2002 when it finalized the purchase of the remaining assets of Ideas Publishing Group (a Miami-based publisher of Spanish-language editions of major American magazines) that it didn't already own. The company had originally acquired a majority interest in IPG in January of 2001. Ideas currently publishes three titles in collaboration with Condé Nast (*Vogue en Espanol*, *Glamour en Espanol* and *Architectural Digest en Espanol*) and six others under licensing agreements: *Newsweek en Espanol*, *Discover en Espanol*, *Teen en Espanol*, *Prevention en Espanol*, *Motor Trend en Espanol* and *Men's Fitness en Espanol*. The IPG magazines reach a monthly audience of five million Spanish-speaking readers in nineteen Latin American countries and in United States.

More print

In March 2004, the company announced plans for a new shopping title all about furnishing and decorating the home. *Domino* is the third shopping-focused glossy from the company. The publisher launched *Lucky*, a women's magazine packed with pictures of the latest shoes, handbags and make-up, in 2000 and came out with a men's version called *Cargo* in March 2004. *Domino* hit newsstands in April 2005.

Visit Vault at **www.vault.com** for insider company profiles, expert advice,
career message boards, expert resume reviews, the Vault Job Board and more.

V/\ULT CAREER LIBRARY   **67**

No doubt the company hopes *Cargo* and *Domino* will be big hits with advertisers just as *Lucky* has proven to be – that magazine racked up a 46 percent gain in ad pages in 2003 compared to 2002.

The announcement of *Domino*'s eminent arrival came just days after the guilty verdict against lifestyle guru Martha Stewart on charges of lying to investigators about a stock sale. Stewart's *Martha Stewart Living* magazine, which takes a how-to approach to decorating and gardening, experienced a sharp advertising drop during her legal travails, nearly 70 percent from 2002 to 2004.

It has also been rumored that the company is looking at ways to replicate the success of *Glamour*, and is considering a magazine targeting women in their 30s. As of March 2004, the as-yet-unnamed title is at dummy stage, according to industry reports. "We haven't made a decision yet," Nicholas Coleridge, the managing director of Condé Nast, told brandrepublic.com, an industry publication. "It's a crowded market and we'd want to be sure that we could bring something out that was vibrant and exciting." In March 2005, the company launched *Easy Living* for women 30-59 in the U.K.

The company entered a new realm – the "over-50" consumer market – in the fall of 2004, with *2*, a British monthly magazine aimed at the baby-boomer generation. Also in the works is an Internet-based radio station, also called "2" which will launch in 2005 to support the magazine. According to *Cavendish Corporate Finance*, *2*'s financial backers, the new glossy is aimed at "grown-up kids" and will be "fun, non-political and informative."

In *Vogue*

After two years, four test issues and rumors about an aborted launch, in January 2003 Condé Nast debuted a younger sister to its *Vogue* magazine: *Teen Vogue*.

For the most part, the magazine emulates its older sibling in design and content, with editors pushing fashion coverage over pieces about sex and boyfriends. Editor-in-chief Amy Astley, former beauty director at *Vogue*, told *Folio* magazine, "We decided that if we were going to do a magazine that had the valuable *Vogue* name on it, we had to offer something that spoke to our heritage and that was different from what's out there."

Also "in vogue" these days is a Chinese edition of the fashion staple, which will be launched in September 2005. Condé Nast will work with the Chinese magazine publisher, China Pictorial, and the General Administration for Press and Publication to cater to the Chinese market, and "celebrate Chinese culture and values."

Comings and goings

College co-eds will no longer be able to find the cure for make-up gone amuck. In October 2001, Condé Nast shut down the women's magazine *Mademoiselle* after six decades of publication. Then-Condé Nast CEO and president Steven Florio said the closing was due to economic difficulties brought on by dwindling advertising and the aftereffects of September 11.

Soon after *Mademoiselle* bid its final farewell, Condé Nast gained a new magazine. In January 2002, it bought *Modern Bride* from Primedia, Inc. for a reported $52 million. As part of the acquisition of the national bridal magazine, Condé Nast also bought a group of smaller, regional magazines collectively called *Modern Bride Connections*. In October 2004, the company expanded its teen offerings with the purchase of Gruner + Jahr USA's *YM* magazine.

Award-winning publications

In March 2004, the National Magazine Awards nominees were announced, and like most years, Condé Nast publications racked up their share of nominations. Teen Vogue, launched by Condé Nast in 2003, was a first-time finalist for general excellence among magazines with circulations between 250,000 and 500,000. *The New Yorker* led the field with 11 nominations in nine categories, raising to 51 the total earned by the magazine during David Remnick's first five years as editor. Remnick's magazine picked up awards for Feature Writing, Public Interest and Essays, while *Gourmet* won general excellence for its circulation base.

The 2005 NMA nominees featured the usual suspects – *Gourmet*, *Wired*, *The New Yorker*, *Vanity Fair* and *Glamour* – for general excellence, and at least one Condé Nast publication in nearly every category, from photo essay to public interest to profile writing to fiction.

New men on top

Advance established the Condé Nast Media Group in 2004 as a new division to support corporate sales and integrated marketing for the company's consumer magazines. Richard D. Beckman, former executive vice president and chief marketing officer of Condé Nast Publications, was named president. One of

Visit Vault at **www.vault.com** for insider company profiles, expert advice, career message boards, expert resume reviews, the Vault Job Board and more.

VAULT CAREER LIBRARY

69

CNMG's first projects was a joint venture with Mazda North American Operations, a contest asking consumers for photographs best representing Mazda's "Zoom Zoom" slogan. A 12-page advertising section published in the October 2004 issues of *GQ*, *Details*, *House & Garden*, *Lucky*, *Cargo*, *Vanity Fair*, *Bon Appetit*, *Condé Nast Traveler* and *Wired* introduced the contest, and a number of prizes, including a 2005 Mazda vehicle.

At the start of 2005, Thomas J. Wallace, former editor-in-chief of *Condé Nast Traveler*, was named editorial director of Condé Nast Publications. Wallace succeeded James Truman, who spent eleven years in the position.

GETTING HIRED

Tough egg to crack

Getting a foot in the door at Condé Nast is tough, but the company does sometimes post job advertisements on various media-related web pages. The company has also launched an employee referral program, in which current employees can receive a sum of money if they refer a candidate that eventually gets hired.

On the CondéNet homepage, click on jobs@CondéNet.com to find out more about openings at the site. Do not send resumes through e-mail. Condé Nast's homepage, www.condénast.com, says the company will discard all electronic queries. Instead, try mailing a paper resume and cover letter to: The Condé Nast Publications, 4 Times Square, N.Y., N.Y., 10036. Make sure ATTN: Human Resources is clearly marked on the envelope.

Cox Communications, Inc.

1400 Lake Hearn Drive
Atlanta, GA 30319
Phone: (404) 843-5000
Fax: (404) 843-5975
www.cox.com

LOCATIONS

Atlanta, GA (HQ)
Abilene, TX
Amarillo, TX
Andrews, TX
Bakersfield, CA
Baltimore, MD
Clovis, NM
Derby, KS
Dodge City, KS
Eureka, CA
Greenville, NC
Hartford, CT
Ketchum, ID
Las Vegas, NV
Manchester, CT
New Orleans, LA
Oklahoma City, OK
Omaha, NE
Orange County, CA
Phoenix, AZ
Providence, RI
Rocky Mount, NC
San Diego, CA
Santa Barbara, CA
Sweetwater, TX
Topeka, KS

THE STATS

Employer Type: Subsidiary of Cox
Enterprises
Chairman: James C. Kennedy
President and CEO: James O.
Robbins
2004 Employees: 22,150
2004 Revenue ($bil.): $6.4

KEY COMPETITORS

Comcast
DIRECTV
Time Warner Cable

EMPLOYMENT CONTACT

www.cox.com/CoxCareer

THE SCOOP

A leader in broadband

Atlanta-based Cox Communications is one of the largest broadband communications company in the U.S., with about 6.7 million customers, including 6.3 million basic cable subscribers across the country. It is the nation's third-largest cable TV company offering both analog cable and digital video, including the new and very popular video-ion-demand service. Cox also provides telephone service, local and long-distance phone service and high-speed Internet access and invests in programming services such as Discovery Communications.

Part of a media family

Cox Communications is a wholly-owned subsidiary of Cox Enterprises Inc., which has interests in newspapers, television and radio stations. The company brought in $11.6 billion in revenue during 2004. Cox traces its roots back to 1898 when James M. Cox bought the *Dayton Evening News*. (Cox later served as Ohio's governor for three terms and ran as the Democratic party's presidential candidate in 1920.)

The company first entered the cable TV business in 1962. After the 1996 Telecommunications Reform Act, it expanded into advanced video, voice and data services. In 2002, the company earned the Cablevision/Multichannel News Operator of the Year Award for the third time in the past 10 years and *CED Magazine*'s Operator of the Year honors. In 2003 and 2004, its western region operations garnered the J.D. Powers & Associates' Customer Satisfaction Award for the company's local and long distance telephone service.

Growth areas

High-speed Internet and telephone services are seen as the next big growth areas for cable companies. Cox has a good lead in both. In 2004, the company's high-speed Internet subscribers surpassed the 2.6 million mark and its growing phone business reached 1.3 million customers.

Cox came up with the idea of offering discounts to customers subscribing to multiple services, a practice called bundling. The company now boasts over 2.7 million bundled customers, and the number's climbing.

The company offers high-speed Internet services, switched voice and long-distance service, and dedicated voice, data and video transport services for businesses, government and military clients through Cox Business Services unit. In 2004, the division had a 23 percent growth in revenue.

The payoff

Thanks to its growing business and the popularity of, among other things, its Internet options, Cox posted some good numbers for 2004. During the year, the company added 268,997 Cox Digital Cable subscribers, an 11 percent increase over the previous year. Cox also added 584,009 high-speed Internet customers. The company continued to expand its telephone segment in 2004, adding more than 76,000 customers and ending the year with just over 1.3 million, a 32 percent growth 2003. Revenue for 2004 reached $6.4 billion, an increase of 12 percent over 2003.

Keeping it together

In February 2004, Cox agreed to a multi-year deal with sports network ESPN that will keep ESPN's channels on Cox systems. The agreement finally put to rest a very public battle between the two sides. The acrimony first bubbled up when Cox claimed that ESPN was boosting the fee Cox was required to pay for the right to carry the sports network's programming by as much as 20 percent over the previous year's fee. The tensions increased when ESPN denied that the rate increases were as high as Cox claimed and said that the rates Cox passes on to its subscribers have more to do with its own overhead expenses than programming costs.

Cox's existing contract with ESPN was to have expired in the spring of 2004, but under the new deal, the Walt Disney-owned ESPN and ESPN2 will stay on Cox's expanded basic cable tier of channels. Originally, Cox wanted to either pay a lower fee for the rights to ESPN or have the right to put the networks on a premium pay tier, where it could then charge customers a higher fee for access to the channels.

Although all the terms of the deal weren't released, it seems that the deal also allows Cox to launch the Spanish-language service ESPN Deportes in markets where it offers a Spanish-language service, and continues the Cox distribution of ESPNEWS, ESPN Classic and ESPN HD. In a related sports programming vein, in December 2003, Cox inked a six-year deal with Fox Sports Net's regional networks that reportedly called for a lower fee to the to Fox owner, News Corp., than Fox had originally demanded.

New deal in the works?

Tongues began to wag in March 2004 when word leaked out that Cox was interested in acquiring some or all of the assets of Adelphia Communications, the beleaguered cable TV system operator. Adelphia founder John Rigas and his two sons are currently on trial on conspiracy and fraud charges, accused of taking company assets and money for personal use. Adelphia filed for bankruptcy protection in 2002, after it was discovered that the company was responsible for billions of dollars in loans taken out by the Rigas family to purchase the Buffalo Sabres NHL hockey franchise, a private golf course and private jets, among other things. Adelphia is currently the nation's fifth-largest cable operator, (one rung below Cox) and despite the financial trouble, is still a highly valuable property with 5.4 million subscribers to its basic cable service.

The speculation started when a report in the trade magazine *Broadcasting and Cable* stated that Cox is "carefully evaluating" how it could buy all or part of Adelphia. The article quoted Cox CEO Jim Robbins as saying that he doesn't want to do a deal with Adelphia until it emerges from its Chapter 11 proceedings, but left the door open to action after the case is settled.

Snooping around

In April 2004, in a sign of our security-heightened times, Cox contracted with infrastructure provider VeriSign to open up its Internet-based telephone service to law enforcement officials looking to eavesdrop on suspected criminal activity. Cox is set to implement the VeriSign NetDiscovery Services for Cox's new voice over Internet Protocol (VoIP) cable service. The move comes as Cox is trying to comply with the 1994 Federal Communications Assistance for Law Enforcement Act, which requires telecommunications carriers to ensure their networks comply with government specifications for wiretapping by law enforcement. Cox first launched its VoIP service in 2003, and as of April 2004, the service is still not widely available.

Private Enterprises

In late 2004, Cox Enterprises, the company's parent, took its cable business private when it bought out all of the stock held by public shareholders. The firm says that by doing this, it can now more freely spend capital to grow bsiness with a long-term growth strategy. The company also believes that it can react more quickly to competition from satellite television, telephone companies and other newly-emerging Internet service providers. To lighten its debt, Cox is exploring options like selling its non-strategic cable systems, which serve about 900,000 subcribers in mainly rural areas in Texas, Louisiana, Arkansas, Oklahoma and North Carolina.

GETTING HIRED

Cox places a listing of all available positions nationwide on its web page located at www.cox.com, where job hunters can search by location or business segment. Those interested can submit an online application through the site as well. The site also offers a list of campus recruiting events the company participates in, and internship information.

Visit Vault at **www.vault.com** for insider company profiles, expert advice, career message boards, expert resume reviews, the Vault Job Board and more.

V∆ULT CAREER LIBRARY

75

Creative Artists Agency

9830 Wilshire Blvd.
Beverly Hills, CA 90212-1825
Phone: (310) 288-4545
Fax: (310) 288-4800
www.caa.com

LOCATIONS

Beverly Hills, CA (HQ)

THE STATS

Employer Type: Private Company
Co-Chairman: Rick Nicita
Co-Chairman and Head of Television:
Lee Gabler

KEY COMPETITORS

IMG
International Creative Management
William Morris

EMPLOYMENT CONTACT

Creative Artists Agency
9830 Wiltshire Blvd.
Beverly Hills, CA 90212-1825

THE SCOOP

A-list stars and the agents who rep them

Michael Ovitz and partners Ron Meyer and Bill Haber founded Creative Artists Agency in 1975 to manage the careers of performers and others in the entertainment industry. The agency's A-list talent includes big-name players such as Steven Spielberg, Madonna and Bruce Springsteen. CAA also boasts a number of top-notch corporate clients such as Coca-Cola and Procter & Gamble. (Other services offered by CAA include strategic counsel, financing, and consulting.) Don't look to find out much more from the company's web site (www.caa.com), though. Privately held CAA only posts basic contact information and there's no actual content. (Gotta love Hollywood.)

Swimming with sharks

In 1995 Michael Ovitz left the agency to become the president of Disney, but was soon fired from the new position. CAA, found itself on the defensive when Ovitz started Artists Management Group three years later, saying it was putatively not an "agency" but a "management group." Ovitz cleaned out more than his desk when he left – he began luring CAA-represented talent to join his management group. While it is not odd for actors and directors to have an agency and a management group, CAA president Richard Lovett believed that AMG was a competitive agency, thinly disguised as a separate and harmless management group. In January 1999, CAA announced that it would no longer represent any star who is also represented by AMG, compelling a number of clients to defect, including actor Robin Williams and director Martin Scorcese. According to company sources, over 90 percent of Creative Artists' clients remained represented by the company.

However, CAA got the last laugh when Ovitz' fledgling "management group" took a nosedive just a few years later, with big-name clients such as Robin Williams, Oliver Stone and Katie Couric leaving for other agencies. In 2002 Ovitz sold off the group's assets to The Firm, an up-and-coming LA-based agency. As an interesting side note: information has recently surfaced that makes one wonder why Ovitz ever left CAA in the first place. Ovitz has been embroiled in a Disney shareholder derivative lawsuit for more than seven years. The shareholders were peeved at the $9 million yearly compensation Ovitz was offered at Disney, as well as the hefty severance package (upward of $140 million) he received after his ouster. Ovitz's defense in court? He says he made $20 to $25 million annually while at CAA and took a massive pay cut when he came to Disney.

The Young Turks

The Ovitz situation is hardly the only saga that's haunted CAA. In the late 1980s, five up-and-coming agents, who were all handsome, twenty-something males infamous for their brazen ambition and cutthroat tactics, became known as "The Young Turks." This powerful, young contingent took the helm when Ovitz and the other founders left in 1995.

Turk golden boy, Jay Moloney, perhaps the most charming of the group, was Ovitz's special protégé. He'd started out as an intern at CAA (although he mostly did nanny duties at Ovitz's home) and Ovitz took him under his wing. As Moloney moved up the ranks, Ovitz guided key clients in his direction, and the wunderkind was soon making over a $1 million bucks a year representing the likes of Steven Spielberg, Martin Scorsese, Tim Burton and Uma Thurman. But when he wasn't charming the A-list, apparently Moloney was using increasingly cutthroat, no-holds-barred tactics to stay on top. (Perhaps the worst incident, as reported in *New York* magazine, occurred when a rumor was spread that an agent at a rival agency had AIDS, and it was eventually discovered that it was most likely started by Moloney.)

In the wake of his father's death and Ovitz's departure, Moloney fell victim to his excessive lifestyle and committed suicide a few days after his 35th birthday.

Tinseltown's revolving door

In 2001 another Young Turk, Patrick Whitesell, left CAA for very different reasons. Whitesell, then co-head of motion picture talent at CAA, accepted an offer to become a partner at Endeavor Talent Agency, taking powerful clients Drew Barrymore, Matt Damon and Ben Affleck with him. It appeared that his former agency would get some revenge when Jennifer Lopez announced in the summer of 2003 that she was leaving Endeavor's Whitesell for CAA. However, the indecisive diva came clamoring back to Whitesell just weeks later, after her film, *Gigli*, bombed. Although CAA wasn't behind the *Gigli* deal, and Lopez didn't cite any particular grievance with the agency, she felt Whitesell was her best bet in getting her acting career back on track. Another big-screen star, Jude Law, left the agency early in 2005, reportedly because of jokes made by comedian Chris Rock about the actor at the 2005 Academy Awards.

A pretty woman comes to CAA

Don't feel too badly for CAA. The powerful "ten-percentery" (slang for talent agency) has also done its share of luring away talent from top competitors. One recent coup came when Julia Roberts defected to CAA from rival ICM in 2003. And she wasn't the first – Cameron Diaz and Lucy Liu had already left ICM to join CAA. Creative Artists now has a virtual lock on representing female leads, with a line-up that includes Nicole Kidman, Sandra Bullock, Renee Zellweger and Gwyneth Paltrow. Although there was initially some rumored concern (especially with Bullock) that Roberts would snag the best roles that came CAA's way, a monopoly does has its benefits: Competitors gripe that CAA gets first look at all the scripts with plum female roles.

Speaking of plum female roles, CAA signed another major actress in March 2005 when Angelina Jolie signed with the agency. Jolie had (and continues to have) a manager, but for nearly 10 years prior to affiliating with CAA, had managed to do something almost unheard of in Hollywood circles – she worked without an agent.

Media-savvy

Repping stars, although perhaps the "juiciest" part of CAA's business, is hardly its only service, and the agency has experienced impressive growth in other sectors. In October 1999, the company acquired 40 percent of Shepardson Stern & Kaminsky, a marketing communications agency. CAA also expanded its business into Internet venues. By September 2000, its new-media division had grown by over 15 agents from just three in the span of a year. It inked deals with Drkoop.com, a site that provides health information, and with DotComGuy, Inc., an entertainment site that traced the every move of an Average Joe who holed himself up in his digital digs for a year. Other new media companies that jumped on board with Creative Artists included TiVo and eStyle. In February 2000, the agency signed an agreement with Bloomsbury Publishing that would allow CAA to screen unpublished books to decide their filmmaking potential. This expansion resulted in the hiring of seven new agents in May 2000. CAA signed eBay in 2003 and has more recently focused on making a big push into the $11-billion-a-year video-gaming sector, signing Xbox architect, Seamus Blackley, as an agent.

In good company(ies)

In September 2004 former CEO of OgilvyInteractive Worldwide, Mike Windsor, was brought on board to head up CAA's promising marketing department, which includes

Visit Vault at **www.vault.com** for insider company profiles, expert advice, career message boards, expert resume reviews, the Vault Job Board and more.

VAULT CAREER LIBRARY   **79**

giants like Coca-Cola, P&G, Motorola, Hasbro and Nextel. Founded in 2000, the marketing division has twenty agents who help create opportunities for corporate clients in film, TV, music, videogames and theater. CAA is credited with such lucrative moves as getting Coca-Cola a sponsorship on hit reality TV show, *American Idol*. In 2005, the agency also signed Starwood Hotels & Resorts as a client. With entertainment industry connections, talent agencies like CAA are proving particularly helpful to corporations in getting prime product placements on television shows or in movies.

A smart subsidiary

In 2003 CAA bought out The Intelligent Group, often known as Youth Intelligence, a N.Y.-based marketing research and consulting company that tracks and forecasts behavior of consumers between the ages of 7 to 35. Youth Intelligence, which operates as an autonomous unit within CAA, publishes *The Cassandra Report*, which details current trends and makes predictions. Intelligence clients have included American Eagle Outfitters, Cosmopolitan, L'Oreal, Levi's and Lancome. The company is often quoted in major publications for its opinion on everything from fashion to pop culture influences shaping the Gen X and Gen Y crowd.

A Bite Out of the Big Apple

Partially due to the Intelligence acquisition, CAA decided to accomplish something that the LA-centric agency thought it would never do: open an office in New York. A number of CAA agents were already working in independent offices throughout the city, and in early 2004 twenty employees from four divisions (including, of course, theater) moved to a building in the Flatiron district. CAA also has a location in Nashville.

Agent abroad

The company seems not to be satisfied with only its east coast expansion and is contemplating making a move into the emerging marketplace in China. CAA agents have made trips over to the country, and they are currently contemplating possible future plans. The company also recently gained a foothold with our neighbors to the north as Telefilm Canada, a federally funded agency responsible for developing Canadian movies, hired CAA in April 2004 to find story material for Canadian movies. (As part of the contract, CAA will also try to persuade Hollywood-based Canadian talent to pursue projects back home.)

Down and out in Beverly Hills

CAA also has plans to move its headquarters from its longtime Beverly Hills location to a spot in Century City. (The move would allow the agency to break its final ties with friend-turned-foe, Ovitz – because Ovitz still co-owns the current CAA property, the company pays him rent.) Due to the constant tug-of-war played out in the talent agency world, it's hard to make concrete predictions about CAA's future plans. If recent history is any indication though, continued expansion is in the cards. Where might the mega-agency direct its high wattage next? Perhaps a merger with IMG, the world's biggest sports-management agency? The two companies already formed a joint venture in 2003, and veteran takeover artist, Theodore Forstmann, who recently purchased IMG for $750 million, is looking to merge with another powerhouse. Apparently, IMG execs told "Teddy" that CAA would be their choice. As of now, CAA prez, Richard Lovett, isn't biting, but who knows what the future will hold. After all, there's nothing Hollywood likes more than a good plot twist.

Visit Vault at **www.vault.com** for insider company profiles, expert advice, career message boards, expert resume reviews, the Vault Job Board and more.

V/\ULT CAREER LIBRARY   **81**

DirecTV Group, Inc.

2230 East Imperial Hwy.
El Segundo, CA 90245
Phone: (310) 964-0700
Fax: (310) 535-5225
www.directv.com

LOCATIONS

El Segundo, CA (HQ)
Boise, ID
Castle Rock, CO
Germantown, MD
Long Beach, CA
Los Angeles, CA

THE STATS

Employer Type: Public Company
Stock Symbol: DTV
Stock Exchange: NYSE
Chairman: K. Rupert Murdoch
President and CEO: Chase Carey
2004 Employees: 11,800
2004 Revenue ($mil.): $11,360.0

KEY COMPETITORS

ComCast
EchoStar Communications
Time Warner Cable

EMPLOYMENT CONTACT

www.directv.com/DTVAPP/aboutus/
 WorkingHere.dsp

THE SCOOP

The dish on entertainment

The DirecTV Group, known as Hughes Electronics Inc. before renaming itself in March 2004, provides digital and satellite TV service to 12.6 million American households. The company also runs Hughes Network Systems, which develops broadband satellite networks for government agencies, businesses and consumers. The DirecTV Group is the third-largest defense contractor in the U.S., and also has the largest non-governmental fleet of communications satellites in orbit. The company is also one of the world's largest suppliers of satellite-based private business networks, and is among the top providers of wireless telephone networks and cellular mobile systems.

A space odyssey

Hughes Electronics was founded in 1932 to construct experimental planes by Howard Hughes, an airspeed world-record holder. The company he founded has a few records of its own: it produced the first laser beam in 1960 and installed the first communications satellite in geosynchronous orbit three years later. Hughes was plagued by canceled defense contracts during the early 1980s. General Motors took over Hughes Electronics in 1985, seeing an opportunity to ride satellite technology into the commercial TV market. But the carmaker never developed a strategy that caught on with investors.

When the company unveiled the DirecTV service in the 1990s, it began to draw the attention of media moguls. After a dizzying series of lawsuits and deals, Rupert Murdoch – the baron behind Fox Entertainment – gained 34 percent of the company's stock in late 2003. The renamed company sells digital and satellite TV service to roughly 12.6 million subscribers under the DirecTV brand – a vehicle for Murdoch's ambitions.

Satellite insight

In December 1998, Hughes merged with satellite television service United States Satellite Broadcasting in a $1.3 billion agreement. Hughes then combined USSB's assets and satellite frequencies with its DirecTV business. Hughes bought PrimeStar Inc., a provider of direct-to-home satellite television for $1.82 billion in January 1999. The deal allowed Hughes to acquire PrimeStar's 160-channel, medium power

Visit Vault at **www.vault.com** for insider company profiles, expert advice, career message boards, expert resume reviews, the Vault Job Board and more.

VAULT CAREER LIBRARY 83

direct broadcast satellite, as well as its Tempo high-power satellite assets. America Online Inc. invested $1.5 billion in Hughes' satellite operations in June 1999 as part of a strategic attempt to increase its visibility in the broadband market. Four years later, however, Hughes terminated the deal. In November 2001, Hughes joined with WorldCom to deliver two-way satellite Internet access.

Deals, deals, deals

Raytheon Co., an industry leader in defense and government electronics, services, and technology, purchased Hughes' defense operations branch in October 1997 for $9.5 billion. Hughes sold off its satellite-making unit to Boeing, the aerospace giant, for $3.75 billion in January 2000.

Hughes Network Systems won a $27 million, 10-year contract with GTECH Corp., an operator of transaction processing systems and services for the lottery industry, in January 2003. That April, Hughes extended a contract with BMW of North America to provide networking services to the car manufacturing giant. Hughes Network Systems also sold off its 55 percent stake in Hughes Software to Flextronics International, a Singapore-based electronics manufacturer, for $226 million in June 2004. Thomas S.A., a French electronics manufacturer, paid $250 million in cash to Hughes for its set-top box manufacturing assets in May 2004.

Broadband explosion

In March 1999, Hughes, sensing the inevitable explosion of broadband data, invested $1.4 billion into the Spaceway global broadband satellite network. Spaceway was a high-bandwidth and high-speed communications system designed to provide bandwidth on demand, with customers paying for only the bandwidth they use. Hughes discontinued its line of cellular and narrowband, local loop communications products at the start of 2000 in an attempt to focus on broadband and high-speed communications systems. By the end of the year, Hughes added to its broadband arsenal with the acquisition of digital service line provider Telocity, Inc. for $179 million. The acquisition allowed Hughes to become the first U.S. provider of both digital multichannel television and wired and satellite broadband Internet access.

Hughes built a 43,000-square-foot, $20 million "nerve center" for its Hughes Network Systems division in July 2001 in Germantown, Md. The opening of the operations center was the start of Hughes' push into the broadband satellite service realm with its DirecWay service, a two-way connection in which users could receive and send data over the same wireless receiver. Over the next two years, the company expanded DirecWay to include satellite services to South America, China, and East Africa through Hughes Telecom Americas of São Paulo, ChinaCast and AFSAT Communications Ltd., respectively.

Ch-ch-changes

General Motors attempted to sell Hughes to EchoStar Communications, but antitrust regulators blocked the deal on competitive grounds in October 2002, claiming the resulting merger would create a monopoly. The two sides worked to restructure the deal, but were again rejected in December 2002; they terminated the merger for good soon after. Hughes let go of nearly half of DirecTV Broadband's employees, and closed its high-speed Internet service business, blaming the failed EchoStar merger for the cuts. GM regrouped, mulled over multiple offers, and eventually sold its interest in Hughes to Rupert Murdoch's News Corp. in September 2003.

News Corp., the Sydney-based media giant, bought Hughes Electronics Corp. and its DirecTV satellite subsidiary in December 2003 for $6.6 billion. Through the deal, News Corp. acquired 34 percent stake in Hughes Electronics, which it then transferred to its Fox Entertainment Group Unit for two promissory notes totaling $4.5 billion and 74.5 million Fox Entertainment shares valued at $27.99 each. Hughes closed its DirecTV Broadband operation in 2003.

Courtroom dramas

During the summer of 2003, DirecTV, along with EchoStar Communications Corp., took on the states of Ohio, Tennessee, and North Carolina in separate lawsuits contending a sales tax that had been placed on satellite television companies, but not on local cable television services. The sales tax was local cable operator's response to a competitive edge lost to faster-growing satellite services; EchoStar and DirecTV declared the tax a direct violation of the Commerce Clause of the U.S. Constitution. No further information on the status of the suits was known as of this writing.

In May 2004, DirecTV won $62.6 million in damages after a federal jury ruled Pegasus Satellite Television Inc. and its Gold Sky Systems Inc. unit violated a marketing contract between the two companies. DirecTV claimed Pegasus did not fairly reimburse it for subscriber acquisition costs.

Visit Vault at **www.vault.com** for insider company profiles, expert advice, career message boards, expert resume reviews, the Vault Job Board and more.

VAULT CAREER LIBRARY   85

I left my wallet in El Segundo

In the first quarter of 2004, DirecTV's $2.5 billion in revenue fell about $90 million short of covering operating costs. The company expects to continue to battle big cable companies for subscribers. It hopes to lure customers by showcasing programs from Murdoch's Fox Entertainment, gussied up with digital effects. (For example, Murdoch boasted of a feature that would let viewers select their own camera angles during NFL games or contests of the *American Idol* variety.)

The battle with the well-capitalized cable companies will take years, so DirecTV has shed expensive businesses during 2004. In March, it sold its stake in XM Satellite Radio. A month later, it sold PanAmSat Corporation, a 25-satellite global communications network, for $3.53 billion in cash to Kohlberg Kravis Roberts & Company, a New York-based private equity firm.

In December 2004, the company sold a 50 percent stake in Hughes Network Systems to SkyTerra Communications, an affiliate of the private equity firm Apollo Management LP, for $251 million. Even though Murdoch has conceded that cable companies reached subscribers early with digital services, some observers expect DirecTV to make a dent in cable's coverage. Murdoch used satellite to create powerful networks in Europe and Asia. He presumably hopes for more lavish rewards in the U.S.

Mission control

DirecTV has been fine-tuning its offerings to suit American audiences. Although satellite TV has been available for years, the service typically did not include local channels. DirecTV is changing that. The company has planned to launch a satellite late 2004 that will enable it to sell local channels in more markets. Chase Carey, a longtime Murdoch deputy who serves as the company's CEO, told *BusinessWeek* that he hopes to serve all 210 local media markets in the U.S. by 2008. The company also aims to carry broadcast networks' enhanced video. In spring 2004, it rolled out high-definition programming from CBS in eight major markets. Moves like this helped DirecTV add 484,000 subscribers in the third quarter of 2004 – an increase of 18 percent over the number of new subscribers during the same period in 2003.

Not-so-darling Darlene

Darlene Investments, a self-proclaimed "significant minority shareholder" in DirecTV Latin America, filed a lawsuit against News Corp. and the DirecTV Group in October 2004, charging the two with fraud and violation of fiduciary and contractual duties. Darlene sought over $1 billion in its attempt to prevent the DirecTV Group from combining DirecTV Latin America with News Corp. affiliates Innova S. de R.L. de C.V., Sky Brasil Servicios, and Sky Multi-Country Partners. Additionally, Darlene complained about transactions it claims improperly benefited DirecTV and subsequently threatened DirecTV Latin America's capabilities, and claimed the Sky transactions disregarded both the company's interests and a previous agreement signed with Sky entities to not compete in Latin America.

SEC investigation

The Securities and Exchange Commission announced in January 2005 it was reviewing several of the DirecTV Group's accounting transactions for the 2004 fiscal year. According to the company, regulators were concerned with the way DirecTV accounted for deals with NRTC, a unit of Pegasus, and with the French electronics company Thomson. DirecTV agreed to fully comply with the SEC.

Corporate change-up

Mitchell Stern, the No.-2 executive at DirecTV Group, abruptly resigned in March 2005. Stern, who reported to CEO Chase Carey, oversaw the day-to-day operations of the DirecTV service, and helped boost subscriber rates. However, sources say Stern was worn down by both the constant travel involved with the job and increasing tensions with Carey. As one insider claims, "There wasn't enough room at the top for two very strong executives."

Carey immediately took over Stern's role, a strong signal that he is not looking for a replacement any time soon. Carey did, however, restructure the group into three new divisions: DirecTV Entertainment; sales and services; and DirecTV Latin America and new enterprises. David Hill, chairman and CEO of Fox Sports, was named head of the entertainment group, while long-time DirecTV employees John Suranyi and Bruce Churchill were placed in charge of sales and new enterprises, respectively. All three men will report to Carey.

Shutting down scammers

DirecTV has been making great strides to catch individuals using illegally activated satellite receivers. In September 2004, the company filed a lawsuit against a Utah couple who allegedly created false subscription accounts and illegally activated multiple access cards and receivers. Then, in February 2005, DirecTV filed a lawsuit in Ft. Lauderdale, Fla., against seven people who also allegedly created fake

Visit Vault at **www.vault.com** for insider company profiles, expert advice, career message boards, expert resume reviews, the Vault Job Board and more.

VAULT CAREER LIBRARY   **87**

subscription accounts for "hundreds" of unnamed individuals. The defendants claimed payment for the illegal services, which DirecTV neither approved of nor received compensation for. Both suits are still pending.

Satellites 'R' Us

Today, The DirecTV Group is a world leader in the design, production, and marketing of advanced electronic systems including satellite technology, its bread and butter. DirecTV is the world's largest communications satellite maker having made nearly 40 percent of the commercial satellites currently in orbit.

New developments

In mid-2005, DirecTV plans to deliver a digital video recorder (DVR) and "video-on-demand" service that will virtually duplicate features available through current partner TiVo, minus the luxury of being able to skip over commercials. The DVR system will offer pay-per-view viewing and will allow DirecTV to "signal a user's DVR to record several movies, making each available for viewing at any time" according to an article in *USA Today*. Also among DirecTV's latest developments are a deal with Walt Disney Co. to offer ABC channel programming in high-definition to customers in 10 markets where ABC owns television stations, and a deal with D.R. Horton, the nation's largest homebuilder, to show off its services in D.R. model homes, showrooms and design centers, with the option for customers to buy "DirecTV-ready" homes from D.R. Horton.

GETTING HIRED

Log on for an out-of-this-world job

Today, the company seeks help developing its network and marketing what the network carries. The company appears at campus job fairs: check with your career services office. The career section of its web site, www.directv.com/DTVAPP/aboutus/WorkingHere.dsp, accepts online applications for posted jobs. Candidates can also use the site to create an employment profile.

Pay-per-(re)view

Whether you're a scientist or a salesperson, DirecTV uses software tools to calculate pay according to a set of benchmarks. The company calls this "performance-based pay" a chance to develop valuable skills, and pairs it with incentive plans. The company offers formal training in performance evaluation, team building, technical projects and leadership.

If the prospect of managerial report cards gets too stressful, workers can find balance in some DirecTV perks. Offices include on-site massage services and mothers rooms for nursing; the company also provides "celebrations of shared successes." Outside the office, the company emphasizes the splendor of its surroundings. Its major operations – in Southern California, metropolitan Denver and Boise – all provide easy access to the great outdoors.

Across the spectrum

The company says it makes a point of "recruiting from diversity-based organizations" and training staff in "diversity awareness." It also says it seeks a "workforce that mirrors our customers, business partners and investors." Customer service positions seem likely to gain importance as marketing grows intense.

Visit Vault at **www.vault.com** for insider company profiles, expert advice,
career message boards, expert resume reviews, the Vault Job Board and more.

VAULT CAREER LIBRARY

89

Discovery Communications, Inc.

1 Discovery Place
Silver Spring, MD 20910
Phone: (240) 662-2000
Fax: (240) 662-1868
www.discovery.com

LOCATIONS

Silver Spring, MD (HQ)
Bethesda, MD

THE STATS

Employer Type: Joint venture of
Advance Publications, Cox
Communications, and Liberty Media
Chairman: John S. Hendricks
CEO: Judith A. McHale
2003 Employees: 5,000 (est.)
2003 Revenue ($mil.): $1,717.0

KEY COMPETITORS

A&E Networks
E.W. Scripps
Time Warner

EMPLOYMENT CONTACT

corporate.discovery.com/careers/
careers.html

THE SCOOP

An entertainment giant

In the early 1980's John Hendricks felt that there just weren't enough documentaries and educational programming on TV. In 1985 he launched a cable channel to fill that void and called it the Discovery Channel. Today, Discovery's worldwide presence encompasses 33 entertainment channels available in 147 countries, reaching a cumulative 1.2 billion people (403 million subscriber households) tuning in to watch volcanic eruptions, science marvels and even neighbors re-decorating each other's homes. Revenues for the company from television and sales – including videos, CD-ROMs, software, and other products – skyrocketed to $1.4 billion in 1999. The privately held company had an estimated market value of $10.6 billion in 2000. The company committed $100 million to create Discovery Health and Discovery Travel & Adventure. The two new channels joined the Discovery Channel, Animal Planet, the Learning Channel and Discovery Kids along with the company's international channels.

In addition, the company has brought big business to the Washington, D.C., area, providing work for local production companies, and igniting a boom in Bethesda's economy. Hendricks tells this anecdote to measure his success: "I had on a Discovery Channel shirt and this Swedish boys soccer team could not believe it. They were asking me for my autograph. These kids watched Discovery all the time. It was their way of learning about the world. It was then I really realized the impact we have. I was proud for our whole company. It's moments like that we become part of the culture."

A history of fast growth

Four years after its debut, Cox Cable Communications, Tele-Communications, Inc. (TCI) and NewChannels acquired controlling interest in the company, and the channel was launched in Europe. In 1991 the company purchased The Learning Channel, which focuses on science, humanities and educational programming. In 1995 the company expanded into Latin America and Asia and began retailing products such as computer software, videos, and science games in Dallas and Chicago.

Visit Vault at **www.vault.com** for insider company profiles, expert advice,
career message boards, expert resume reviews, the Vault Job Board and more.

VAULT CAREER LIBRARY

91

An aggressive expansion strategy

The company also owns a controlling interest in the U.S. component of the Travel Channel and is looking to acquire its European and Latin American divisions. Discovery continued its aggressive expansion by collaborating with the BBC to launch three jointly owned satellite channels in Europe and Latin America. And in March 1998, the pair launched BBC America, a digital cable channel featuring BBC drama, sitcoms, live world news and documentaries. Discovery is also test-marketing Your Choice TV, a digital service that would allow viewers to watch the shows they want, when they want. Implementing a method similar to pay-per-view, the same program would begin at different times on different channels so viewers would get more than one shot at catching the shows they want to see. Discovery expects this service to be available to the general public by 2000. The company is also launching two new 24-hour global channels in March 2000 with the help of a $100 million investment from Discovery Networks International.

Store front

Discovery first entered the retail business with multimedia and home-video products based on the Discovery Channel and the Learning Channel, and branched out into the storefront market in June 1995, when it bought a 16-store chain based in Dallas, called Discovery Store Inc. A year later, the company acquired Berkeley, Calif.-based The Nature Co., a 117-store chain. The next piece of the puzzle was the launch of a new retail format at its mall stores, including overhauling The Nature Co., and changing its store brand name to The Discovery Channel Store. After an initial test run of 11 stores in the San Francisco area, the Discovery Channel Store rolled out to 20 cities nationwide in 1998. New merchandise included educational books, CDs, videos and artifacts from other cultures, as well as products relating to aviation, the universe, the animal kingdom, geology, travel, dinosaurs, science and gardening, under the theme, "Explore your world." The stores also offered key cross-promotional opportunities for new television shows and specials on the company's cable channels.

A flagship retail store was launched in the heart of Washington, D.C. in March 1998, hoping to translate capital-district tourism into sales profit. The $20 million, 30,000-square-foot D.C. store featured four floors, representing underground, the seas, culture and the sky, as well as a theater offering an overview of the city, and interactive exhibits. Retail items included standard beanie babies and typical gift shop knick-knacks, in addition to more sophisticated displays seen in natural history museums. A second 15,000-square-foot "destination" store was opened in San

Francisco in October 1999. However, the downtown D.C. location failed to attract a large quantity of retail shoppers and shut down in September 2001, three and a half years after it first opened its doors. The company reassigned "many of the employees and much of the inventory" to newly opening Discovery Channel Store stores in the Virginia area.

Feeling the bust of the multimedia boom

In February 1997, Discovery Communications announced it was cutting down its Discovery Channel Multimedia division, eliminating half of its staff. The division had previously developed 25 CD-ROM software applications since its inception in 1994 in three major areas: games, childrens' products and reference products. Although all were critical successes, Discovery decided to reduce product lines to focus strictly on software games, saying it no longer wanted to develop new childrens' and reference titles on its own.

Twenty-five jobs were affected by cut; Discovery was able to move most displaced employees to other positions. A spokesman for the company said, "If we had continued down the road we were on, we would not have met our five-year business plan of breaking even," blaming the high cost of developing quality CD-ROMs and waning consumer interest in interactive computer forums as the Internet gained popularity.

Discovering the Internet

In 1995 the company launched its $10 million web site. Discovery Communications strengthened its web site in 1997 by investing several million dollars in Omniview Inc., the innovator of the technology that creates 360-degree photo images of environments that can be explored online in real time. Discovery used this technology on its web site to explore the remains of the Titanic in 1996. In 1999 the company signed a multi-year deal with Wink Communications to provide shows on the Discovery Channel and the Learning Channel with interactive programming options like e-mail and e-commerce. And in early 2000 the company detailed a $500 million web strategy which included the creating of vertical portals (known as "vortals") that pair topical content and virtual communities with relevant e-commerce opportunities. Later that year, Discovery.com entered into an agreement with SpaceRef.com in which Discovery will host the space buff's destination, which includes "the world's only dedicated space search engine." Some analysts speculate that Discovery.com will eventually seek an intial public offering. Discovery

Visit Vault at **www.vault.com** for insider company profiles, expert advice, career message boards, expert resume reviews, the Vault Job Board and more.

VAULT CAREER LIBRARY   93

Communications is also the largest shareholder of online retailer petstore.com. In May 2000 the company announced the launch of an Indian dot-com subsidiary and said that the company's current Indian subsidiary was well on its way to breaking even.

Channel surfing

CBS Corp. joined with Discovery in July 1998 in a 50/50 venture to operate the 24-hour cable channel, CBS Eye on People. Paxson Communications has sold its remaining 30 percent interest in the Travel Channel to Discovery Communications for $57.3 million in February 1999, giving Discovery full control of the Travel Channel. In April 2002, The New York Times Co. and Discovery announced a joint venture, in which the newspaper company invested $100 million for a 50 percent stake in Discovery's Discovery Civilization Channel. Also included in the deal was a separate, $40 million deal in which the Times television unit agreed to produce programming through 2007. Civilization was originally introduced in 1996, along with five other Discovery-brand cable channels; it's programming ranges from ancient history to current events. In June 2002, Discovery debuted a 24-hour high-definition cable channel, called Discovery HD Theater, which featured programs covering several categories including nature, history, travel and children's programming. The June 17th launch celebrated the 17th anniversary of the first day The Discovery Channel aired, June 17th 1985. Discovery revealed plans to produce a new fitness channel called FitTV that would showcase "Body By Jake" fitness guru Jake Steinfeld. The channel, a rebranding of The Health Network debutted in 2004, and features exercise and wellness programs.

Recent developments

The Discovery Channel became the corporate sponsor for the Lance Armstrong-led U.S. cycling team in June 2004. Through the agreement, Armstrong became an on-air personality for Discovery's global networks, including the Discovery, Travel and Science channels. Discovery Channel logos were also placed on the team's jerseys. Also in the works for the company are plans for a new, state-of-the-art command center for the transmission of programming for its 14 cable networks in the United States in June 2004. The Discovery Television Center-Virginia is expected to start operations in late 2005, and will employ 100 people.

GETTING HIRED

As a fast-growing company, Discovery Communications has been hiring at a fast clip for the past several years. The company's expansion into retail means that in addition to television production there will be far more opportunities in advertising, marketing and sales. Across the board, the increasingly international nature of the company translates to a need for candidates with foreign language skills. While not a requirement for many non-production positions, a background or interest in documentaries or natural sciences is definitely a plus at Discovery Communications. Young applicants should not be discouraged; insiders report that entry-level positions are often given to talented recent graduates as first jobs. The company's human resources department does not accept blind applications, so call the switchboard at the Bethesda HQ (301-986-0444) after 6p.m. EST for information on openings and how to apply.

Visit Vault at **www.vault.com** for insider company profiles, expert advice,
career message boards, expert resume reviews, the Vault Job Board and more.

VAULT CAREER LIBRARY

95

Dow Jones & Company, Inc.

1 World Financial Center
200 Liberty Street
New York, NY 10281
Phone: (212) 416-2000
Fax: (212) 416-4348
www.dj.com

LOCATIONS

New York, NY (HQ)
South Brunswick, NJ

London
Hong Kong

THE STATS

Employer Type: Public Company
Stock Symbol: DJ
Stock Exchange: NYSE
Chairman and CEO: Peter R. Kann
2004 Employees: over 7,000
2004 Revenue ($mil.): $1,671.5

KEY COMPETITORS

Bloomberg
Gannett
Reuters

EMPLOYMENT CONTACT

www.dj.com/Careers/Careers.htm

THE SCOOP

That's a lot of publications...

Dow Jones & Company's flagship publication, *The Wall Street Journal*, started selling for 2¢ in 1889. Now more than 100 years later, Dow Jones is truly a global multimedia empire, encompassing extensive print, online and TV holdings. The company employs over 2,400 reporters and editors around the world, has more than 130 news bureaus worldwide and is No. 1 or No. 2 in market share with all of its products. *The Wall Street Journal*, which now sells for $1 on newsstands, has a more than 2.6 million paid circulation in print and online.

Dow's index finger

Before discussing Dow's many media holdings, let's take a moment to explore one other thing the Dow Jones name is synonymous with: its indexes. In 1884 Dow Jones launched its first stock indicator, an index mainly composed of railroad stocks that would later become known as the Dow Jones Transportation Average.

In 1896 Dow introduced what would become the world's most widely followed stock-market indicator, the Dow Jones Industrial Average (DJIA). Comprised of 30 blue-chip U.S. stocks, such as General Electric and IBM, the DJIA is a widely used barometer of the U.S. stock market. Tradable instruments based on the DJIA, including futures, options and structured products, were licensed beginning in 1997. The Dow Jones Utility Average, which debuted in 1929, is the youngest of the three core averages.

The Dow Jones Global Index family is comprised of more than 4,000 separate indexes tracking stock prices of more than 5,000 companies in 48 countries. The Dow Jones STOXX index family, launched in 1998, is the European component of the Dow Jones Global Index family. STOXX Ltd. is a joint venture of Deutsche Boerse, Dow Jones & Company and the SWX Group for developing, maintaining, distributing and marketing the Dow Jones STOXX indexes.

What about Bergstresser?

Three young reporters founded Dow Jones & Co. in 1882: Charles Dow, Edward Jones and Charles Bergstresser. Stationed near the New York Stock Exchange, the three young men produced handwritten newsletters and delivered them to subscribers in the Wall Street area. The business thrived and by 1889 Dow had a team of 50 employees. They decided to turn their "Customers' Afternoon Letter" into a newspaper, calling it *The Wall Street Journal*. When the paper debuted on July 8, 1889, it was just four pages long.

Charles Dow died in 1902, and Clarence W. Barron, a long-time employee who'd been hired to be Dow Jones' first out-of-town correspondent, decided to purchase control of the company. At that time, *Journal* circulation had already reached about 7,000. By the end of the 1920s that total had grown to more than 50,000 copies printed daily. Expansion began with the debut of *Barron's National Business and Financial Weekly in 1921*.

A flagship publication

The Wall Street Journal, which has always been the company's flagship publication, is second only to *USA Today* as the most widely read U.S. paper. Although the paper was founded in 1889, it wasn't until 1941 when Bernard Kilgore took over as managing editor of the *Journal* (he was later named president of Dow Jones in 1945) that the paper became what it is today. Kilgore expanded coverage to include all aspects of business, economics and consumer affairs, as well as the impact of different aspects of life that affected business. In the 1960s circulation flew past one million, and coverage of social issues, science, education and foreign affairs was added or expanded.

Weekend update

In 1999, *The Wall Street Journal Sunday* was launched in 10 U.S. papers, achieving a circulation of over four million. Today the *Sunday Journal* can be found in over 82 newspapers across the U.S. and its circulation is 10.1 million. The *Journal* also announced it would begin publishing its own weekend edition, which is set to launch in September 2005. The *Journal* used to have a Saturday edition, but went to a five-day-a-week schedule in 1953 after the New York Stock Exchange ceased trading on Saturdays. Subscribers will not be charged an additional fee for the weekend edition.

Venturing into new territory

Dow Jones first expanded overseas in 1973 when it bought a stake in the *Far*

Eastern Economic Review (more commonly known as just *The Review*), a Hong Kong-based weekly magazine providing news and analysis on Asian business, economics and politics. *The Review* initially was founded in 1946.

In the 1970s, the *Journal* became interested in expanding its global reach, introducing *The Asian Wall Street Journal* in 1976. The *Asian Journal*, edited in Hong Kong, was the first daily newspaper to provide business and economic news to an Asia-wide audience. In 1983 Dow Jones began publishing *The Wall Street Journal Europe* in Brussels, and in 1994 DJ launched *The Wall Street Journal Special Editions*, a collection of *Journal* pages, in local languages, printed in 39 leading newspapers around the world.

Dow ventured over into Russia in 1999, partnering with *Financial Times* and Independent Media to publish, *Vedomosti* (*The Record*), a Russian-language business daily, which became profitable ahead of schedule in 2002, and had 66,477 subscribers by the end of the first quarter of 2005.

Journal is teacher's pet

Another niche market the Journal has entered is the classroom: In 1991 Dow began publishing *The Wall Street Journal Classroom Edition*, published monthly from September through May and geared toward U.S. middle school and high school students. The publication reaches over 750,000 students in more than 5,000 secondary schools each month.

WSJ.com: the *Journal* goes online

In 1996 the *Journal* decided to jump into the quickly emerging online medium, launching *The Wall Street Journal Online* at WSJ.com. As of the first quarter of the fiscal year 2005, www.wsj.com had 731,000 paid subscribers, the largest paid subscription site on the entire Web. Fans include business luminary Warren Buffett, who remarked in a 2003 *Fortune* interview, "I still really pay for only three things on the Internet: *The Wall Street Journal*, online bridge and books from Amazon.com."

A weekly dose of business

In 1921 Clarence Barron decided if Charles Dow and Edward Jones could have the company named after them, he could at least get a publication. Or perhaps he just saw the need for a weekly business publication. Whatever the case, in 1921 he launched *Barron's National Business and Financial Weekly*, serving as the first editor of the magazine. The publication, 10¢ an issue, was an immediate success, reaching a 30,000 circulation by its sixth year. With a tag line, "News Before the Market Knows," it targets an influential audience of businessmen and investors. Today the publication, known simply as *Barron's*, still has a weekly print version (circulation is

Visit Vault at **www.vault.com** for insider company profiles, expert advice, career message boards, expert resume reviews, the Vault Job Board and more.

VAULT CAREER LIBRARY   99

around 300,000), as well as an online version at www.barrons.com that currently costs $79 per year. The magazine also has a new digital delivery service through which a reader can pay to receive the newest print issue of *Barron's* downloaded to their computer each Saturday morning. Although Dow has experienced its share of woes during the economic downturn of the past few years, *Barron's* enjoyed a terrific quarter in the second quarter of 2004 with an increase in advertising pages of 21.1 percent. In 1992 Dow Jones also began publishing (through a joint venture with Hearst Corp.) a monthly magazine named *SmartMoney* to help intelligent, professional workers manage their finances.

Telerate

Dow's markets subsidiary, Telerate, was sold to Bridge Information Systems Inc. in May 1998 for $510 million in cash and convertible preferred stock. The sale forced Dow to take an after-tax charge of $98 million in the second quarter ($123 million for the year), causing a second-quarter net loss of $51.7 million for the quarter ended that June. Previously, the company recorded a charge of more more than $900 million in 1997 to write down the unit. Despite the trouble with Telerate, Dow Jones' other businesses continued to prosper, increasing second quarter revenue in its print publishing unit by 6.7 percent to $307.9 million, while advertising revenue rose to $216.5 million from $199.6 million the previous year.

All the way with Ottaway

Even as Dow was expanding into a global market it got smaller in one sense, gaining a presence in the local newspaper market with the 1970 acquisition of Ottaway Newspapers, Inc. (ONI), a group of nine community newspapers in New York, Pennsylvania, Connecticut and Massachusetts.

By the first quarter of 2005, ONI had grown to encompass 15 daily and 18 weekly newspapers, and over 20 other publications in nine states. Ottaway newspapers have a daily circulation of 428,568 – reaching 1.3 million readers – and Sunday circulation of 470,041 – reaching 1.4 million readers. In 2003 it acquired *The Record*, a daily newspaper out of Stockton, Calif.

Just the Factiva

In 1999 Down Jones partnered with Reuters Group PLC to pool their online business-news and research services in a single site, Factiva. The site offers users an archive of business and news information from nearly 9,000 sources to aid in in-depth business research. The site also covers more than 10 million public and private companies worldwide and offers a customized news-tracking tool that filters information to a user based on their individual needs. Used by 78 percent of Fortune Global 500 Companies, it has 1.6 million subscribers.

Feeling wired

The Dow Jones News Service has been the leading electronic provider of comprehensive business and stock markets news to the securities for more than a century. The Dow Jones Newswires grew out of the Dow Jones News Service, and provides real-time news for financial professionals in the equities, fixed-income, foreign exchange and energy markets. The division also offers news for financial firms' web sites and Dow Jones Newsletters' sector-specific content. As of the first quarter of 2005 the service reaches more than 390,000 paid subscribers worldwide.

Dow launched a "Newswire of the Future" initiative, which launched its first product Dow Jones NewsPlus, in March 2003. The product is a web-format enhancement allowing users to move more efficiently through the roughly 10,000 daily headlines.

Ready for a close-up

In 1997 Dow Jones decided to make its presence known over the airwaves through a global business-television alliance with NBC Universal and its CNBC cable network. Business news channel CNBC was launched in 1989 and reaches roughly 197 million households in the U.S., Asia and Europe. Dow Jones is co-owner with NBC Universal of CNBC-TV operations in Asia and Europe and also provides news content to CNBC in the U.S.

The Wall Street Journal Radio Network provides news content for 213 radio stations covering 92 percent of the U.S. Founded in 1980, it is the leading provider of business news information for radio stations.

Ad woes

Dow Jones counts on advertising to generate well over half of its revenue and with an economic downtown, advertising budgets are often one of the first things to go. In Dow's wild ride, the company's revenue grew 15 percent in 2000, only to plummet 20 percent in 2001. The stock hit a high of $77 in mid-2000 and was down to $43 in October 2001. (As of June 2005, the stock was in the mid-$30 range.)

In 2002 the bleeding continued and total revenue dropped from $1.77 billion in 2001 to $1.56 billion in 2002. Ad revenue continued to take a nosedive as well from $1.05 billion in 2001 to $878 million in 2002, a fall of nearly 17 percent. Circulation revenue was also down slightly. In 2003 things steadied off with revenue dipping only slightly under that of 2002.

Stopping the bleeding

In an effort to curb the slide Dow Jones unveiled a comprehensive three-year business strategy at the beginning of 2002. Called "Business Now," the plan was outlined in three steps: Horizon 1, to be accomplished during the three-year plan; Horizon 2, to be begun during the three-year plan; and Horizon 3, longer-term initiatives that extended beyond the scope of "Business Now." Although Dow Jones wasn't able to realize its ambitious overall revenue growth goal of 8 percent to 10 percent during this period, it was successful in some individual goals like substantially increasing its color ad revenue, improving growth and profitability at the online *Journal* and enhancing its Ottaway portfolio by unloading some unprofitable papers and making the Stockton newspaper acquisition. In the next phase of the plan (Horizon 2) primary objectives were set to begin expanding into new business-to-business markets and extending reach to non-core customers. Chief among long-term objectives (Horizon 3) was further globalizing *The Wall Street Journal* and Dow Jones brands.

Financial forecast

The first quarter of 2005 saw revenue growth of 3 percent to $412 million but advertising linage at *The Wall Street Journal* fell over 8 percent. Spending in the financial services sector was down 24 percent and there was a 10 percent increase in color premium revenue. (The *Journal* spent more than $200 million during a four-year long color capacity expansion that was completed by the beginning of 2002. Color ads were up 28 percent in 2003 and 20 percent in 2004, and the trend is expected to continue.) Technology advertising was down 23 percent, although improved trends are expected in the second quarter. Dow CEO and chairman, Peter Kann, sees some clouds on the horizon. According to Kann, "We still see inconsistent trends in monthly *Wall Street Journal* advertising and ad levels, and results remain well below what we consider normal levels. We'll continue to control all we can to maximize financial results in any advertising environment." The numbers for May 2005, for example, bore out Kann's prediction as advertising for *The Wall Street Journal* fell by 2.6 percent, *Barron's* declined 6.9, according to a June 2005 report by

Internet news service Business Wire. *The Wall Street Journal Europe* increased by 12.1 percent, and *The Asian Wall Street Journal* proved to be a bright spots: Advertising linage increased by 12.1 percent and 4.6 percent respectively during May 2005.

As the Dow turns

The Dow got a minor facelift in April of 2004 when it dropped AT&T Corp., Eastman Kodak Co., and International Paper from its list, and replaced the companies with Verizon Communications, American International Group, Inc. and Pfizer. Paul Steiger, managing editor of *The Wall Street Journal* and the man in charge of the Dow Jones index, said the changes were meant "to recognize trends within the U.S. stock market, including the continued growth of the financial and health sectors." As recently as the late 1980s, two-thirds of the components of the Dow came from heavy manufacturing and oil industries; currently, the two make up only one-third of companies listed.

An integral part of Dow's future plan rides on the September 2005 debut of *Weekend Edition*. In addition to being delivered with no additional charge to subscribers, it will also be found on newsstands. Dow hopes it will help the company diversify its ad revenue. One concern is that it will take away subscribers from sister publication, *Barron's*, also received by many subscribers on Saturday. Another big part of the company's future stems from its January 2005 purchase of San Francisco-based MarketWatch Inc., which owns the news web site CBS MarketWatch. Dow Jones beat competitors Viacom Inc. and the New York Times Co. to gain access to the site, which will give Dow Jones a stronger presence online, and make it the third-largest presence in the online financial news industry, behind Yahoo Finance and MSN Money. With the good news came a bit of bad though – Dow announced it would cut 97 positions at MarketWatch and Dow Jones following the finalization of the acquisition. Dow was ready for further expansion in May 2005 when it announced that it would establish the Dow Jones Bahrain Stock Exchange Index, featuring all the stocks available on the Bahrain Stock Exchange, in June 2005.

GETTING HIRED

A foot in the door

Don't count yourself out if you're not a writer. It takes many different skill sets to make a multimedia organization tick. Dow has thousands of employees in fields that include sales, marketing, advertising, finance, customer service, and more. Go to the careers at www.dowjones.com/careers to learn more. Applicants will also find links to information pages devoted specifically to careers in Asia and Europe. Dow Jones also prides itself on a comprehensive internship program in journalism, production and technology. There is a specific *Wall Street Journal* internship program run by the company, but there are also opportunities to work at the venerable paper through the Newspaper Fund Interns Program. Also, Dow Jones recruits heavily from colleges, so check out the web site to see if they might be coming to your campus soon.

Top-notch benefits

Dow offers a number of options for medical plans and there is no required employee contribution for its basic life insurance or long-term disability. Medical and dental plans cover unmarried domestic partners and Dow also offers an extensive 401(k) plan. Dow also offers to pay 60 percent of physical fitness activities for employees up to an annual maximum of $400 per year. A number of work/family programs are also available to help employees balance work and family.

DreamWorks SKG L.L.C.

1000 Flower Street
Glendale, CA 91201
Phone: (818) 733-7000
Fax: (818) 695-7574
www.dreamworks.com

LOCATIONS

Glendale, CA (HQ)
Beverly Hills CA
Nashville, TN
New York City, NY
Universal City, CA

London
Toronto

DEPARTMENTS

Domestic Home Entertainment
DreamWorks Television
International Marketing & Distribution
Marketing
Motion Picture
Production
Theatrical Distribution
Worldwide Home Entertainment

THE STATS

Employer Type: Private Company
Principals: David Geffen, Jeffrey Katzenberg, and Steven Spielberg (Principal), President and COO: Rick Sands
2003 Employees: 1,100
2003 Revenue ($mil.): $1,250

KEY COMPETITORS

Fox Filmed Entertainment
Lucasfilm
Miramax

EMPLOYMENT CONTACT

www.dreamworks.com

Visit Vault at **www.vault.com** for insider company profiles, expert advice, career message boards, expert resume reviews, the Vault Job Board and more.

VAULT CAREER LIBRARY   105

THE SCOOP

Lights, camera, SKG

If raw talent were a measure of prestige, DreamWorks SKG would be the most respected entertainment company in the world. DreamWorks SKG first grabbed headlines in 1994 when acclaimed movie producer Steven Spielberg, music industry force David Geffen, and animation producer Jeffrey Katzenberg (who was responsible for revitalizing Disney's film department) announced that they were joining forces. Each partner contributed $33 million to the company. The resulting company has since moved at breakneck speed into the multimedia production of movies, television programming, interactive software, toys and records.

Life unlike the movies

In the beginning, the company scored a series of coups: a 10-year, $1 billion licensing agreement with HBO; a $100 million programming partnership with ABC; a $50 million animation studio co-founded with Silicon Graphics; and a $30 million joint venture with Microsoft to produce interactive software. (Microsoft co-founder, Paul Allen, also owns a stake.) But then the company started churning out some weak-performing products, turning the dream into something less workable. Its first three movies, *The Peacemaker*, *Mouse Hunt*, and *Amistad*, were mediocre performers at the box office, though they were successful compared to DreamWorks' TV programming. TV highlights included *High Incident*, *Champs*, *Ink* and *Arsenio*, none of which are still on the air. Moreover, the DreamWorks-produced George Michael album (his first in five years) was a bomb, and the company's interactive software received less-than-rewarding notice.

In October 1999 Dreamworks worked with Imagine Entertainment to unveil Pop.com, which acquired the rights to short films and animation for online distribution. However, even this foray into cyber space didn't jumpstart new revenue streams, and the struggling netcaster was scrapped after a failed merger with ifilm.com.

Shifting focus

However, at least DreamWorks films were starting to do improved box-office business, and the studio put out such summer 1998 hits as *Deep Impact*, *Small Soldiers*, and *Saving Private Ryan*. Further success in the 1999 and 2000 box offices spurred a series of other promising partnerships. The claymation *Chicken Run*, one of the company's chief summer releases for 2000, prompted a continuing partnership with Aardman Animations, the British studio responsible for the lovable Wallace and Gromit shorts. (*Wallace & Gromit: Tale of the Were Rabbit* is set for release in October 2005.) And after working in conjunction with Montecito Picture Company to produce the Tom Green comedy *Road Trip*, the two companies decided to continue their relationship over the next three years. When *American Beauty* brought DreamWorks five Oscars, including Best Picture, in 1999, the company proved it was not a fluke, following it up with another Best Picture nod for box-office darling, *Gladiator*, in 2000. Scoring a triple play, the studio followed this with a 2001 Best Picture win for *A Beautiful Mind*, a picture it co-produced with Universal Pictures.

DreamWorks began streamlining its operations to rid itself of less lucrative ventures and focus on these gains. In 2000 Dreamworks and Microsoft sold DreamWorks Interactive, the video game studio responsible for Playstation titles like *Lost World: Jurassic Park* and *Medal of Honor*, to Electronic Arts. In 2001 the company also sold its floundering gameworks venture, and in late 2003 it sold DreamWorks Records, which produced soundtracks to all the company's films and albums for popular artists, to Universal Music's Interscope Records for an estimated $100 million. However, another round of financing in 2002 allowed the studio to increase its more successful live-action film production and expand animation production facilities.

An animated offering

Animation has proven to be the studio's real cash cow: In 1998 an enthusiastic audience welcomed *The Prince of Egypt*, a not-necessarily-for-kids animated work that had been intensely researched for accuracy by the DreamWorks staff. The hits kept on coming, and the success of computer-generated, full length feature films like *Antz* (1998), *Shrek* (2001), *Shrek 2* (2004) and *Shark Tale* (2004), led the company to spin off its high tech DreamWorks Animation unit in an October 2004 IPO where 29 million shares priced at $28 were offered for the newly formed DreamWorks Animation SKG Inc.

Jeffrey Katzenberg serves as CEO of this new company, and the stock had soared to roughly $37 as of February 2005 due to record DVD sales for *Shrek 2* (home video sales of 12.1 million units its first three days out), the third-highest grossing domestic film of all time. Third Quarter earnings for DreamWorks Animation were $13.7 million, up from the $35.9 million loss the division had experienced from the quarter a year ago. However, the new company's future may not be all smooth sailing, and challenges include the increasing competition from studios like Pixar, and the high production costs and long turn-around time of making computer-generated films. *Shrek 3*'s release date has been pushed back from November 2006 to May 2007 and the studio's next release was *Madagascar* in the spring of 2005.

The show must go on

DreamWorks may have engineered a successful spin off with its lucrative animation unit, but TV has been a continued sore spot for the parent company – its only notable hit was *Spin City*, which went off the air in 2002. (Even its one animated offering, *Father of the Pride*, tanked in prime time and was quickly cancelled.) The company has signed a development pact with NBC, and programming includes weekly, one-hour drama, *Las Vegas*, and the boxing reality show, *The Contender*, a Sylvester Stallone and Mark Burnett co-production, which debutted in March 2005.

The Contender experienced a fair share of buzz for some unfortunate reasons. The actual competition recently took back seat to personal tragedy when 23-year-old contestant, Najai Turpin, took his own life after production on the show had ended. Various reports have suggested his suicide was related to personal problems and not the show itself, and the creators decided to air the program as planned. A trust fund will be created for Turpin's family. Says Burnett, "All of us at *The Contender* mourn the loss of a great fighter with tremendous heart and courage. His death comes to a shock to all of us. We all came to love Najai, and the episode in which he was most depicted will stand as a wonderful testament to who he was – it will not be changed."

DreamWorks biggest issue remains generating steady profit in what has been a very hit-and-miss venture in its first decade. Revenue has steadily shrunk over the past three years from $2.2 billion (2001) to $1.8 billion (2002) to $1.25 billion in 2003 and DreamWorks is counting on films like *The Ring Two* (March 2005) and strong DVD sales to bring in some big numbers for the studio.

GETTING HIRED

Where the jobs are

DreamWorks has operations in Glendale, Calif.; Beverly Hills; Universal City, Calif; Nashville, Tenn.; New York City; London, U.K.; and Toronto, Canada. The company's shrinking revenue has meant shrinking employee numbers for the studio, which downsized from 1,600 to 1,100 employees in 2003. However, DreamWorks is still hiring and openings are posted on the job section of its web site, www.dreamworks.com, for positions in departments ranging from business affairs to marketing. To check out job offerings at DreamWorks Animation, go to the new company's web site at www.dreamworksanimation.com, and peruse the list of available positions in its job section. (The most opportunities seem to be in Feature Animation Technology.)

DreamWorks also has internship opportunities posted on its web site in various departments, including archives/theaters, business affairs, domestic theatrical distribution, finance/accounting, international theatrical marketing, marketing, television, theatrical creative/production and worldwide technical services. Requirements include full-time enrollment in a university, an academic major related to the department of interest, and the ability to work a minimum of 10 weeks. Students who intern during the fall or spring semesters must work from 12 to 24 hours/week and receive class credit, while summer interns work a minimum of 40 hours/week and receive an hourly wage of $7. Make sure to check out the site if interested, because different internships have specific requirements that should be considered before applying. If animation is a main interest, go to the DreamWorks Animation web site, which also has a section on internships, although not as extensive.

Visit Vault at **www.vault.com** for insider company profiles, expert advice, career message boards, expert resume reviews, the Vault Job Board and more.

VAULT CAREER LIBRARY   **109**

Fox Entertainment Group

1211 Avenue of the Americas
New York, NY 10036
Phone: (212) 852-7111
Fax: (212) 852-7145
www.fox.com

LOCATIONS

New York, NY (HQ)

THE STATS

Employer Type: Subsidiary of News Corp.
Chairman and CEO: Rupert Murdoch
2004 Employees: 12,500
2004 Revenue ($mil.): $12,175.0

KEY COMPETITORS

Time Warner
Viacom
Walt Disney

EMPLOYMENT CONTACT

www.fox.com/corporate/jobs.htm

THE SCOOP

Putting the "biz" in "showbiz"

Fox Entertainment Group, Inc., the film and television arm of media mogul Rupert Murdoch's News Corporation Ltd., is one of the biggest entertainment conglomerates in the world. News Corp. owns 81 percent of Fox Entertainment, which has close to 13,000 employees and is headquartered in New York. Fox Entertainment produces and distributes feature films and TV shows largely through subsidiary Fox Filmed Entertainment. The company also owns the Fox Broadcasting Company, which runs 37 television stations throughout the U.S., and Fox Cable Networks. With the 2003 acquisition of a significant stake in Hughes Electronics (which now goes by the name of its satellite service, DirecTV), Murdoch's News Corp. is poised to make Fox Entertainment ringmaster of the American media circus.

Wilhelm Fried's Nickelodeon

Born in 1879, Wilhelm Fried left Hungary as a youngster with his family, settled in New York and in 1904, purchased a nickelodeon theatre for $1,600. The entrepreneur also changed his name to William Fox. Fox started making his own films and was ahead of his time in reaping the benefits of vertical integration. His Fox Film Corporation, founded in 1915, was the first to collectively produce, lease and distribute films. In the late 1920s, the studio moved to L.A., and William Fox was forced out of his company in 1930.

Fox Film Corporation merged in 1935 with Twentieth Century Pictures, started two years earlier by erstwhile Warner Brothers mogul Darryl Zanuck. With Zanuck at the helm, the newly formed Twentieth Century Fox blossomed in the 1930s and 1940s, but lost ground in the 1950s to the increasingly popular medium of television. Zanuck briefly left in 1956, but returned in 1962 and clashed so much with his son Richard, the president of the studio, that they both resigned in 1971. Nevertheless, the 1970s proved an auspicious decade for Twentieth Century Fox: Who hasn't heard of George Lucas and his little film about political unrest in space? When Fox released *Star Wars* in 1977, at that time the biggest box office smash in movie history, merchandising and entertainment became linked forevermore.

Visit Vault at **www.vault.com** for insider company profiles, expert advice, career message boards, expert resume reviews, the Vault Job Board and more.

VAULT CAREER LIBRARY   111

Stacking the deck

In 1981, Twentieth Century Fox was purchased by oilman Marvin Davis for $722 million. The studio changed hands again four years later when Australian-born-billionaire-turned-U.S.-citizen Rupert Murdoch bought the company. Not content to rest on Fox's movie-making laurels, Murdoch aggressively pursued other media outlets (namely, the small screen). Fox – now known as Fox Entertainment Group – is divided into four, powerhouse units: Filmed Entertainment; Television Stations; Television Broadcast Network; and Cable Network Programming. Fox went public in 1998 and raised over $2.8 billion for Murdoch's News Corp., one of the biggest public offerings in U.S. history.

Bread 'n butter

Fox may have diversified into other media outlets, but its filmed entertainment division has remained a big piece of the financial pie (it generated $967 million income in 2004 alone.) Perhaps the studio's biggest coup during the Murdoch era has been bonanza blockbuster, *Titanic*, but the hits have kept on coming. George Lucas' three *Star Wars* prequels have proven to be a cash cow for the studio, and the *X-Men* franchise and first *Daredevil* flick have been two comic-book hits. (The 2005 follow-up to *Daredevil*, *Elektra*, didn't fare so well, however.) Disaster movies like 1996's *Independence Day* and *The Day After Tomorrow* (the 2004 film grossed $530 million worldwide) have also proven lucrative. Other recent box-office winners are a diverse stable of movies, including *Ice Age*, *Dodgeball* and *I-Robot*. *Minority Report* and the less lucrative, but critically acclaimed, *Road to Perdition*, were both films co-produced with Steven Spielberg's DreamWorks SKG.

In April 2002, Fox withdrew from Movies.com, a proposed joint venture with Disney Corp. that would provide "content on demand" to customers in the U.S. via cable or the Internet. Soon after that announcement, Fox expanded a relationship with In Demand, a pay-per-view provider, to include a long-term agreement for video-on-demand offerings. The agreement included video-on-demand rights to recent Fox releases such as *Shallow Hal*, *Behind Enemy Lines* and *Ice Age*. Partially due to the increased contribution of this market, Fox's film entertainment operating income jumped from $717 million in 2003 to $967 million in 2004.

Successful like a Fox

It wasn't so long ago that CBS, NBC and ABC stood as the "big three" of network broadcasting. When Murdoch purchased Twentieth Century Fox, he introduced a new three-lettered competitor, buying six TV stations from Metromedia and launching the Fox Broadcasting Network. In the 1990s, president of prime time, Peter Chernin (president and chief operating officer of News Corp. since 1996) successfully steered Fox from a fledgling network only airing shows two nights of the week, to a perennial leader in the coveted 18-49 demographic.

Fox steadily carved its own niche by programming cutting-edge, quirky shows (*King of the Hill*, *The X-Files*, etc.) that embraced the sensibilities of Generation X and still had a crafty appeal to adults under 50. During the 1990s, young viewers flocked en-masse to prime-time teen soap, *Beverly Hills 90210*, sketch comedy show, *In Living Color*, (Jim Carrey, Jamie Foxx and Jennifer Lopez – one of the Fly Girl dancers – all got their start there) and raunchy sitcom, *Married with Children*. But nothing has eclipsed the staying power of crowd-pleasing, critical-favorite, *The Simpsons*, a pop culture staple still going strong after 16 years. And the continued success of long-running *Cops*, which follows real-life men in blue as they bust belligerent "Bad Boys" shows that the network knew how to tap into viewers' voyeuristic tendencies long before the reality craze even hit.

All the "reality" you can stand

Steady gains by the network were interrupted in 2001 when stalwarts like quirky-lawyer-show, *Ally McBeal* and *The X-Files* finally went off the air, and the broadcast network took a beating in the ratings war against its rivals. Fox's ratings among the coveted 18-to-49 year old demographic declined 11 percent in the 2001-2002 viewing season, according to Nielsen Media research. New shows slated for fall 2002 included the short-lived *Girls Club* from David E. Kelley, the producer behind *Ally* and *Boston Public*, and *The Grubbs*, a sitcom about a dysfunctional-family. But more successful offerings included the reality-TV dating-and-mating show *Joe Millionaire*, and the wildly popular singing contest, *American Idol*, whose popularity, along with the returning hit drama 24, bolstered ratings by 16 percent during fiscal year 2003. The fall 2003 lineup included critic's favorite, *Arrested Development*, an off-beat sitcom that experienced poor ratings, but picked up an Emmy nod for outstanding comedy series, helping stave away cancellation. *Arrested* has continued to be a ratings-challenged critical darling: As the 2004-2005 season drew to a close, it was once again the subject of cancellation speculation. However, *Arrested* beat the odds for a second time, and was renewed in May 2005 for the upcoming season. The five Emmys the show won in 2004, as well as its growing fan base are likely to have played a role in the renewal.

For ratings winners, the network has come to rely heavily on reality series, and while all of the *American Idol* installments have been big winners, a second installment of Joe Millionaire fizzled, and primetime ratings declined 10 percent in fiscal year 2004. In an effort to find that next-big-show, the network has repeatedly come under fire for its questionable taste (plastic-surgery-makeover, beauty pageant, *The Swan* comes to mind), most recently due to the premise behind reality show, *Who's Your Daddy*. Deemed "destructive, insensitive and offensive" by one adoption agency executive, the show asks a woman adopted years earlier to determine which of eight men is her father. (If she guesses right, she gets a cool $100,000.) Backlash hasn't hindered Fox's reality lust though: A Fox Reality Channel is set to premiere in more than 17 million homes in 2005.

A good sport

Fox has aggressively courted sports fans while expanding its TV presence. The network continually pays eye-popping sums to broadcast NFL games. According to a November 2004 *Boston Globe* report, Fox will pay $4.3 billion to extend its contract to broadcast Sunday NFL games for an additional six years.

In addition, Fox has created a number of other outlets to broadcast a variety of sports. In 1996 Fox joined with Liberty Media to compete with Disney's ESPN, and in 1998 News Corp. purchased the 50 percent share of Fox/Liberty Networks that it didn't already own. The sports division of the company, whose ownership was transferred to Fox, has since been renamed the Fox Sports Network. (Liberty Media came away with an 8 percent interest in News Corp.) Revenue growth for FSN's Regional Sports Networks was one of the reasons cited behind the impressive overall growth the cable networking segment experienced (operating income increased 39 percent over the year before) in 2004.

Fox also has 20 percent stakes in the New York Knicks and Rangers teams through a partnership with Cablevision, as well as interests in various sporting venues. Fox also sold the cash-draining L.A. Dodgers baseball team – it consistently bled about $40 to $50 million a year – to South Boston Seaport parking lot owner, Frank McCourt, in March 2004 in a deal valued at $430 million. Fox has striven to appeal to niche sports markets with auto racing channel, SPEED, and by introducing a network dedicated to extreme sports (called Fuel), in July 2003.

One pleasant sports surprise for Fox was the 2004 Major League Baseball postseason, broadcast by the network. A history-making comeback by the Red Sox against the Yankees in the ALCS, and the Sox' subsequent curse-breaking win in the

World Series, fueled ratings that culminated in a 23 percent increase over the Series the year before.

Fair and balanced?

Sports are only one part of Murdoch's cable empire. Other FCN (Fox Cable Networks) holdings include National Geographic Channel and FX, a general entertainment channel that's started to gain respect and viewers with critically acclaimed original programs like *The Shield*, *Nip/Tuck*, (basic cable's No.-1 series among adults 18-49) and *Rescue Me*.

The real coup came in an inspired decision to go head-to-head with news channel, CNN, in 1996. The Fox News Channel, which overtook CNN in the ratings to become the number one cable news channel in the U.S. by 2002, attributes its success to a "Fair and Balanced" (its tag line) approach. But others feel that Fox has a distinctly right-leaning tone that actively courts conservative viewers disillusioned by a perceived liberal bias in the media. Whatever the reason, few quibble about the channel's success. Ratings for coverage of the Republican National Convention in August 2004 defeated even those for the three major networks (presented by some as evidence as to its conservative viewership), and the presidential election of 2004 turned out to be Fox New's biggest victory to date. FNC's 8.05 million viewers, its biggest prime-time audience ever, was up a whopping 235 percent from prime time coverage in 2000. (Fiscal year 2004 operating income for the channel grew a whopping 86 percent.) Fox News Channel is also poised to become a significant player in radio as a result of a deal to provide news to radio stations owned by Clear Channel Communications Inc. It estimates that as many as 500 Clear Channel affiliates will broadcast Fox News by the middle of 2005.

Fox News has touted itself as a scrappy underdog, but with these powerhouse numbers, can it take this approach in the future? Said Fox News Chairman Roger Ailes, in a recent interview: "Being in the establishment has nothing to do with numbers. We'll always be the kids with the nose up against the glass." His next goal? To be the top-rated cable network, period. To do so, Fox News would have to nearly double its average daily viewership to beat Nickelodeon – a lofty goal any way you look at it. But love or hate Fox, few people are counting it out.

Fox News in the news

A fair share of recent controversy has also kept Fox News in the news itself. In 2003 Fox News slapped a trademark-infringement lawsuit against liberal humorist Al

Visit Vault at **www.vault.com** for insider company profiles, expert advice, career message boards, expert resume reviews, the Vault Job Board and more.

VAULT CAREER LIBRARY **115**

Franken and his publisher, the Penguin Group, for titling his book *Lies and the Lying Liars Who Tell Them: A Fair and Balanced Look at the Right*. The company claimed the title violated a 1998 trademark on the term "fair and balanced." Fox also argued that the prominent display of the words "fair and balanced" on the book cover would trick consumers into believing the network condoned Franken and his work, which satirizes Fox News and its rating darling "*The O'Reilly Factor*," helmed by opinionated, controversial Bill O'Reilly. The injunction sought by Fox News to halt the sales of the book was flatly denied on August 22, and Fox finally dropped its complaint.

O'Reilly became the subject of headlines again in September 2004 as the target of a sexual harassment suit filed by a former producer, Andrea Mackris, who outlined numerous inappropriate sexual comments she alleged the TV personality made towards her. (Due to her extremely detailed presentation of the accusations, many believed Mackris had tapes of O'Reilly committing the alleged harassment.) Vocal family-man, O'Reilly, who often uses his show and best-selling books to condémn questionable moral standards, immediately came under fire. O'Reilly, who initially countersued his accuser, ultimately decided he didn't want to drag out the situation and settled for an undisclosed amount.

Wheeling and dealing on TV

Fox's television stations have grown rapidly in recent years. In July 2001 Fox sold the Fox Family Channel, which they co-owned with Saban Entertainment, to Walt Disney for about $5.3 billion. Days later, parent company News Corp. obtained approval from the Federal Communications Commission (FCC) to buy Chris-Craft Industries for $4.4 billion. The merger raised News Corp.'s interest in Fox Entertainment to over 80 percent and helped Fox snap up nine new TV stations from competing broadcast networks. Eight of those stations belonged to UPN in top TV markets like New York and Los Angeles, while the ninth, KMOL in San Antonio, was an NBC affiliate. With a newly enlarged 41 percent share of U.S. viewers, News Corp. was able to obtain a temporary stay of enforcement on federal prohibitions against a single company owning stations that combined, reach more than 35 percent of the general audience.

In October 2001, Fox exchanged two TV stations, KTVX in Salt Lake City, a former affiliate of ABC, and KMOL in San Antonio with Clear Channel Communications Inc. for Fox affiliate WFTC in Minneapolis. In November 2001, Fox television stations switched several large news stations with media titan Viacom. Fox took over Viacom's WDCA-TV in Washington, D.C., and KTXH-TV in Houston, while

Viacom scored Fox's KBHK-TV in San Francisco. With the two acquisitions, Fox gained ownership of 33 stations, including several in nine of the top 10 U.S. markets. Then, in June 2002, Fox television stations swapped KPTV in Portland, Ore., a UPN affiliate, for Meredith Corporation's WOFL (Fox) in Orlando, Fla., and WOGX (Fox) in Gainesville, FL. Also that summer, Entertainment Group and Fox television stations acquired WPWR-TV, a Chicago affiliate of rival broadcast company UPN, from Newsweb Corporation for $425 million in cash. Subject to regulatory approval, the acquisition would give Fox Entertainment a grand total of 35 stations and nine duopolies in major markets, including the top three markets of New York, Los Angeles and Chicago. Already the owner and operator of WFLD-TV, a Fox affiliate in the Chicago TV market, the station group would be adding to its rapidly growing list of cities where it currently operates media duopolies: New York, Los Angeles, Dallas, Washington, D.C., Houston, Minneapolis, Phoenix and Orlando.

Market manuevers

With all this property at stake, Murdoch has been a vocal opponent of the regulations limiting a single company's holdings in individual markets. It looked like he might get his wish when a June 2003 vote in Congress to ease FCC regulations prescribing media ownership raised the cap for a single company's ownership of U.S. audience share from 35 percent to 45 percent. However, the backlash against the controversial rule change ultimately resulted in an appeals court settling at 39 percent.

The FCC also granted News Corp. a two-year waiver to shuffle its holdings in New York, where the acquisition of Chris-Craft added WWOR-TV and tabloid newspaper, *New York Post*, to News Corp.'s stable. A longstanding FCC rule barring companies from owning both a TV station and a newspaper in the same market had already been waived for News Corp.'s holdings in New York. However, long-term legislation still remains shadowy, and Fox's New York future is still in question.

Send up the satellites

In 2003 News Corp. acquired Hughes Electronics, the parent company of top satellite-TV service DirecTV. News Corp. announced its agreement in April 2003 to shell out $6.6 billion in cash and stocks for the 19.9 percent stake in Hughes that General Motors had held, along with a further 14.1 percent of Hughes from public shareholders and GM's pension and other benefit plans. Murdoch gained a 34 percent interest in Hughes, and has access to DirecTV's many millions of satellite-

TV subscribers, a move that must give head honchos at Fox competitors like Disney and AOL Time Warner cause for concern.

With DirecTV as the biggest portion of a global media armada that already broadcasts news, sports and entertainment shows throughout Britain, Asia and parts of South America, Murdoch is poised to become the world's top-dog media powerhouse; he'll have a huge say in deciding which content gets delivered to millions of households, not to mention which new services get to reach those audiences. Although News Corp. publicly declared its desire to honor FCC regulations, thereby granting rival cable TV operators like HBO and the Disney Channel a place on DirecTV, Murdoch has the potential to cut out programmers and gain access to even more viewers for features like his on-demand movie service or interactive sports channels of his design.

While DirecTV has added about 1.4 million subscribers in calendar year 2004, and currently stands at 13.5 million (more subscribers than all other satellite companies combined), this growth has definitely come with a high price tag. Net income for Fox Entertainment for the first quarter of fiscal year 2005 decreased to $320 million compared to net income of $401 million in the prior year, largely due to equity losses from the DirecTV group.

But Murdoch is looking at the long-term benefits, which most likely include using DirecTV as the launching pad for his next wave of cable channels: Fox hopes to launch a business channel, possibly as early as summer 2005, to go head-to-head with CNBC. There's also a Reality Network in the works, and a weather channel, as well as other sports channels, are possibilities.

Looking ahead

Financially, besides the 1Q2005 hiccup, Fox Entertainment has had a more-than-healthy economic profile in the last few years: In June 2003, the company reported record profits at its film, TV station and cable segments and achieved a record breaking fiscal year. Fiscal year 2004 was another banner performance, with net income increasing from $1 billion to $1.4 billion. If Murdoch doesn't get too bogged down in keeping control of the News Corp. empire – in late 2004 his longtime investing partner, John Malone, unexpectedly raised his stake in the company and Murdoch is busy crafting a poison pill to keep him from gaining a majority position – all this wheeling-and-dealing may not only shape Fox's future, but ultimately that of the entire media industry.

GETTING HIRED

Hiring overview

Interested applicants can check the web site, www.fox.com/corporate/jobs.htm, for employment opportunities and detailed job descriptions. The site features links for different divisions throughout Fox with more specific instructions for applying, which vary according to division. Click on the link for Twentieth Century Fox, for example, and you'll be taken to www.Foxcareers.com. Here you'll find a searchable database listing job opportunities and access to an online response form, which the company requires before officially considering applications. Jobseekers hoping to work with the Fox Sports Networks, on the other hand, can submit their resumes online or mail them to Human Resources at the Fox Cable Networks office in Los Angeles. The best bet is to consult the online resources with individual contacts.

Visit Vault at **www.vault.com** for insider company profiles, expert advice, career message boards, expert resume reviews, the Vault Job Board and more.

VAULT CAREER LIBRARY 119

Gannett Company, Inc.

7950 Jones Branch Drive
McLean, VA 22107-0910
Phone: (703) 854-6000
Fax: (703) 854-2046
www.gannett.com

LOCATIONS

McLean, VA (HQ)
Offices in 43 states and in the U.K.

THE STATS

Employer Type: Public Company
Stock Symbol: GCI
Stock Exchange: NYSE
Chairman and CEO: Douglas H. McCorkindale
2004 Employees: 53,000
2004 Revenue ($mil.): $7,381.3

KEY COMPETITORS

Cox Enterprises
Dow Jones
Knight-Ridder

EMPLOYMENT CONTACT

www.gannett.com/job/job.htm

THE SCOOP

Pushing journalistic integrity?

Frank Gannett started his media empire by purchasing a half-interest in upstate New York's *Elmira Gazette* in 1906. As of the summer of 2005, the Gannett family included 101 daily newspapers and 21 television stations. Despite the diversity of Gannett's corporate holdings, newspapers still generate about 75 percent of the company's revenue, and Gannett's crown jewel is *USA Today*, the largest newspaper in America, with a circulation of more than 2.3 million.

Derisively called "McPaper," *USA Today*'s mix of catchy graphics, splashy colors and entertainment news was initially widely denounced by many in the journalistic community. However, few can question the paper's influence upon the newspaper industry since it first hit newsstands in 1982.

In the past several years, *USA Today* has improved its reporting and writing, and while a Pulitzer may not be imminent, the paper's reputation within the industry has also improved quite a bit. Like many major papers, however, *USA Today* has had its share of misfires. In 1998 the paper suffered a blow to its credibility when it ran a Glaxo-Wellcome advertisement posing as a full-fledged *USA Today* issue. In another Gannett blunder, *The Cincinnati Enquirer* ran a lengthy expose of Chiquita Brands International, alleging dirty business practices. After protests from Chiquita, the paper admitted that the article relied on illegally obtained voicemail messages and retracted the story. Gannett immediately apologized and offered Chiquita an unsolicited settlement of about $15 million. A former editor, however, has sued Gannett over the way the company treated him regarding the Chiquita incident. Lawrence Beaupre claimed that he was made to be the scapegoat in the situation, so the company could avoid responsibility.

Crossing borders

Although approximately 87 percent of its revenue comes from domestic operations in 43 states, the District of Columbia and Guam, the company is more than just a group of American newspapers. It has foreign operations in the United Kingdom and in several European and Asian markets, including Belgium, Germany, Italy and Hong Kong. Overall, Gannett publishes *USA Today* and 100 other U.S. newspapers, operates 21 television stations, (which cover about 18 percent of the United States),

Visit Vault at **www.vault.com** for insider company profiles, expert advice, career message boards, expert resume reviews, the Vault Job Board and more.

VAULT CAREER LIBRARY   **121**

owns several British publications and has 500 non-daily publications. All of this adds up to 2004 revenue stream of over $7.3 billion.

Newspaper behemoth

Gannet has undertaken several deals to enlarge its market share. It joined with other newspaper groups to form new national online newspaper services, and it launched an Internet complement to *USA Today*. However, a partnership with The New York Times Company and the Times-Mirror Company, called The New Century Network, was disbanded in March 1998.

In June 2000, Gannett announced that it would pay close to $1.125 billion for 19 newspapers owned by Thomson Corp. The dailies are located in Louisiana, Maryland, Ohio, Wisconsin and Utah. Together, the newspapers have a combined circulation of 466,000. Additionally, the company unveiled a broadcast and Internet initiative, USA TODAY LIVE; it bought British publisher Newsquest Plc; it purchased East Coast publisher Tucker Communications, Inc.; and, shortly after news that Douglas McCorkindale would replace John Curley as CEO, Gannett announced plans to acquire another British publisher, News Communications & Media Plc. In July 2000, for $2.6 billion in cash, Gannett also added to its army of publications Central Newspapers Inc., whose flagship newspapers are *The Arizona Republic*, based in Phoenix, and the *Indianapolis Star*.

Expansion?

Gannett revealed in March 2004 that it was considering whether to make a bid for the assets of Hollinger International Inc., the troubled newspaper company that owns the *Chicago Sun-Times* and several British papers. Hollinger's prize asset is the U.K. newspaper, the *Telegraph*, which would operate under Gannett's Newsquest division, a group publishing newspapers in the United Kingdom, and is the U.K.'s second largest regional newspaper company. The company said that it is currently studying Hollinger's books to see if it would be a good fit. Because several other media companies are looking at making bids as well, a deal between Gannett and Hollinger is still up in the air.

In the U.K., Newsquest has been aggressively expanding its stable of local newspapers. It owns more than 300 regional newspapers, including the *Glasgow Herald*, which it bought earlier this year when it acquired the local newspaper assets of Scottish Media Group for £216 million. In February 2004, Newsquest was blocked by the U.K.'s Competition Commission in its planned £60 million purchase of Independent News & Media's local London newspapers. Undaunted, Gannett also announced that it is interested in acquiring the *Financial Times* if its publisher, Pearson, puts it up for sale. In working toward the deal, Gannett announced in March 2004 that its Gannett Offset division will begin to print the *Financial Times* in Springfield, Boston and Atlanta in November. Other cities will follow in 2004. Terms of the deal were not disclosed.

Chief Executive Douglas McCorkindale had also noted that Gannett was interested in acquiring Dow Jones, publisher of *The Wall Street Journal*, in a December 2003 interview in *Barron*'s, which incidentally, is also owned by Dow. As of March 2005, however, no steps had been taken toward acquiring the company.

Oops

In March 2004, *USA Today* was forced to admit that a former star foreign correspondent, Jack Kelley, made up parts of at least eight stories between 1993 and 2003, committing "journalistic sins" that were "sweeping and substantial." Gannett said a team of reporters and an editor found evidence of repeated fabrications during an examination of 720 articles written by Kelley. Its evidence "strongly contradicted" Mr. Kelley's stories that he had spent a night with Egyptian terrorists; met a vigilante Jewish settler; taken part in a dangerous hunt for Osama bin Laden; visited a terrorist gathering point on the Afghan-Pakistani border; and watched a Pakistani student "unfold a picture of the Sears Tower and say, 'This one is mine,'" in a thinly veiled reference to another impending terrorist attack.

Kelley, 43, is also accused of using at least two dozen passages from the work of other news organizations without attribution and trying to subvert *USA Today*'s investigation by concocting scripts–complete with phony identities-for associates to follow if editors tried to substantiate his work. Kelley had previously been nominated him five times for the Pulitzer Prize. Kelley, who resigned in January after admitting to editors that he had misled them, insisted that he did nothing wrong. The paper said that he told the staff on Thursday: "I feel like I'm being set up."

Government issues

In June 2003, the Federal Communications Commission cast a controversial vote to change the rules that bar ownership of a newspaper and television station in the same market. The FCC wanted to expand the percentage of media a company could own in a region to 45 percent saturation, a move multimedia companies like Gannett

Visit Vault at **www.vault.com** for insider company profiles, expert advice, career message boards, expert resume reviews, the Vault Job Board and more.

V∆ULT CAREER LIBRARY   **123**

applauded. The changes were blocked almost immediately by court action and Congress, however.

Congress eventually settled on a partial change, allowing companies to own stations that cover up to 39 percent of the country. But the cross-ownership part of the rule (owning both newspapers and broadcast stations in the same region) remains on hold by the courts.

In a separate move in 2003, Congress enacted the very popular Do Not Call Registry, which blocks cold calls from businesses to private citizens. The law had a direct impact Gannett, since the company sells about half its subscriptions through phone solicitation. In response, the company dropped all telemarketing efforts and has said that it is "seeking out other means of getting customers." Yet another act had an effect on Gannett in 2003. The new, complicated campaign-finance rules Congress set forth left political parties and candidates a bit confused about what spending they could and could not do, leading to a dearth of election-year advertising that newspapers and television stations normally count on to boost the bottom line. As of March 2004, Gannett has yet to report any significant impact from political ad spending for the year.

GETTING HIRED

Gannett's employment web page, www.gannett.com/job/job.htm, is updated weekly and list current positions in the corporate headquarters only. For jobs with Gannett's newspapers, broadcast stations and newspaper web sites across the U.S., including *USA Today*, check out the company's site for the appropriate contact person and submission requirements. Editorial applicants sending applications via e-mail must mail supplementary materials submission according to the directions on the web site.

HarperCollins Publishers, Inc.

10 E. 53rd Street
New York, NY 10022
Phone: (212) 207-7000
Fax: (212) 207-7145
www.harpercollins.com

LOCATIONS

New York, NY (HQ)

THE SCOOP

The Harper brothers

The earliest incarnation of HarperCollins was founded in New York City by two of four Harper brothers in 1817 and called J&J Harper. In addition to an endless list of bestsellers, the Harper Brothers were responsible for the ever-popular *Harper's Monthly* and *Harper's Bazaar* magazines. In 1962 the company (renamed Harper & Brothers when the other two brothers joined) merged with textbook publisher Row, Petersen & Co. to become Harper & Row. In 1987, the company was acquired by Rupert Murdoch's News Corp., and two years later it strengthened its textbook unit with the purchase of Scott, Foresman. When News Corp. acquired William Collins in 1990, the two were merged to form HarperCollins Publishers, which currently brings in revenue that tops $1 billion annually. In 2004, the company boasted 97 titles on *The New York Times* bestseller list, including nine books that made it to No. 1. HarperCollins also benefited from media tie-ins with the releases of films based on of J.R.R. Tolkien's *The Lord of the Rings* trilogy, Meg Cabot's *The Princess Diaries*, Ira Levin's *The Stepford Wives* and Daniel Handler's *Lemony Snicket's A Series of Unfortunate Events*.

Bestsellers

HarperCollins today boasts successful authors like John Gray (*Men are From Mars, Women are From Venus*), Wally Lamb (*I Know This Much Is True*), Barbara Kingsolver (*The Poisonwood Bible*), Dennis Lehane (*Mystic River*) and Michael Crichton (*Jurassic Park*). Imprints within the company include HarperCollins Adult Trade, Cliff Street Books, Regan Books and HarperPerennial, which reprints classic pieces of literature with scholarly commentary. The company has also published bestsellers *Divine Secrets of the Ya-Ya Sisterhood* (and its sequels), by Rebecca Wells and the Dilbert books. The company's e-book imprint is called PerfectBound.

HarperCollins is no stranger to the pitfalls that have plagued the publishing industry in the past few years. In the mid-1990s, the company had to write off huge advances when books by celebrities such as Jay Leno didn't sell well. Anthea Disney, formerly the editor-in-chief of *TV Guide* (then controlled by News Corp.), was brought in by Murdoch as HarperCollins' CEO in 1996 to turn the unit into a moneymaker.

By June 1997, Disney had led the most expensive restructuring in publishing history. (In the first half of 1997, the company's operating profit fell almost 50 percent, despite an 11 percent increase in sales.) In the restructuring, the company took a $270 million charge, laid off 420 employees and canceled contracts with 106 authors. This event was soon dubbed the "manuscript massacre" by the media. With her eye on the bottom line, Disney also revised HC's publishing goals. The company began to focus on "high-concept" books in six areas: self-help and psychology; fiction; "headline-grabbing," sensational non-fiction; business; science fiction; and children's books. Needless to say, literary purists had a field day criticizing HarperCollins' business strategy.

Successful business strategy

But it was HarperCollins' turn to gloat by the time the restructuring was over. The unit had more books on the bestseller list in the summer of 1997 than any other publisher. By September 1997, Rupert Murdoch rewarded Disney for her economic belt-tightening by promoting her to lead his new publishing division, News America Publishing Group. One month later, Murdoch named Jane Friedman, a former top exec from Random House's prestigious Knopf imprint, as head of HarperCollins. Despite continuing worries among company insiders that Murdoch would sell HarperCollins and trigger another round of changes, the talk at the publishing house eventually returned to the business of books. Under Friedman, HarperCollins boasted 11 *New York Times* bestsellers in August 1998, including several titles in No.-1 spots.

HarperCollins also acquired Avon Books and William Morrow & Co. from the Hearst Corporation, in 1999 for about $200 million. That same year, HarperCollins made another acquisition, bringing Amistad Press, one of the country's leading publishers of works by and about African-Americans, into the fold, as well as The Ecco Press, a prestigious literary publisher. The acquisition of these imprints solidified HarperCollins' position as the second-largest publisher in the United States behind Random House and made the company the third-largest publisher of children's books. The HarperCollins children's division is responsible for favorites from author Shel Silverstein and the *Lemony Snicket* book series. Upon merging operations, Friedman divided HC into two divisions: HarperCollins General Books Group and HarperCollins Children's Book Group (located in different midtown Manhattan offices). Other changes included cutting 17 imprints and 74 people from the HC lineup. The company now publishes about 1,700 titles, which is about 20 percent fewer than the former entities combined.

Visit Vault at **www.vault.com** for insider company profiles, expert advice, career message boards, expert resume reviews, the Vault Job Board and more.

VAULT CAREER LIBRARY   127

More rights for writers

In January 2001, HarperCollins agreed to partner with the web site, Rightscenter.com, which allows writers, publishers and agents to meet (via cyberspace) and negotiate deals. HarperCollins lists 500 of its international frontlist and backlist titles on the site. Although many independent publishers and agents are members of the site, HarperCollins became the first major print label to come aboard.

In a service designed to enhance publicity opportunities for its authors, HarperCollins announced the launch of a speakers bureau service in May 2005 that set up appearances for its writers. The speakers bureau is the "first major new program" in the company's Author+ initiative, according to a press release.

Good year

HarperCollins enjoyed a great year in 2003. The publisher had a record 111 adult and children's titles on *The New York Times* bestseller list during the year. Thirteen of these titles reached the No.-1 spot, including *Prey* by Michael Crichton, *Stupid White Men* by Michael Moore and *Dr. Atkins' New Diet Revolution* by the late Dr. Robert Atkins. During a week in February 2003, HC had 27 titles on *The New York Times* bestseller list – the company's best week ever.

In addition to this, Perennial, an HC imprint, published *A Problem From Hell* by Samantha Power, which won several awards, including the Pulitzer Prize for General Nonfiction and the National Book Critics Circle Award. *Everything Is Illuminated*, a novel by Jonathan Safran Foer, won the National Jewish Book Award for Fiction, among others. And *Bel Canto* by Ann Patchett won the Book Sense Paperback Book of the Year Award.

Rumblings at ReganBooks

In February 2004, the company's imprint, ReganBooks was the subject of both good and bad news. The good news was that Sean Hannity's *Deliver Us from Evil: Defeating Terrorism, Despotism and Liberalism*, had just hit No. 1 on *The New York Times* bestseller list. The bad news was that four employees of the famously sharp-tongued editor Judith Regan quit the imprint. The departure of longtime marketing director Carl Raymond and his assistant left the imprint without a marketing department. Also gone were a junior editor and Regan's personal assistant.

According to the *New York Daily News*, Raymond and the others were the newest departures in what had been a "mass exodus" from ReganBooks in the past two years

– nearly a dozen employees in all. One former ReganBooks staffer told the paper, "She is the boss from hell." Regan, however, didn't seem to mind, telling the paper, "I run a tight ship, work with very creative and hardworking people, who are really smart and really aggressive. We also produce at a very high level. Some people can't do that. Some people don't have the work ethic, the creativity, the drive, the ambition, the desire – and that's why they don't make it."

More big books

Armed with a proposal that ran just two-and-a-half pages, Jack Welch, the former chairman of General Electric, sold the world rights for a how-to business manual to HarperCollins for an estimated $4 million in February 2004. The book, *Winning* (which was written with Welch's wife, Suzy), was released in 2005. It didn't quite fetch the advance of *Jack: Straight From the Gut*, which he sold in 2000 without any written proposal for an advance of $7.1 million, but hey, $4 million is nothing to sneeze at.

Winning grew out of Welch's extensive post-retirement experience on the lecture circuit, he said. "I've been talking to armies of people and I realized that I had answers to questions about managing that people at lower levels could really use." Although he has been out of the public eye for several years, HarperCollins still seems willing to bet (with a hefty advance) that Welch's name is powerful enough to propel sales of a business how-to book.

The company announced another potential blockbuster in April 2005 after acquiring the rights to publish the diaries of former President Ronald Reagan. The diaries, scheduled to be released in 2006, are cover the years Reagan spent in the White House and will include his observations of both "the historic and the routine day-to-day events of his presidency."

Reaching out to readers

Over the years, HarperCollins has put forth a concerted effort to provide quality literature to targeted minority audiences who have been historically underrepresented in the literary marketplace. The revival of the Amistad imprint brought the publishing house a Pulitzer Prize through Edward P. Jones' *The Known World* in May 2004. In addition, HarperCollins picked up nine awards at the Latino Book Awards for its Rayo imprint, earning the title of No.-1 publisher for the Latino market.

Visit Vault at **www.vault.com** for insider company profiles, expert advice, career message boards, expert resume reviews, the Vault Job Board and more.

VAULT CAREER LIBRARY   **129**

HarperCollins has also created a number of programs for readers that have been very successful. Invite the Author allows book group participants chosen at random to interact with authors via telephone to enhance their book discussions. First Look ships advance reading copies of select books to customers before publication, generating early buzz for a number of titles. In addition, the HarperCollins web site boasts message and discussion boards where readers can talk about new and classic fiction, and tips for making the most of local reading groups.

GETTING HIRED

Hiring overview

HarperCollins lists all available positions, with instructions on how to apply, on its web site at www.harpercollins.com/hc/aboutus/careers.asp. Other than job openings, HaprerCollins' career site is mum on other career-related info like benefits, compensation and life at the company.

The publisher does offer a Career Development Program for candidates with "a college degree or equivalent work experience." Successful candidates become rotational associates at HarperCollins and spend time rotating among various departments to learn about the publishing business and find an appropriate position that aligns with the associate's skills and interests. Those interested in applying should view the company's career web page for more details.

Hiring advice from insiders

HarperCollins employees "suggest using an active approach" to get your foot in the publishing door. The company advertises job openings in *Publishers Weekly* and *The New York Times*, in addition to listing openings on the career portion of its web site. If you don't see an ad that fits your skills, consider just sending a resume and cover letter to HR, expressing an interest in an entry-level position (in editorial, publicity, production, etc.). Another good tip: "If there's a publishing program offered at your college, take it. Publishing people look for this – it shows you mean it when you say you have an interest in publishing." Insiders say that contacts are truly the best way to get your foot in the door. Their applications are placed on top of all other unsolicited resumes.

Interviews

The interview process begins with HR, and if they feel you're right for a certain department, they'll set up a meeting with someone from that area. There are usually only two interviews, and they're generally "very relaxed." In some cases, "one job doesn't work out but HR thinks they can place you in another department, so they might contact you again later on," insiders tell us. "After your interviews, be sure to send letters thanking the interviewer for his or her time," advises one source. "This shows that you're interested and aggressive enough to pursue the job by writing a letter."

"As for technical stuff," one insider reports, "Microsoft Word, Filemaker, Quark and Excel are about as technical as it will get." Though "if you're going for a copy editor's job, you'll have to take a test. Your English grammar has to be well above average, and you should be very familiar with the *Chicago Manual of Style*."

Visit Vault at **www.vault.com** for insider company profiles, expert advice,
career message boards, expert resume reviews, the Vault Job Board and more.

VAULT CAREER LIBRARY   131

Hearst Corporation, The

959 8th Avenue
New York, NY 10019
Phone: (212) 649-2148
Fax: (212) 649-2108
www.hearstcorp.com

LOCATIONS

New York, NY (HQ)

THE STATS

Employer Type: Private Company
Chairman: George R. Hearst, Jr.
CEO: Victor F. Ganzi
2003 Employees: 20,000
2003 Revenue ($mil.): $4,100.0

KEY COMPETITORS

Advance Publications
Gannett
Viacom

EMPLOYMENT CONTACT

www.hearstcorp.com/human_resources

THE SCOOP

All in the family

The Hearst Corp. is a media juggernaut with a stable of newspapers, magazines, TV and radio stations and online properties. The company has been in the Hearst family for more than 100 years, and the Hearst's seem to be completely happy keeping it in the family for another 100 more. Among its print publication roster, the company owns the *San Francisco Chronicle*, 14 weekly papers and 189 magazines in the U.S., including *Cosmopolitan* and *Good Housekeeping*, and 138 international editions, including 18 magazines in the United Kingdom. According to statistics from Mediamark Research Inc., Hearst's magazines reach a larger number of adults (72 million), both women (53 million) and men (18 million) than any other publisher of monthly magazines.

Hearst also has stakes in 27 local news channels and several cable station networks, including such stalwarts as A&E, Lifetime and ESPN. The company has also moved into the world of online content with interests in Netscape, genealogy.com, Exodus Communications and a minority stake in iVillage, a web network geared toward women. Victor Ganzi, a longtime employee of Hearst, has led the company since June 2002.

A new brand of journalism

William Randolph Hearst introduced his own brand of journalism to the world when he was given control of the faltering *San Francisco Examiner* in 1887 by his father George, a rancher and career politician. The younger Hearst's flashy revamping of the *Examiner* and his jingoistic print-based promotion of the Spanish-American War helped give birth to sensationalistic "yellow journalism." Early on Hearst realized that his brand of dynamic, splashy reporting sold papers and set out to capitalize on this, filing his papers with juicy journalism and revolutionizing the media industry in many ways. Hearst papers can boast of featuring the first multi-colored page, the first half-tone photographs on newsprint and the first full-color comics section. Not satisfied with his burgeoning newspaper business, in 1903 Hearst entered the magazine business and his honeymoon – an automobile trip across Europe – gave birth to *Motor* magazine, still appearing on newsstands today.

Visit Vault at **www.vault.com** for insider company profiles, expert advice, career message boards, expert resume reviews, the Vault Job Board and more.

VAULT CAREER LIBRARY   133

Growing an empire

By 1913, Hearst had acquired *Cosmopolitan* and *Good Housekeeping* magazines. The company branched out into other media forms soon after, with the creation of Hearst Metronome News in 1929 (which churned out newsreels seen in movie theaters) and the acquisition of radio stations in the 1920s and WBAL-TV, one of the first television stations in the country, in 1948. In 1980, the company bought a group of business publications, which eventually grew into Hearst Business Media (formed in August 1999), which includes publications such as *Electronic Products* and *Floor Covering Weekly*. In 1989, the company formed its Hearst Entertainment and Syndication unit, which includes some of the company's cable television interests and also the largest comics syndication business in the world, with stalwarts such as "Blondie" and "Beetle Bailey" in its lineup.

Hearst the diverse

Today, Hearst is a media/entertainment empire with 19 top-selling magazines targeting just about every audience, from the sensible *Good Housekeeping* to the glam *Harper's Bazaar*. Hearst also publishes 12 U.S. daily newspapers, including the *San Francisco Chronicle* and 14 weekly newspapers. The company has even branched out into book publishing, and all Hearst books are co-branded with one of Hearst's magazines. Each year Hearst Books publishes about 30 new titles, including: *The Good Housekeeping Illustrated Cookbook*, *Country Living Country Quilts*, *Country Living Country Gardens*, *Victoria Business of Bliss* and *House Beautiful Decorating Style*.

The company also publishes 110 overseas editions of its popular magazines, including 45 versions of *Cosmopolitan*. The most recent addition is in Latvia, which began publication in February 2002. The company owns 20 percent of ESPN and partnered with ABC to launch Lifetime network, the History Channel and the Arts & Entertainment channel in 1984. In April 2000, in a joint venture with Oprah Winfrey's Harpo Inc., Hearst launched *O: The Oprah Magazine*. Also in 2000, Hearst and rival publisher Condé Nast entered into an agreement for joint ownership of a newsstand distribution and marketing company.

In April, 2003, Lifetime Entertainment Services-jointly owned by The Hearst Corporation and The Walt Disney Company-and Hearst Magazines introduced a new women's magazine, called, fittingly enough, *Lifetime*. The magazine launched as a bimonthly with a rate base of 500,000 and went monthly starting with the September 2003 issue, though it was cancelled a year later due to disappointing results. Also that April, Hearst picked up *Seventeen* magazine, the No.-1 title in the teen market, from PRIMEDIA Inc. for an undisclosed amount. As part of the deal, Hearst also received a number of related businesses, including seventeen.com, *Seventeen*-branded licensing initiatives, 14 international editions, special editions of *Seventeen* and *Teen* magazine-branded publications, and Cover Concepts, an in-school marketing unit. Hearst called the deal a "strategic investment" and "extraordinary opportunity."

Hearst premiered *Town & Country TRAVEL*, a spin-off of *Town & Country* magazine, in September 2003. The travel edition is published quarterly, and covers "upscale information and quality advice on the world of luxury travel." Another new women's magazine, *SHOP Etc.*, debuted in August 2004. Covering fashion, home and beauty, *SHOP Etc.* was printed three times in 2004, and is expected to increase frequency to 10 issues in 2005. In September 2004, Hearst picked up White Directory Publishers Inc., the fourth-largest independent yellow pages publisher in the U.S., for an undisclosed amount. The same month, Hearst announced it would pair its British magazine division with one of Australia's biggest magazine publishers to create a weekly consumer publication for Britain. On the slate for the summer of 2005 is *Quick & Simple*, a weekly publication covering "real" women and featuring articles on home, family, food, health, nutrition, fitness, fashion and beauty.

Oprah overseas

In January 2002, Oprah's two-year old magazine crossed the ocean. *O* was launched in South Africa as the first international edition of the successful title. The South African edition is a joint venture among Hearst Magazines, Harpo Print LLC and Associated Magazines South Africa. Then in July 2002, the company unveiled yet another example of the cross-pollinating of its print and TV properties. Hearst launched a TV channel in Latin America based on its *Cosmopolitan* magazine. Hearst is mulling a similar channel in the U.S., a company executive told *The Wall Street Journal*. Though Hearst did not provide financial details of the Spanish-language channel's launch, the *Journal* reported that the costs are estimated to be $10 million to $15 million over five years.

Hearst tower

In April 2003, Hearst held a ceremonial groundbreaking at its six-story headquarters, 959 Eighth Ave. at 57th Street in Manhattan. The new building, to be competed in 2006, will be a 42-story glass and steel expansion built on top of the existing structure, and will be one of most environmentally-friendly buildings ever constructed in New York City. The original structure was built by W.R. Hearst in 1928. The expansion will permit Hearst to consolidate its New York operations. From the project's inception, Hearst set as its goal the attainment of LEED certification (or Leadership in Energy and Environmental Design) from the U.S. Green Building Council. The "green building" designation is bestowed upon those projects that employ pioneering solutions to fully utilize renewable sources of energy while offering substantial reductions in pollution and energy consumption. Hearst will be the first office building in New York City to achieve "green" status for the exterior and interior of its tower. New York Governor George Pataki praised the company for its "dedication to sustainable design which is sure to set an example for corporations across the country."

In addition to construction of the tower, Hearst will implement a series of public improvements to the Columbus Circle-59th Street subway station, which serves 100,000 subway riders a day. The company will construct a new entrance, install and maintain three elevators, reposition turnstiles and add or move stairwells. Hearst has already begun the process of temporarily relocating its employees out of 959 Eighth Avenue to prepare the site for construction. Considered an "important monument in the architectural heritage of New York" the original building was designated a Landmark Site by the Landmarks Preservation Commission in 1988.

Troubled Times in Seattle

Hearst filed a lawsuit against *The Seattle Times* in April 2003, after the *Times* announced plans to put into action a clause that would dissolve a joint operating agreement between the Seattle paper and the multimedia conglomerate's *Seattle Post-Intelligencer*. According to the JOA under which the two papers operate, either could renegotiate or dissolve the agreement if they reported three consecutive years of losses. Terms of the JOA established a plan in which both companies could publish one newspaper, or Hearst could publish *P-I* as a stand-alone paper. As part of the deal, both papers operate separate newsrooms, with *The Times* providing *The P-I* with back-office functions. Hearst would be forced to sell the paper if the JOA dissolved. *The Times* claimed it had lost money since 2000 due to a strike by the Newspaper Guild, Sept. 11th terrorist attacks, and the subsequent recession. Hearst argued that a "Force Majeure" clause in the JOA prohibited the papers from backing out of the partnership due to unforeseen events beyond control. According to *The Times*, its intention was not "to kill the *P-I*" but acknowledged that, under the JOA with Hearst, the *P-I* would "yield substantial losses for the foreseeable future."

A judge ruled in favor of Hearst in September 2003, but the decision was overturned in April 2004 by the Washington State Court of Appeals. The company is currently pursuing an appeal "to prevent the Seattle Times Company from ceasing JOA-publication of the *P-I* and achieving its goal of turning Seattle into a one-newspaper town."

Catering to teens

iVillage Inc., The Internet For Women, a leading women's media company, expanded a relationship with Hearst Magazines in 2004 to produce and host a new Hearst Teen Online Network of magazine web sites. The network is comprised of the *Seventeen, CosmoGIRL!* and *Teen* magazine web sites; iVillage provides design, production, hosting services, ad services, metric tracking, and reporting for all three. Additionally, a new reality television series is currently in development between MTV: Music Television and *Seventeen*. The 10-episode series is set to premiere on MTV in the fall of 2005, and will feature the quest for the lucky girl most deserving of the title "America's Sweetheart." The winner will receive a college scholarship, paid internship at *Seventeen*, and a cover story for the magazine.

Corporate face-lift

Two new executive positions were created in March 2004 at Hearst to enhance circulation and consumer marketing. Kenneth Godshall was named senior vice president, consumer marketing, while Lindsay Valk was named senior vice president, analysis and planning. In other news, Hearst announced at the start of 2005 that it would consolidate consumer marketing operations in New York City, including the relocation of consumer marketing employees from the Hearst Service Center in Charlotte, N.C., (roughly 60) to the company's Manhattan offices. The move was made to integrate all aspects of Hearst's overall publishing operations, including consumer marketing, editorial and advertising.

Award-winning journalism

In March 2005, the National Magazine Awards released its nominations for the year's best articles, interviews, photo essays and fiction pieces. *Esquire*, published by Hearst, gained three nominations. The NMAs, established in 1966, are awarded annually to "honor editorial excellence" and are sponsored by the ASME in association with the Columbia University Graduate School of Journalism.

Visit Vault at **www.vault.com** for insider company profiles, expert advice, career message boards, expert resume reviews, the Vault Job Board and more.

VAULT CAREER LIBRARY   **137**

GETTING HIRED

Lots of opportunities

The company's diverse array of operations means job positions are constantly opening-and closing. New hires are brought aboard most frequently in the marketing, sales and editorial departments of Hearst's numerous publications. Hearst's publications regularly rely on newspaper and trade journal advertisements to advertise positions. One insider advises, "Watch the trade publications, but apply fast-jobs are often filled very quickly." Another contact agrees, saying "You almost need to know about the job as soon as it comes out, because there'll be 100 other people just as hungry as you pulling all the strings and calling in all the favors they can to land it."

Aside from newspapers and the trades, the company's web site also lists job links by department, enabling applicants to e-mail resumes. The employment site can be found at: www.hearstcorp.com/human_resources. The company does not accept phone calls and though you can e-mail your resume, Hearst prefers that you snail mail it to the specific department or publication you are interested in.

Getting in

Breaking in to publishing is often a difficult process. "Unless you're some kind of wunderkind you're probably going to have to start at the bottom and work your way up." One contact says, adding, "And when I say bottom, I mean it. You'll work long hours for little pay and little recognition, but once you begin to move up the ladder, it's an incredibly rewarding and exciting place to work." Another insider says that "While publishing isn't necessarily an 'old-boys network', your best bet for getting in is to know someone on staff or to have interned at one of Hearst's publications. Many magazines and newspapers are loathe to take a chance on someone, and without at least some college newspaper of internship experience, you might as well forget it."

Home Box Office (HBO)

1100 Avenue of the Americas
New York, NY 10036
Phone: (212) 512-1000
Fax: (212) 512-1182
www.hbo.com

LOCATION

New York, NY (HQ)

THE STATS

Employer Type: Unit of Time Warner
Chairman and CEO: Chris Albrecht
2003 Employees: 2,000
2003 Revenue ($mil.): $3,003.0

KEY COMPETITORS

NBC
Starz Entertainment Group
Viacom

Visit Vault at **www.vault.com** for insider company profiles, expert advice,
career message boards, expert resume reviews, the Vault Job Board and more.

VAULT CAREER LIBRARY   139

THE SCOOP

Cable mammoth

A division of Time Inc., Home Box Office has been a driving force in the cable television industry since it was launched in 1972. The HBO network, the company's primary service, boasts almost 39 million subscribers in the U.S. alone and generates the highest prime-time ratings of all cable networks. Home Box Office founded the second-leading network, Cinemax, in 1980. That channel currently offers over 1,200 movies a year, more than any other premium network. Home Box Office also owns 50 percent of Comedy Central, manages E! Entertainment Television and produces its own programming through HBO Downtown Productions and HBO Independent Productions.

Since it founded Home Box Office, Time has grown into entertainment conglomerate Time Warner. However, in the wake of its parent company's expansion, HBO has not let the quality of its programming flag. In addition to presenting the cable premiers of films that feature big-name stars like *Titanic* and *The Mexican*, the company also produces films and miniseries, such as *Angels in America*. HBO also continues to produce award-winning original series such as *Curb Your Enthusiasm* and *The Sopranos*.

Sex and the Sopranos

In 1999 HBO began to cash in on a three-year effort to find and develop original drama series. The cable network's *Sex and the City* became a huge success that ran for six seasons. HBO went on to garner even more hype and praise for the popular mobster hit, *The Sopranos*. Both shows have taken home their fair share of Emmys and Golden Globes.

Along the same vein of in-your-face-commercial-free quality programming, HBO has continued to launch unique new series. Debuting in 2001, HBO broadcast *Six Feet Under*, developed by the Academy-award winning writer of *American Beauty*, Alan Bell. *Six Feet Under* depicts the trials and tribulations of a family who manages a funeral parlor, a bold departure from the occupations typically seen on television, like lawyers, cops and doctors. *Six Feet* joined its HBO cohorts when it took home the Golden Globe for Best Drama Series in early 2002. Other successful shows like the prison drama *Oz* and sports-centered *Arli$$* are certainly not hurting the company, either. A couple of the network's most recent series focus on the world of show business. *Entourage*, a comedy about the Hollywood misadventures of a young actor and his childhood buddies, and *Unscripted*, which follows a trio of would-be actors in search of their big break, both debuted in 2004. In addition to all this original comedy and drama, the network has also broadcast live concerts from such megastars as Madonna and Janet Jackson, stand-up comedy from Chris Rock, theatrical movies and even sporting events (primarily boxing).

Of course, not every show is destined to become a break-out hit. *The Mind of the Married Man*, which debuted in 2002, was no doubt aimed at the male demographic complementing the female *Sex and the City* viewers, but the show didn't catch on and was cancelled.

High-tech HBO

The kid-friendly HBO family channel, launched in 1996, features children's shows, "G" and "PG"-rated films before 9 p.m. and PG-13 rated films after 9 pm. The service is available to HBO subscribers at no extra charge. In 1998 the company launched "HBO the Works" and "MultiMAX," two new "multiplexing" services. With the increased capacity afforded by upgrades to digital services, the company can now offer larger suites of channels instead of just one or two versions (HBO has actually been multiplexing since 1991, with HBO2 and HBO3). The HBO suite includes HBO Signature, featuring original films, theatrical pieces and documentaries; HBO Family; HBO Comedy; and HBO Zone, which shows independent films, music specials and more "edgy" original films. HBO Latino offers versions of HBO's regular series and movies dubbed in Spanish, as well as new Spanish-language movies in their U.S. debut.

Following a good lead

After HBO launched the multiplexing concept, its little sister, Cinemax soon followed. Cinemax now offers a four-channel "MultiMAX" suite, including the original Cinemax; MoreMAX, with more movies; ActionMAX, a channel for action films; and ThrillerMAX, with mystery and horror films. In March 1999, the company launched its first high-definition TV (HBO HDTV) service. HBO HDTV follows the same schedule as the main HBO channel, yet offers a greater selection of feature films and HBO original programming shown in wide-screen format.

Good will greenlight

In 2000, HBO signed on with Matt Damon, Ben Affleck and director Chris Moore, to become a part of *Project Greenlight*. Founded by the three partners, *Project Greenlight* is a contest that selects one submitted screenplay and helps its writer produce the film and introduce it to Hollywood high society. The project funds the film with $1 million and acts as a producer and distributor. HBO debuted the first *Project Greenlight* film, *Stolen Summer* by Pete Jones, in December 2001.

Dueling networks

HBO fell into heated debate with NBC in early 2002 when both networks unveiled their schedules for the month of March. NBC had produced a made-for-TV-movie based on the life of Matthew Shepherd, the young man killed a hate crime in Laramie, Wyo., because he was gay. It was scheduled to air on the same day as HBO's interpretation of the off-Broadway play, *The Laramie Project*, which was based on interviews of people involved with the murder and living in the town. The debate ceased when HBO moved its film one week ahead of NBC's.

Emmy avalanche

In 2003, HBO took provocative comedian Bill Maher (who had been ousted from his late-night ABC talk-fest *Politically Incorrect*) under its wing and gave him another late-night talk show. The program, *Real Time with Bill Maher*, premiered in February of that year to a fair amount of critical acclaim.

HBO received 18 Emmy Awards (and 109 nominations) in 2003, the most of any network. The big winners were *The Sopranos*, *Live from Baghdad* and feature film *Hysterical Blindness* (awards for supporting stars Ben Gazzara and Gena Rowlands) which collectively took home 10 of the statues.

The network appeared to be on the right track during 2004 also, as it was honored with a record breaking 124 Emmy nominations and 20 Golden Globe nominations. Out of the 124 potential awards, HBO took home 32 awards with Mike Nichols' *Angels in America* as the standout performer. The two-part, six-hour film, an adaptation of Tony Kushner's Tony- and Pulitzer Prize-winning play, starred Al Pacino, Meryl Streep and Mary Louise Parker and was awarded with no less than 11 Emmys.

HBO Films

In 2004, HBO Films showcased stars such as Hilary Swank and Anjelica Huston in *Iron Jawed Angels*, the story of women's suffragists Alice Paul and Lucy Burns; Alan Rickman and Mos Def in *Something the Lord Made*, based on the true story of unlikely partners, a black lab technician and a white surgeon, who pioneered cardiac surgery in 1940s; and Geoffrey Rush and Charlize Theron in *The Life and Death of Peter Sellers*. All of the aforementioned productions were honored with Golden Globe nominations.

Financials

Employing some 2,000 people, HBO has seen its revenue grow at a steady pace since the late 1990s. Revenue for 2004 totaled more than $3 billion, compared to $2.78 billion for the year before and it marks a 50 percent increase in revenue since 1999. Since its inception, HBO has truly gone global and has a presence in some 50 markets worldwide. Its 16 million international subscribers are primarily located in Asia, Latin America and Central Europe.

For 2005, HBO has announced it is producing new seasons of its richly imaginative cult series *Carnivale* and Western series *Deadwood*. Collaborating with the BBC, the network is also hard at work on a series called *ROME* which is set to premiere in 2005. The historical epic is a story of two soldiers set in, you guessed it, ancient Rome.

GETTING HIRED

The online connection

HBO jobs are listed on careers section of the Time Warner web site (www.timewarner.com/corp/careers), where openings are searchable by division, location, area of interest and position type. Applicants can also submit a resume to the Time Warner database without applying for a specific job. Openings for positions at America Online, Time Inc., Time Warner Cable, Home Box Office, New Line Cinema, Turner Broadcasting System and Warner Bros. are also listed on the same site.

Visit Vault at **www.vault.com** for insider company profiles, expert advice, career message boards, expert resume reviews, the Vault Job Board and more.

VAULT CAREER LIBRARY   **143**

Houghton Mifflin Company

222 Berkeley St.
Boston, MA 02116-3764
Phone: (617) 351-5000
Fax: (617) 351-1105
www.hmco.com

LOCATIONS

Boston, MA (HQ)

KEY COMPETITORS

Harcourt
McGraw-Hill
Pearson

EMPLOYMENT CONTACT

www.hmco.corporate.com/hr.job
   postings.html

THE SCOOP

Educating America

Whether they are the products of a private or public education, students everywhere are reared on a steady diet of Houghton Mifflin textbooks. The company began in 1832 when John Allen and William D. Ticknor bought the Old Corner Bookstore in Boston. When the partnership dissolved, Ticknor tried again with James T. Fields; the pair went on to become American publishing legends by selling classic works by authors such as Ralph Waldo Emerson, Nathaniel Hawthorne and Mark Twain.

Ticknor and Fields began working with Henry Houghton's Riverside Press in 1852; by 1880 the two firms merged into a partnership called Houghton, Mifflin & Company. The company established an Education Department early in its history, but the department did not begin to dominate the company until the baby boom swelled the number of students at all levels of schooling. Now textbooks and other educational material account for 90 percent of the company's sales.

Testing the textbook

Houghton Mifflin went on a buying spree during the 1980s and 1990s, acquiring Rand McNally's education unit, McDougal, Little & Company, and D.C. Heath. As a result, Houghton Mifflin incurred short-term debts and saw frequent turnover in its top management. However, the company successfully absorbed Heath and was headed into a more stable period.

As evidence of this stability, Houghton Mifflin acquired two companies to beef up its divisions. Virtual Learning Technologies became part of HM's Riverside Publishing, an academic and clinical assessment unit based in Illinois. With VLT's educational Internet testing expertise, Riverside can now focus on the growing web-based K-12 testing market.

The French are coming ... and they're gone again!

Even though Houghton Mifflin denied rumors that it would be sold for years, the company did eventually give up its independence. French media giant Vivendi Universal bought the company in 2001 for some $2.2 billion, which included about half a billion dollars in assumed debt. However, Houghton Mifflin, which was incorporated under Vivendi's publishing umbrella, was sold to an investment consortium (consisting of Bain Capital, The Blackstone Group and Thomas H. Lee) a year later. The 2002 deal was part of Vivendi's huge $10 billion asset sale.

That same year, an ill wind blew into Houghton Mifflin from the estate of Margaret Mitchell. Alice Randall's *The Wind Done Gone*, which made the bestseller lists in 2001, retells Mitchell's classic *Gone With the Wind* from the perspective of a slave but Mitchell's camp argued that it was a case of not just retelling but plagiarizing. The case was settled out of court in May 2002. The company also gained much success with the publication of *The Lord of the Rings* books and the children's favorite, *Curious George*.

Acquisitions

Houghton Mifflin was branching out and away with its acquisitions in 2003. In October 2003, the company purchased Cognitive Concepts, a firm focusing on early literacy and reading performance products. Cognitive Concepts' Earobics package (including CD-Roms, audiotapes, videotapes and printed materials) is a research-based early literacy package designed to ensure that all students have the fundamental skills they need to be successful readers. Earobics is used in over 7,500 schools in the U.S. Two months later it acquired San Francisco-based Edusoft which offers an assessment platform that helps school districts improve student achievement through better access to performance data and instructional tools.

Houghton Mifflin posted a $790 million loss in 2002, which was related to Vivendi selling the company to the investment consortium in late 2001. Bain Capital's Mark Nunnelly remarked in a pre-release that "the loss reported is not a reflection of the company's performance. Ironically, it is a result of the favorable price we paid when acquiring Houghton Mifflin in 2002, and reflects the loss Vivendi Universal took on the transaction." In 2003, Houghtin Mifflin showed an increase in revenue of $70 million and lowered expenses – including a reduction of its employee count by some 100 people – and declared a $70 million loss for the year.

Staying on track

Houghton Mifflin's K-12 revenue accounts for almost two-thirds of the company's revenue and in 2004, it seems to have steadied the ship. College publishing is growing progressively for Houghton Mifflin and the trade market is a cash cow that performs steadily. The company reported net sales of $570 million for the quarter ended September 30, 2004, a 2 percent increase over the $558 million in the third quarter of 2003. The K-12 publishing segment's net sales increased 2 percent to

$397.2 million for the third quarter of 2004, up from $390.3 million for the same period in 2003. The segment has benefited from the school division's sales of its reading programs and Houghton Mifflin Leveled Readers, as well as McDougal Littell's success in the secondary school markets for math, language and social studies programs.

The college publishing segment's net sales were $116.1 million for the third quarter of 2004, up slightly from $115.2 million for the same period in 2003. Results were marred by lower sales of backlist titles and smaller quantity orders by college bookstores. The college publishing segment has been affected by market-driven issues of used textbook sales and Internet availability of textbooks and supplements.

The trade and reference publishing segment's net sales were $41.1 million for the third quarter, an 8 percent increase over the $38 million for the same period in 2003. The increase was due primarily to the higher sales of adult, children's and cookbook titles, offset by the decline in sales of Tolkien titles, following the run of the movie trilogy, which ended in 2003.

GETTING HIRED

Make the connection

Houghton Mifflin lists current job openings on its employment web page, located at www.hmco.corporate.com/hr.jobpostings.html. Resumes and cover letters can be e-mailed to jobs@hmco.com, mailed to the human resources department at the above address or faxed to (617) 351-1106. Or job seekers can apply online through the web site. One editor gives encouraging advice: "Ignore the requirements listed in the job posting. Houghton Mifflin tries to get the best candidates, and so it often puts what seem to be insurmountably high requirements into their job listings." Houghton Mifflin favors candidates who demonstrate a strong interest in book publishing, academic achievement, superior verbal and writing skills, and computer proficiency. "Most of the recent college graduates that work for Houghton Mifflin begin as freelancers," a source says. "They are put on six-month contracts, and eventually – hopefully – are hired." Says another, "Make sure that the human resources people know that you are willing to accept contract work."

Expect two or three interviews before being offered a full-time position: "Interviewing basically comes down to an initial interview with the HR rep, before you move on to the next phase, an interview with the hiring manager." The second

Visit Vault at **www.vault.com** for insider company profiles, expert advice, career message boards, expert resume reviews, the Vault Job Board and more.

VAULT CAREER LIBRARY   **147**

("real") interview varies widely: "I've known friends who interviewed with a manager in a local restaurant over a couple of beers, and managers who made an interview into the Spanish Inquisition." A word of caution: "I have not seen a lot of cross-department shifting, though so if you are interested in trade books, don't accept a job in school or college division, because you might never transfer laterally."

Student ops

Each year, Houghton Mifflin offers some limited opportunities for students to work in temporary positions during the summer. In May and June, the company hires in administrative and editorial positions, primarily in the Boston office. Students interested in applying for these positions should send cover letters and resumes to: jobs@hmco.com.

The company also has internship programs for its editorial, marketing, art and design, production, rights and permissions, and custom publishing departments. The internship includes a full-time appointment from June through August. To participate, students must have completed their sophomore or junior year in college or be in graduate school. Candidates should contact:

Houghton Mifflin Company
College Division, Internship Coordinator
222 Berkeley Street
Boston, MA 02116

International Data Group

1 Exeter Plaza, 15th Floor
Boston, MA 02116-2851
Phone: (617) 534-1200
Fax: (617) 423-0240
www.idg.com

LOCATIONS

Boston, MA (HQ)

THE STATS

Employer Type: Private Company
Chairman: Patrick J. (Pat) McGovern
CEO: Pat Kenealy
2004 Employees: 13,510
2004 Revenue ($mil.): $2,500.0

KEY COMPETITORS

CNET Networks
United Business Media
Ziff Davis Media

EMPLOYMENT CONTACT

careers.idg.com/www/home.nsf/
CareersAtIDGForm?OpenForm

THE SCOOP

Information and technology

International Data Group has become the go-to source for those looking for cutting-edge information about the inner workings of the IT community. The Boston-based publishing company prints up 300 high-tech magazines and newspapers in 85 countries, and is the world's No.-1 publisher of computer-related periodicals. To keep up at this pace, IDG employs more than 13,000 people worldwide. In 2004 the company brought in revenue of $2.5 billion.

IDG offers the widest range of magazines, events and web sites targeted to the IT professional in the world – in fact, the company estimates that some 120 million technology buyers read its publications. The company's diverse product and services portfolio spans six key areas including: print publishing, online publishing, events and conferences, market research, education and training, and global marketing solutions.

Insight into the future

Patrick McGovern became interested in the computer industry while working as a part-time editor at *Computers and Automation*, the first U.S. computer magazine, during his undergraduate days at MIT After graduation, McGovern founded International Data Corporation in 1964 – way before computing became a commonplace activity in American life – as a way to provide the burgeoning computer industry with timely information and statistics. The company got a jump on the competition by first publishing *Computerworld* magazine in 1967 and took its product to the global marketplace soon after.

Throughout the 1970s, IDG expanded worldwide, reaching markets in Japan, France, the U.K., Germany, Brazil and Australia. McGovern's concept of "think globally, act locally" carried over into these foreign countries, where titles like *Shukan Computers* and *Computerwoche* offered culture-specific information tailored to local technology concerns and needs, and were edited and managed by an indigenous staff.

By 1982, IDG's computer magazines could be found in stores from Spain to Sweden, and the company maintained 11 offices worldwide. For its 20th anniversary in 1984, IDG published the first issue of *Macworld* the same week Steve Jobs introduced the Macintosh home computer to the market. IDG next conquered Eastern Europe and

Asia, launching the first publishing deal in the Soviet Union between the former U.S.S.R. and the U.S. in 1987, and expanding into Hong Kong, Korea and Taiwan.

When the computer industry took off in the 1990s, IDG was there right along side it, sponsoring independent studies on the dynamics of IT purchasing processes, developing PC and Mac expos worldwide, creating IT forums, adding to its cache of technology publications, building web sites and IDC Internet services, and launching an ad campaign focusing on "Answers in the Information Age."

Award-winning publications

IDG's print publishing division consists, logically enough, of the 300 periodicals the company publishes in various languages around the world. IDG's five global publication product lines – *Computerworld/InfoWorld*, *CIO*, *Macworld*, *Network World* and *PC World* – account for more than 175 of these titles. Not only are the titles widely read, but they're pretty well respected in the industry, as well.

In October 2003, IDG cleaned up at Folio Awards, (an annual event at which the magazine industry awards the year's top achievers) winning 18 Gold, Silver and Platinum awards for superior editorial and design work. IDG's award winners were *Bio-IT World*, *CIO Magazine*, *CSO Magazine*, *Computerworld*, *InfoWorld*, *Macworld*, *Network World* and *PC World*. The awards included a Silver Award for Computerworld for the second consecutive year for editorial excellence and a Silver Award in online business-to-business. *InfoWorld* took home a Gold award for best online site design in the business-to-business category and a Platinum award for best site design from among consumer, business-to-business, and association/non-profit/custom award winners. *InfoWorld* also won a Gold award for editorial in 2002. *Macworld* won a Silver for best use of an illustration in a single article. *Network World* won a Gold for best table of contents and two Silver awards for editorial excellence in telecommunications and best use of an illustration. Finally, *PC World* won Gold for the second straight year for best consumer/computing magazine and two Silvers for best use of digital imagery and best site design. *CIO* magazine also holds the distinction of winning the Grand Neal Award at the National Business Journalism Awards in March 2003. *CIO*'s article, *Making it in 2002*, beat out 1,091 other entries to snag the award. *PC World* also took home several awards from the 2004 Folio Awards.

In July 2004, IDG dominated the American Society of Business Publications Editors competition, winning 116 awards, including "Magazine of the Year" for both *Computerworld* and *CSO* magazine, a security-focused publication. In addition, *PC*

Visit Vault at **www.vault.com** for insider company profiles, expert advice, career message boards, expert resume reviews, the Vault Job Board and more.

VAULT CAREER LIBRARY

151

World was named as one of the "Top 10 Magazines of the Year." Founder and Chairman Patrick J. McGovern also took home the "Lifetime Achievement Award."

Selling For Dummies

Not all of the company's publishing endeavors have met with such success, however. In 2001 the firm sold its 75 percent stake in Hungry Minds (formerly IDG Books Worldwide), to publisher John Wiley & Sons for $182 million. With the sale, IDG dropped the *"For Dummies"* how-to book series, *Webster's New World* dictionaries and *CliffsNotes* study guides, Frommer's travel guides and the *Betty Crocker* and *Weight Watchers* cookbooks. The unit had a higher ratio of bestseller books than any other technology publisher, covering technology, business, computer-based learning tools and how-to books. The *"For Dummies"* series had also been translated into 31 languages with more than 60 million books in print. Despite all this, however, Hungry Minds had been losing money for IDG. For the six months ending in March 2001, sales fell 22 percent to $95 million and net losses totaled $9.5 million. Net revenue for the quarter ending in June 2001 was also reported to be down to $41 million, from $55 million a year earlier. IDG had only purchased Hungry Minds in August 2000 for about $5 million, but decided to dump the subsidiary when it couldn't maintain profitability. IDG Books Worldwide had also acquired an array of books and online brands from the Macmillan General Reference Group of Pearson Education for $83 million in 2000, but decided to combine the newly acquired reference books with the *"For Dummies"* and sell them off as a group.

Online presence

IDG's online network, centered around the company's www.idg.net web site, includes 400 web sites based in 85 different countries, which are staffed by some 2,000 journalists. The network also runs a global ad network that offers enhanced web marketing programs including custom webcasts, e-mail newsletters and micro networks to interested parties. In addition to this, the network is supported by the world's only 24-hour global technology news organization, the IDG News Service, reporting the latest technology news and analysis in multiple languages around the world.

IDG's online empire is pretty extensive, offering career development sites www.jobuniverse.com and www.itcareers.com, which offer content on career enhancement, along with career opportunities for those in the IT industry. There is also www.pcworld.com which provides an interactive version of the print magazine's

"Top 100" product reviews, and www.idc.com, which provides market research that offers insight, trends, and forecasts by industry. In 2002, the company launched digital versions of its print magazines through a partnership with Brisbane, Calif.-based Zinio Systems Inc. The electronic reprints contained the same content, fonts, graphics and advertisements as print versions in an Internet-accessible interactive format, allowing users to zoom, search, hyperlink and make electronic notations.

They do research, too

IDG also owns International Data Corporation, found at www.idcresearch.com, which is the world's leading provider of global marketing information on IT market and technology trends. With research centers in 43 countries and more than 575 research analysts worldwide, IDC serves a stable of more than 3,900 clients worldwide. The company can also lay claim to being the leading provider of worldwide market research in consumer computing, including personal computing, interactive entertainment and online services. One of the largest computer training companies in the world is IDG's subsidiary, ExecuTrain, which offers 785 courses in more than 230 locations, specializing in the computer education of business professionals.

IDG - event planners?

Among its many other business interests, IDG is also the leading producer of more than 168 globally branded conferences and events in 35 countries. Some of the international events the company sponsors include LinuxWorld Conference & Expo, *Macworld* Conference & Expo, and *BioITWorld* Conference & Expo. Leading conferences include Agenda and Demo, in addition to hosting and creating customized online events and webcasts on www.ITworld.com. Having expanded its reach in recent years, IDG now also produces 17 conferences and events in China alone, and was the first company to offer expos in emerging markets throughout Asia, Eastern Europe and Latin America as those economies became increasingly privatized and joined in the global tech economy.

In October, 2003, IDG announced an addition to its already large roster of conferences – "Mac IT" – a new conference for enterprise IT managers that will debut at the upcoming *Macworld* Conference & Expo in January 2004. The new conference will offer sessions on servers, services, security, IT management, integration and networking.

Visit Vault at **www.vault.com** for insider company profiles, expert advice, career message boards, expert resume reviews, the Vault Job Board and more.

V∧ULT CAREER LIBRARY   **153**

The *Macworld* event ran into some trouble earlier this year when IDG announced that it wanted to bring the event back to Boston in 2004, after having moved it to New York in 1997. But Apple Computer didn't want the event moved to Beantown, and informed event organizers that it was scaling back its participation in the conference. Then, the city of Boston announced it wasn't so sure about letting IDG use its Convention center (for free) for the Expo. IDG responded by canceling the blocks of rooms that it had tentatively reserved at hotels for conventioneers, forcing the city's hand, and by August, Boston relented. The event was eventually held in Boston July 12-15, 2004. Without the presence of Apple Computer (who pulled out), the Expo had a more general focus than usual, focusing more on graphic designers and other creative professionals.

Customized gatherings

In October 2004, IDG announced the advent of the Custom Events Group, a new group to create "small exclusive gatherings" for a company's prospects or customers. IDG World Expo, the company's tradeshow-producing arm, developed the group as a way to expand on IDG's event planning experience with its larger, open events (such as *Macworld* and LinuxWorld). Mike Healy, the group's vice president, said the Custom Events Group will personalize each event, working closely with clients for recruitment and registration, and coordinating from start to finish, including topic development, audience mining, logistics and marketing. "The events are energizing," Healy said, "and provide clients with a productive and intimate environment where vision, ideas and strategies are shared, and where clients get the opportunity to meet their most important prospects and customers."

IDG looks east

In December 2002, IDG announced that it was planning on investing $100 million to expand its presence in Vietnam by 2010. The publisher launched a handful of IT titles in Vietnam in 2003, including *Network World, Telecom World* and *Electronic Tech World*. The company first entered the Vietnamese market in 1992 with the launch of PC World, which now has a paid circulation of 52,000. But Vietnam isn't the only Asian country IDG has established a foothold in. The company has been in China since 1980 and has invested more than $200 million in 120 technology companies there over the last 10 years. IDG is now so established in the Chinese market that it publishes the Chinese versions of more general American and European magazines, including *Cosmopolitan, Harper's Bazaar* and *Esquire*. In March 2004, IDG's Chinese subsidiary announced a publishing deal with Nikkei

Business Publications to publish a new magazine under both companies' logos. Overall, IDG publishes 30 magazines through partnerships in the Chinese market.

The trouble with deep linking

In August 2003, Patrick Kenealy, CEO of IDG, began an in-house assessment of the company's web sites to see where its traffic comes from. In June 2003, the company first noticed what it deemed to be an excessive amount of traffic coming from Boston-based TechTarget, a four-year-old Internet portal for IT professionals. The company then blocked all visitors coming from the upstart business. Kenealy is upset because he contends that small and large publishers, as well as technology companies, are profiting directly or indirectly from IDG's intellectual property through deep linking – the practice of clicking on a link from one site directly to another's content – thereby bypassing the homepage. IDG says it has put a halt to traffic from 15 additional competitors. Lots of companies, Kenealy claims, are generating sales leads, getting registration data or otherwise re-purposing IDG's intellectual property, and he plans on putting a stop to it.

GETTING HIRED

Hiring overview

In 2003, the company announced that for the third year in a row, *Fortune* magazine selected it as one of the "100 Best Places to Work for in America." Those interested in seeking employment can start by visiting the company's web site at www.idg.com, where they can look for open positions throughout the company. The company offers standard benefits, including medical, dental and vision care, as well perks such as paid maternity and adoption leave.

John Wiley & Sons, Inc.

111 River St.
Hoboken, NJ 07030
Phone: (201) 748-6000
Fax: (201) 748-6008
www.wiley.com

LOCATIONS

Hoboken, NJ (HQ)
New York, NY
Somerset, NJ

THE STATS

Employer Type: Public Company
Stock Symbol: JW.a, JW.b
Stock Exchange: NYSE
Chairman: Peter Booth Wiley
CEO: William J. (Will) Pesce
2004 Employees: 3,300
2004 Revenue ($mil.): $923.0

KEY COMPETITORS

Pearson
Reed Elsevier Group

EMPLOYMENT CONTACT

www.wiley.com/WileyCDA/Section/
id-101311.html

THE SCOOP

Specialization: launching literary giants

The oldest independent publishing company in America, John Wiley & Sons has published the works of writers who would later go on to become literary giants. Since then it has moved on to become a giant publisher in its own right, particularly in science and technology. The company specializes in three areas: professional and consumer books; textbooks and educational materials, and scientific, technical, and medical publications. This third category accounts for roughly half of the publisher's sales. Although Wiley is a publicly traded company, as of 2005 the family retains 70 percent of the company's shares and 49 percent of its voting power.

History

Charles Wiley started off with a small printing shop in Manhattan's West Village in 1806 when he was 25 years old. Five years later, Charles joined Cornelius Van Winkle to create "The Den," the store's back room where many of the writers it published, such as James Fenimore Cooper, were known to congregate. In 1814, Charles became a publisher, and by 1819, he was publishing the works of the city's literary jet set, including Nathaniel Hawthorne and Washington Irving. Charles parted ways with Van Winkle in 1820 and continued to build his company until his death in 1826. Wiley's son John took over the business, and George Palmer Putnam became a junior partner of the company 10 years later. Together, the men published the works of many famous American and European authors of the time, including Herman Melville, Edgar Allan Poe, Hans Christian Anderson, Victor Hugo, Charles Dickens and Elizabeth Barrett Browning. Putnam left the company in 1851, and Wiley began publishing books in architecture, agriculture and rural affairs. By 1875, both of Wiley's sons had come on board, and the company name was changed to reflect their contributions. Five years later, the publisher shifted its focus from general interest books to science and technology, influenced by William Wiley's passion for engineering.

At the start of the 20th century, John Wiley & Sons, Inc. was incorporated; by 1929, sales had eclipsed $1 million. The company went public in 1962, and within four years, the company had expanded into Europe, Mexico, South America, Australia and Japan.

Visit Vault at www.vault.com for insider company profiles, expert advice, career message boards, expert resume reviews, the Vault Job Board and more.

VAULT CAREER LIBRARY   157

Hey, big spender

In 1984, to strengthen its position in science publishing, the company purchased Scripta-Technica, a scientific journal publisher and translator. Five years later, Wiley added Alan R. Liss, Inc., which specializes in life science books and journals, to its family. In 1991, Wiley strengthened its standing in law publishing with a number of acquisitions, including the law publications division of Professional Education Systems Inc., London-based Chancery Law Publishing Ltd. and James Publishing Group's paralegal line. The publisher has also branched out into software, multimedia, and Internet businesses, largely through acquisitions. It has also formed strategic alliances with a wide variety of companies, including The Gallup Organization, Internet publisher Mecklermedia, and the publishers of *Upside* magazine, *Forbes* and *Adweek Magazines* Group.

New avenues

In 1996, the company acquired a 90 percent stake in VCH Publishing Group, a German company specializing in scientific and technical journals. The following year, the company launched Wiley InterScience, an online service that provides access to nearly 400 of the company's scientific, technical, medical and professional journals. Wiley continued to focus on the sciences during the last half of the 1990s, acquiring Van Rostrand Reinhold, a publisher of environmental/industrial science, culinary arts/hospitality and business technology books from Thomson Corp. for $28 million, in addition to acquiring Chronimed (health care) publishing, the Preservation Press and the Clinical Psychology Publishing Company. Wiley also became the publisher of *Cancer*, the journal of the American Cancer Society, in 1997.

President/CEO William J. Pesce took his post in January 1998. It was also quite a year for co-development deals at the company: Wiley signed deals for the development of various types of interactive educational software with companies including Zoologic Inc., Question Mark Corporation, AccountingNet.com and SAS Institute Inc. In addition Wiley began publishing the *Ernst & Young Tax Guide* on America Online and the *Journal of Image Guided Surgery* online. By the end of Pesce's first year, the company had earned a spot on the "top 40 most respected companies" list conducted by the *Financial Times* and a global survey of CEOs. Wiley was the only publisher to make the list.

In 1999, Wiley spent more than $1 billion dollars in acquisitions, striking three key deals to increase its holdings. First, Wiley made a deal with Pearson, acquiring 55 college textbook titles and instructional packages in biology/anatomy and physiology; engineering; mathematics; economics/finance; and teacher education for $58 million. Next, the company bought Jossey-Bass, a San Francisco, Calif.-based publisher of business, psychology, education and health management books for journals, professionals and executives, for $81 million. Finally, Wiley acquired the J.K. Lasser tax and financial guides to solidify its footing in the financial planning market. The company's buying binge paid off: Between the fiscal years 1990 and 2002, Wiley more than doubled its revenue and increased market capitalization from $100 million to $1.3 billion.

Coursepack scandal

Wiley, along with University of Chicago Press, Princeton University Press, Elsevier Inc., SAGE Publications and Pearson Education Inc., sued BISI Inc., an Austin, Texas-based owner of multiple copy shop chains in February 2004. The publishers charged the company with copyright infringement, alleging that BISI copy shops, including Abel's Copies and Speedway Copy and Printing, duplicated and distributed copyright materials for print and electronic forms of "coursepacks," or packs of journal articles, selected materials, book excerpts and other reading required by local universities, without obtaining permission from the publishers or the Copyright Clearance Center, a non-profit copyright licensing and management company. BISI and representatives from the publishing companies are currently working to settle the case.

The Texas case was not the first time Wiley battled copyright infringement related to coursepacks. The previous summer, the publisher joined with HarperCollins, Pearson, Princeton, and SAGE to battle a similar lawsuit in Indiana. Wiley also joined with Elsevier and MIT Press in July 2003 in a lawsuit aimed at Gainesville, Fla.-based Custom Copies, alleging the company with producing coursepacks for the University of Florida without authorization. A lawyer for Wiley noted that "lawsuits like this are the last resort in minimizing copyright infringement, yet we are willing to take this step when needed to protect our interests."

Brand expansion for dummies

In recent years, Wiley has continually broadened its horizons within the nonfiction publishing sector. The company purchased Hungry Minds, Inc. in 2001, its biggest acquisition to date, gaining the popular "*For Dummies*" series, *Webster's New World Dictionaries*, *CliffsNotes* study guides, Frommer's travel guides and cookbooks by Betty Crocker and Weight Watchers. The same year, Wiley also purchased Frank J.

Fabozzi Publishing, a publisher of financial titles, and created a multimedia geology web site through a partnership with Columbia University Press.

In July 2002, Wiley's corporate headquarters moved across the Hudson River to Hoboken, N.J. The company added GIT Verlag, a chemistry, drug, biotechnology, security and engineering journal publisher, as well as A&M publishing, a publisher of pharmaceutical and health care content. In 2003, Wiley gained publication rights to the *British Journal of Surgery*, and joined with the American Institute of Chemical Engineers to publish the *AIChE Journal*; *Environmental Progress* and *Process Safety Progress*.

Utilizing the Internet

Wiley has recently turned to the Internet as a new outlet for publishing ventures. In April 2002, Wiley and GlobalMentor, Inc., an international education technology company, published *Graph Theory* and *Geography*, an e-book using animation, interaction and full color graphics to provide "a new realm" of learning. It was the first e-book released by a major publisher containing extensive user interaction, and was published by the Wiley Interscience Series in Discrete Mathematics and Optimization.

In March 2004, the company signed a deal with San Carlos, Calif.-based Aplia, an education technology solutions provider, to develop an electronic textbook, incorporating intermediate economics and interactive web tracking tools, which allow students to be linked to new stories, analysis and problem sets as economic policies change. Wiley plans to release the product in January 2006, and hopes to jumpstart the burgeoning college e-textbook market, which was established in 2001, through the Aplia deal.

In December 2004, Wiley and rivals Reed Elsevier and Blackwell Publishing teamed up with the American Cancer Society, American Diabetes Association and American Heart Association to create patientINFORM, a consortium designed to distribute scientific publishing content free of charge through the patient-advocacy groups' web sites. The project is expected to launch during the spring of 2005, and was created by Brian Crawford, a vice president at Wiley, who noted that the scientific publishing industry was getting "a bad rap for not having original research information available to the general public."

Record results

Wiley rounded out the fiscal year 2004 with record results, increasing its net income by 12 percent to $86 million, excluding tax benefits and charges. Revenue improved 8 percent to $923 million, driven by strong sales in the professional/trade division in the U.S., and the scientific, technical and medical divisions on a global scale.

GETTING HIRED

Wiley looks for responsible, energetic individuals with an interest in publishing. Most of its entry-level hires are recent grads, but if you're looking to change industries, don't rule it out. The company does seek to hire candidates with office experience, either through a previous job or an internship. Look for job information under the "About Wiley" section of Wiley's web site for job descriptions, qualifications, and internship opportunities. Post, fax, or e-mail resumes to the addresses listed on the web site.

Visit Vault at **www.vault.com** for insider company profiles, expert advice, career message boards, expert resume reviews, the Vault Job Board and more.

VAULT CAREER LIBRARY   161

Liberty Media

12300 Liberty Blvd.
Englewood, CO 80112
Phone: (720) 875-5400
Fax: (720) 875-7469
www.libertymedia.com

LOCATIONS

Englewood, CO (HQ)

DEPARTMENTS

Interactive Group
Networks Group
Tech/Ventures Group

THE SCOOP

Freedom of communication

Liberty Media Corp. is a holding company owning interests in a variety of e-tailing, media, communications, and entertainment businesses broken down into three core groups: Interactive, Networks, and Tech/Ventures. Among Liberty's holdings are QVC, Court TV, Encore, STARZ!, Discovery, IAC/InterActiveCorp, and The News Corporation Limited. Today's Liberty Media Corp. was created in August 2001 from a spin off by AT&T as part of a larger restructuring plan to boost stock value at the telecom giant. AT&T gained Liberty as part of a March 1999 acquisition of former Liberty parent TCI.

Not so fast ...

The split from AT&T was not without a hitch. Current Liberty chairman (and former TCI chairman) John Malone resigned from the AT&T board in August 2001 after two events reportedly sparked fury in the media titan. First, news surfaced that Malone would be excluded from talks related to Comcast Corp.'s bid for AT&T's cable-TV unit. To add insult to injury, AT&T also questioned the validity of a contract with the Starz network inherited through its acquisition of TCI. Following Malone's departure from the board, Starz filed a lawsuit in a Colorado district court, accusing AT&T of failing to pay $44 million in licensing fees to the network as outlined in a 1997 deal. Comcast went on to acquire AT&T's cable service in 2002, and, in September 2003, hammered out a deal with Starz in which Comcast agreed to pay the network per subscriber base rather than by the flat fee Starz proposed. But, as a concession, the company agreed to distribute Starz Encore's video-on-demand and high-definition services in new markets and areas where Starz Encore offered service.

From high to low

Initially, traders had a love affair with the new Liberty stock. Malone quickly got to work trying to boost the company's holdings abroad, entering into negotiations with British and German cable giants in a quest to create the world's largest cable company. In February 2001, Malone announced a plan to acquire six cable-TV companies in Germany from Deutsche Telekom, and to invest an additional $543 million in UnitedGlobalCom. However, a year later, Germany's Federal Cartel Office squashed the deal, prohibiting Liberty from acquiring the cable channels.

Visit Vault at **www.vault.com** for insider company profiles, expert advice, career message boards, expert resume reviews, the Vault Job Board and more.

VAULT CAREER LIBRARY   **163**

Then, a deal between Liberty and NTL, Britain's largest cable operator, fell through. Meanwhile, in the midst of a recession back at home, Malone's media holdings tanked on the market. By May 2002, Liberty's shares slid 58 percent from their 52-week high.

New ventures

Malone moved to a new prospect: interactive television. In May 2002, the company formed Liberty Broadband Interactive Television Inc., which then, in turn, picked up a controlling stake in OpenTV. The move closely mirrored the creation of Liberty Digital, another Malone-driven project executed in 1999, which acquired minority stake in OpenTV but then went private two years later after interactive TV failed to attract widespread public interest. LBIT would focus on the interactive advertising and T-commerce arenas, areas Liberty Digital had previously skimmed over.

In July 2003, Liberty paid $7.9 billion for Comcast's 57 percent stake in the QVC, giving the company full ownership of the home-shopping network. The next month, Liberty picked up Class B shares of UnitedGlobalCom it didn't already own for $141.2 million in stock, granting it 96 percent of voting rights for UnitedGlobalCom shares. In one last deal to close out 2003, Liberty acquired outstanding shares of TP Investment, a private investment vehicle run by Malone, for $60.7 million in Liberty stock.

Going global, finally

Despite all the moving and shaking on Malone's part to boost Liberty's bottom line, the company reported a first-quarter loss in May 2004 of $10 million compared with a gain of $132 million the year prior after some investments declined in value, including the Starz network, whose operating income slipped 41 percent on increased marketing spending.

The next month, the company announced it had successfully spun off its international holdings into a new publicly held company, Liberty Media International Inc., which would hold Liberty assets in Europe, Japan and Latin America worth roughly $9 billion. That November, Liberty's international arm further increased its presence in the global marketplace through a joint venture with Sumitomo Corp. The newly created LMI/Sumisho Super Media LLC held majority stake in Japan's largest cable provider, managed by a committee consisting of one LMI and one Sumitomo member.

At the start of 2005, LMI and UnitedGlobalCom combined businesses under one name, Liberty Global Inc., and converted shares for each company into one share of the new company, which then became one of the largest owners and operators of broadband communications systems outside the U.S., with ownership interests in companies with more than 14 million customers in 17 countries. Michael T. Fries was named president and CEO of Liberty Global. One of Liberty Global's first big deals involved the July 2005 acquisition of Astral Telecom SA, one of Romania's largest broadband telecommunications operators, for a total of $404.5 million. As of the summer of 2005, the company is also in the midst of an IPO process with Japan's Jupiter Telecommunications Co., a Japanese cable operator in which it owns more than 45 percent.

Still spinning

The transformation continued into March 2005, when the company announced a plan to spin off interests in Ascent Media and Discovery Communications Inc. to shareholders, thus creating a new publicly traded company called Discovery Holding Co., made up of Liberty Media's 100 percent ownership of Ascent and 50 percent ownership in Discovery. The consolidations followed an ongoing trend of spin-offs and consolidations designed to simplify Liberty's balance sheet and reorganize its portfolio as the company's loss margin widened from $5 million to $21.1 million during the fourth quarters of 2003 to 2004, respectively.

Malone is currently weighing a deal to swap the 18 percent voting stake he has built up in News Corp for News Corp's National Geographic Channel. News Corp. chairman Rupert Murdoch is reportedly eager to reclaim the stake. Meanwhile, first-quarter profit hit $254 million on increased sales at QVC and Discovery. Liberty also raised its 2005 forecast based on increasing international sales at QVC on apparel items.

Uncertain future

Liberty has performed worse than rival media stocks like News Corp and Time Warner over the past two years, and Malone is aggressively seeking to increase growth and stock value. Analysts are wondering if Malone's slow disbanding of the company's assets is a steppingstone to his ultimate departure, and what the next major spin off will be, if any. Still up for grabs are the QVC home shopping channel, minority shareholdings in News Corp and the IAC Interactive Corp, the Starz Encore television channel, and a number of other telecom investments.

Visit Vault at **www.vault.com** for insider company profiles, expert advice, career message boards, expert resume reviews, the Vault Job Board and more.

VAULT CAREER LIBRARY   165

GETTING HIRED

The Liberty web site lists job openings as they become available at www.libertymedia.com/careers/default.htm.

Martha Stewart Living Omnimedia, Inc.

11 W. 42nd Street
New York, NY 10036
Phone: (212) 827-8000
Fax: (212) 827-8204
www.marthastewart.com

LOCATIONS

New York, NY (HQ)

THE STATS

Employer Type: Public Company
Stock Symbol: MSO
Stock Exchange: NYSE
Chairman: Thomas C. Siekman
CEO: Sharon L. Patrick
2003 Employees: 544
2003 Revenue ($mil.): $245.8

KEY COMPETITORS

Advance Publications
Meredith
Time Warner

EMPLOYMENT CONTACT

www.marthastewart.com/page.jhtml;
    jsessionid = MVPS15BUVCU0PWCK
    UUXCIIWYJKSS0JO0?type = page-
    cat&id = cat663&navLevel = 3&nav
    History =

THE SCOOP

More than your average chef

Like it or not, if you live in America, you've unmistakably heard of Martha Stewart. The million-dollar-woman is the impetus behind Martha Stewart Living Omnimedia's creation and success. Martha, who considers herself "one of the original feminists," is proud to "help give women back a sense of pleasure and accomplishment in their homes." Martha Stewart, born Martha Kostyra and of Polish decent, made her publishing debut in 1982 with her first book, *Entertaining*. The book, which has sold over 500,000 copies in thirty printings, was issued exactly 10 years after Stewart opened her own catering business in Westport, Conn., one of the cities now home to her television show *Martha Stewart Living*.

Stewart, far past her stockbroker and modeling career days, became lifestyle consultant to discount store, Kmart, in 1987, and soon after, began publishing *Martha Stewart Living* magazine for Time Inc. Her already successful career was only just beginning to flower. In 1992, Martha coupled with Sherwin Williams to add a line of paints to her operation, then known as Martha Stewart Enterprises. Her television show, *Martha Stewart Living*, began broadcasting the following year. The TV series embraced everything associated with the home, from gardening to entertaining, and has earned a total of five Daytime Emmy Awards and 16 nominations. By 1999, Martha Stewart Living Omnimedia was a multi-million-dollar success, encompassing an Emmy-award winning television show, successful monthly magazine, Internet site, catalog sales and profitable merchandising deals.

Taking the reins

Still wanting to expand further, Martha Stewart premiered a catalog business, Martha by Mail, and commenced a weekly syndicated newspaper column in 1995. Two years later, however, Martha Stewart Enterprises had grown to what Stewart believed was too much for Time Inc. to handle. Stewart extracted her operation and created Martha Stewart Living Omnimedia (MSLO). Soon after, the company embarked on several expansions. It united with Kmart to sell the Martha Stewart Everyday collection, landed Stewart a weekly spot on television show *CBS This Morning*, started national radio show askMartha, and created marthastewart.com.

Zellers, the Canadian division of Hudson's Bay Company, linked with MSLO in 1998 to vend the Martha Stewart Everyday Home line in its stores. Other retailers that carry MSLO products include Sears, Canadian Tire and Jo-Ann Fabrics. The company later took another leap forward, deciding to go public in fall 1999. The date of its IPO, October 20, amusingly turned out to be the same date as that of the World Wrestling Federation.

Rising like yeast

In April 2000, MSLO introduced a plant encyclopedia to the gardening section of its web site. The encyclopedia, which can be accessed free of charge, has information and tips on over 1,000 flora. Some of the plants can even be purchased at the web site's online store. The company announced more growth in early June when it expressed interest in expanding operations into Japan, England and Germany. Plans also included adding new publications, television shows, merchandise and special magazine issues. Partially due to a new houseware line that debuted in fall 2000, MSLO's annual growth was expected to reach 34 percent. To accommodate her sprouting company, Martha Stewart purchased a new headquarters in the Chelsea district of Manhattan mid-year. The gigantic 150,000 square foot space, used previously by Stewart for a holiday party and several photo shoots, will house roughly 350 of MSLO's 450 employees for its catalog, retail, and web site operations. A prop library, test kitchen, and several photo studios will also be included.

Multimedia marketing

MSLO teamed up with DaimlerChrysler for an undisclosed amount in April 2002. Chrysler became the sole automotive advertiser in "Road Trips," a section in *Martha Stewart Living* magazine. "Road Trips" content can also be found in the *Martha Stewart Living* television program, the "*Ask Martha*" radio show, and MSLO's official web site.

Red light, yellow light, green light, blue light

MSLO acquired 5 percent of Kmart's web site and Internet service provider, BlueLight.com, in 2000, for $13 million. Kmart, which is contracted with MSLO until 2007, now provides over 350 Martha Stewart Everyday products via BlueLight.com. The home and garden collection, which has been at Kmart since 1997, is only available at BlueLight, marthastewart.com and Kmart stores. In October 2002, MSLO introduced a line of holiday decorating products, called Martha Stewart Everyday Holiday, specifically for Kmart. MSLO has proudly brought

Visit Vault at **www.vault.com** for insider company profiles, expert advice, career message boards, expert resume reviews, the Vault Job Board and more.

VAULT CAREER LIBRARY 169

Kmart well over $1 billion in sales, and is credited for helping the outlet store get back on its feet.

However, the relationship between the two went sour in February 2004, when Kmart – once known as "Kmartha" – sued MSLO over "how royalties under the minimum originally stipulated in the contract were calculated." Kmart, which filed for bankruptcy in January 2002, closed 316 stores in 2003, and was not able to sell enough MSLO products to meet contracted minimums. Kmart claimed MSLO was "double-counting" royalties as MSLO products failed to meet guaranteed targets. Kmart pulled the suit in April 2004, after the feuding companies resolved to expand and extend an exclusive merchandise contract through 2009. Product category minimums were absent from the deal.

The scandal that shocked a nation

On December 27, 2001, Martha Stewart sold nearly 4,000 shares of ImClone Systems the day before the biotechnology company released a damaging report in which the FDA publicized its rejection of ImClone's Erbitux, a drug developed to fight colo-rectal cancer. An investigation as to whether or not Stewart was guilty of insider trading ensued. Stewart publicly denied charges of insider trading, lying to investigators, conspiracy and obstruction of justice. She insisted she had an arrangement with her broker, Peter Bacanovic of Merrill Lynch, to sell ImClone if stock dipped below a certain amount, which was exactly what she did.

Stewart's face and namesake company became daily staples in media outlets across the country. Martha Stewart Living Omnimedia took the brunt of the negative publicity. In October 2002, Stewart stepped down from her position on the board of the New York Stock Exchange.

On June 5, 2003, Stewart was indicted on charges of securities fraud and obstruction of justice arising from the controversial ImClone stock sale. Immediately following the indictment, Stewart resigned as chairman and CEO, and MSLO posted a loss for the first time since it went public in 1999. On March 5, 2004, Stewart was convicted of lying to government investigators about the reasons she sold the shares, and sentenced to five months in prison and five months of home detainment. On October 8, 2004, Stewart began her sentence at a minimum-security prison in Alderson, W.V., located in the foothills of the Allegheny Mountains, and nicknamed "Camp Cupcake."

Ironically, since Stewart sold those fateful shares, the FDA has approved Erbitux, and shares in ImClone have recently increased, while MSLO has continued a downward spiral.

Media makeover

In the spring of 2004, following Stewart's trial, MSLO announced it was "revamping" its *Martha Stewart Living* magazine. The new design featured Stewart's name in a much smaller font size than before, with the inside of the magazine containing significantly fewer pages concerning Stewart. Her "Remembering" column was also removed. The new version of the magazine represents MSLO's attempt to slowly decrease its dependency on the image of its former CEO and founder, and to become a media enterprise in its own right. Advertising shares in the magazine were down 50 percent in the first half of 2004.

Expanding a publishing empire

MSLO acquired *Body & Soul*, a New Age journal of health, spiritual well-being, natural therapies, and stress reduction, in August 2004, for $6 million. Also included in the deal was a newsletter called *Dr. Andrew Weil's Self Healing*. Lauren Stanich, the MSO president of publishing, later announced plans to redesign the magazine, advertise it on a national scale, and expand its cross-promotional range to a "much larger 'how-to' omni-brand with companion television and merchandising programs." Publishing remains the company's largest segment.

Survivor: Westport?

Shares of MSLO soared to a two-year high in September 2004 after the company confirmed a collaboration with Mark Burnett, the ace producer behind reality television successes *Survivor* and *The Apprentice*. The rise in stock was also attributed to the announcement that Stewart would begin serving her prison sentence that October. The prime-time reality series will debut in the fall of 2005 and feature the domestic diva as its star, but no other word regarding the show has been made public.

Uncertain future

Following Stewart's sentencing, industry observers wondered how the diva's jail time would affect MSLO's relationships with long-time partners Sears and Kmart. The two retail giants remained tight-lipped, offering best wishes to Stewart in her troubled time. Sears indicated it would closely watch developments in the case against Stewart, but did not indicate that any changes were in the works. (Interestingly, in November 2004, the two retail giants announced plans to merge.) Vincent Power, a Sears Canada director of corporate communications, suggested that the fate of MSLO in the coming months rests not on public speculation, but on consumer loyalty to the Martha Stewart brand. "I don't think personal things matter to the consumer," he said. "If you like her stuff, you like her stuff."

Original episodes of *Martha Stewart Living* were put on hiatus, and MSLO introduced a new television cooking show, *Everyday Food*, featuring five cooks – but not Martha. The changes were part of the company's strategic plans to invest in non-eponymous products in the future.

MSLO expected to lose money before the end of 2004, but less than it had originally projected. Martha Stewart's decision to begin her prison sentence in October 2004 also provided some relief to the company, which hopes to rebound once Stewart's legal woes fade from the public's memory. New CEO Sharon Patrick, who took over after Stewart stepped down, is increasingly optimistic about the future of MSLO, and expects a financial turnaround in the second quarter of 2005, Now that Stewart has been released from prison.

GETTING HIRED

Job listings, and descriptions are available at marthastewart.com. Applications and information for submitting resumes are also on the site.

McGraw-Hill Companies, Inc.

1221 Avenue of the Americas
New York, NY 10020
Phone: (212) 512-2000
Fax: (212) 512-3840
www.mcgraw-hill.com

LOCATIONS

New York, NY (HQ)

THE STATS

Employer Type: Public Company
Stock Symbol: MHP
Stock Exchange: NYSE
CEO and Chairman: Harold W. (Terry) McGraw III
2003 Employees: 16,068
2003 Revenue ($mil.): $4,827.9

KEY COMPETITORS

Moody's
Pearson
Reed Elsevier Group

EMPLOYMENT CONTACT

www.mcgraw-
   hill.com/careers/careers.html

THE SCOOP

A history of trend-spotting

The McGraw-Hill Companies produces everything from textbooks to television stations. Its vast holdings includes *BusinessWeek*, McGraw-Hill educational materials and corporate-ratings provider Standard & Poor's. The company started in 1909, when two trade magazine publishers, James McGraw and John Hill, joined forces to publish scientific and technical books under the name The McGraw-Hill Book Company. The next 50 years saw the ambitious and successful publishing company pump out dozens of new trade magazines. The company has a history of uncannily accurate predictions – two months before the Great Depression, McGraw-Hill's *BusinessWeek* went against current public opinion by expressing concern over the state of the economy. In addition, the publisher has consistently demonstrated an ability to use technological breakthroughs to its advantage. It began producing educational software and textbooks on CD-ROM before they were in high demand from schools across the country. Today, McGraw-Hill is a $5 billion corporation with roughly 16,000 employees worldwide.

Continuing to expand, carefully

Now the nation's leading textbook publisher, McGraw-Hill continues to expand its range of products to include, among others, financial services. The company swapped its legal publishing arm for the Times-Mirror's Higher Education Group in 1996, and sold its multimedia publications (including the popular computer trade magazine *BYTE*) to CMP Media in 1998. One of the company's high tech arms, McGraw-Hill Lifetime Learning, bought U.K. multimedia training and intranet technology company Xebec in June. Also in 1998, McGraw-Hill president Harold "Terry" McGraw III replaced the retiring Joseph Dionne as CEO. The great-grandson of the company's co-founder reaffirmed the company's mission to expand as a global information, education and financial services provider. To that end, the company acquired Tribune Education and medical publisher Appleton & Lange. However, these acquisitions have been balanced with carefully planned divestments, including that of five digital printing centers and Tower Group International, a transportation logistics company.

How to become a textbook giant, 101

The nation's leading producer of textbooks has learned a thing or two about sales and acquisitions throughout its almost century-long history. Offering a wide arrange of educational materials in both print and electronic format, McGraw-Hill publications educate and inform teachers and students alike, from the pre-kindergarten level through college. The company has a long history of strategic business maneuvers that have contributed to its success.

McGraw-Hill bought Tribune Education, an educational publisher, from the Tribune Company for $635 million in June 2000. The sale helped strengthen McGraw-Hill's already flourishing education publishing business. The next month, the company posted second-quarter earnings that surpassed Wall Street expectations, and jumped 22.2 percent in net income, driven by a surge in textbook sales and *BusinessWeek*'s most successful quarter in its history.

In January 2001, Orlando-based Digital Owl, a provider of secure and controlled transfer technology for protected electronic books and documents, signed with McGraw-Hill's Professional division to expand its distribution of electronic books. Also that January, McGraw-Hill acquired Mayfield Publishing Company, a leading college-level publisher in humanities and social science disciplines. Hal Leonard Corp., a Milwaukee-based music print publisher, signed on with McGraw-Hill Education in April 2001 to create and distribute a line of multimedia music education products. The next year, McGraw-Hill bought Realty-Based Learning Co., a Redmond, Wash.-based Internet education software developer, and later acquired software licensing rights to Finale Workbook, a music notation software from Net4Music, Inc. McGraw-Hill planned to bundle the software with its college-level music theory textbooks.

Continued success

In December 2001, McGraw-Hill announced it would trim 925 jobs, roughly 5 percent of its workforce, to cut costs. Out of that number, 575 jobs came from its education business, while the information and media side released 300. The financial services segment cut 50 jobs. Despite the cuts, the company insisted profit growth remained on track.

The company acquired Nashville-based Bredex Corp., an educational technology company, in August 2002. Bredex, an Internet based system of tracking and enhancing student performance in the elementary and middle school market, was integrated with McGraw-Hill's Digital Learning Unit to increase McGraw-Hill

Education's ability to help educators assess and improve student performance through technology. That October, McGraw-Hill's stock and total returns were up, due in part to the success of its textbook division and a diversified publishing portfolio. By focusing on business and educational publishing, McGraw-Hill was able to generate sales through a constant demand for textbooks, which historically require less advertising. Platts, the company's energy industry news service, also generated revenue through subscriptions.

McGraw-Hill sold off its retail educational book business to Greenville, Wis., based-School Specialty Inc. in January 2004. The educational book business includes workbooks, teacher's guides and educational games for grades pre-kindergarten through eighth, and has annual sales of $60 million to $65 million. But ridding itself of this arm allowed McGraw-Hill to focus on selling its books through schools directly, rather than bookstores.

In June 2004, CTB/McGraw-Hill signed a five-year deal to provide testing services to the state of Ohio. Ohio joined McGraw-Hill's growing list of contracts with other states, as well as the Defense Department, for testing services, bringing in a total of $112.5 million.

New ventures

In February 2001, McGraw-Hill Education signed with Time Inc. and Infraworks Corp., an Austin, Texas-based firm which helps protect creative and intellectual property, to join its Lighthouse Partner Program. The program helps companies evaluate ways to securely deliver digital information through the Internet, a rising concern within the financial sector.

In October 2004, McGraw-Hill announced the publication of a new bi-monthly regional magazine, *My House*. The magazine's distribution covered Colorado, Utah, Wyoming and Montana in its first month, with additional states to follow. My House is geared toward high-end homeowners and design and building professionals.

Management musical chairs

Promotion fever swept through McGraw-Hill in November 2004: Geoffrey A. Dodge was promoted to senior vice president and North America publisher of *BusinessWeek*, Paul Maraviglia was named vice president and international publisher of *BusinessWeek*, and Peggy White was named vice president of *BusinessWeek* online.

Rewarding the pursuit of education

The Harold W. McGraw Prize in Education was created in 1988 to celebrate the company's 100th anniversary and to honor McGraw's lifelong commitment to education. Judged by a panel of prestigious educators, the award annually recognizes individuals dedicated to the field of education whose accomplishments make a difference in the world today.

Diverse assets

McGraw-Hill currently owns a wide variety of media, including KMGH-TV (Denver), KGTV (San Diego), KERO-TV (Bakersfield), WRTV (Indianapolis), *BusinessWeek* magazine, McGraw-Hill Education, McGraw-Hill Construction Group, McGraw-Hill Construction, Healthcare Information Group, Aviation Week Group, Platts, Standard & Poor's Rating Service and Standard & Poor's Financial Information.

GETTING HIRED

Hiring overview

Most McGraw-Hill divisions hire through the company's main office in New York, which accepts resumes via regular mail and fax. Applicants should indicate the specific division in which they are interested. For detailed information regarding specific openings, contact McGraw-Hill's headquarters in writing, by regular mail. McGraw-Hill also offers a variety of consulting positions for those already in the industry, and company representatives visit college campuses each fall for on-campus interviews. For most general management positions, McGraw-Hill requires five years of prior business experience as well as a degree in finance, marketing, media or general management. McGraw-Hill insiders say the firm prefers MBAs with concentrations in finance, marketing, media and general management. The interview process is described as "laid-back," with the interviewer more interested in "personality and initiative and independent thought than in specific skills." It is McGraw-Hill policy to have at least two interviews before granting a job offer, "although sometimes they combine it into one interview with both people at the same time."

Visit Vault at **www.vault.com** for insider company profiles, expert advice, career message boards, expert resume reviews, the Vault Job Board and more.

VAULT CAREER LIBRARY   **177**

Metro-Goldwyn-Mayer Inc. (MGM)

10250 Constellation Blvd.
Los Angeles, CA 90067
Phone: (310) 449-3000
Fax: (310) 449-8857
www.mgm.com

LOCATIONS

Los Angeles, CA (HQ)

THE STATS

Employer Type: Public Company
Stock Symbol: MGM
Stock Exchange: NYSE
Chairman and CEO: Alex Yemenidjian
2003 Employees: 1,280
2003 Revenue ($mil.): $1,883.0

KEY COMPETITORS

Disney Studios
Sony Pictures Entertainment
Warner Brothers

EMPLOYMENT CONTACT

www.mgm.com/corp_employment.do

THE SCOOP

Star-studded history

In 1924 Loew's Inc. bought Louis B. Mayer's nine-year-old production company, Samuel Goldwyn's studio (United Artists), and Metro Pictures Corp. to form MGM. The company was consistently profitable, despite the introduction of "talkies" and declining attendance during the Depression. In the 1930s, MGM brought to life *A Tale of Two Cities*, *Gone With the Wind* and *The Wizard of Oz*. Fred Astaire, Joan Crawford, Clark Gable, Judy Garland, Greta Garbo, Katharine Hepburn, Mickey Rooney and Spencer Tracy were all under contract with the studio. Trouble set in after World War II, with the advent of television and federal antitrust action which forced movie companies to break from their theater chains. Despite attempts at revitalization with *Singin' in the Rain* and *An American in Paris*, finances lagged and Mayer resigned in 1951. In 1969 Kirk Kerkorian sold off the company's assets, but the studio's production still slowed to three or four films a year.

Goldwyn Mayer, Metro-Goldwyn-Mayer

The company's saving grace was United Artists, which struck a gold mine with the James Bond series in the 1960s and 1970s. In 1986 Ted Turner bought MGM/UA (which became MGM again in 1992) and kept the film library for his cable operations, including the jewel in the crown, *Gone With the Wind*. In 1992 Credit Lyonnais infused money into the flailing company and brought in new management, restabilizing MGM. The company backslid in 1995 with an $18 million investment in *Cutthroat Island*, the biggest box office bomb in the history of film. In 1997 MGM purchased most of John Kluge's entertainment assets for $573 million, acquiring Orion pictures, Goldwyn Entertainment, Motion Picture Corp. of America, and its 4,100-title film and television library in the transaction. That same year, MGM went public and was valued at $1.4 billion.

The MGM comeback

Metro-Goldwyn-Mayer (MGM) chairman Frank G. Mancuso, financier Kerkorian (who surfaced again), and Australian broadcaster Seven Network came together to breathe new life into the motion picture leviathan. The triumvirate, led by Kerkorian, bought MGM from French bank Credit Lyonnais in 1996 for $1.3 billion. Kerkorian has long been held responsible for ruining the studio in the 1980s, but since his return MGM has grown, thanks to the $573 million purchase of film operations from

Metromedia International (MIG). The company has yet to resuscitate its production facilities and still occupies an office building in Santa Monica. In addition to MGM Pictures, the company operates United Artists Pictures, Orion Pictures, Goldwyn Entertainment, the MGM 4,100-film library (the largest in the world), and other multimedia operations. In August 1998, Kerkorian bought out Australian-owned Seven Networks' stake for $389 million – his company, Tracinda Corp., currently holds about 75 percent of MGM stock.

Any takers?

The studio's tepid performance (and shrinking credit line) inspired layoffs of seven percent of the company in 1998. That same year, MGM curtailed its television and studio projects. MGM's newer releases have been a shot in the arm – *Tomorrow Never Dies* marked continued strength in MGM's James Bond franchise, and *The Man in the Iron Mask* benefited from the post-*Titanic* Leonardo DiCaprio mania, despite less than glowing reviews. In October 1998, Tracinda Corp invested almost $600 million in MGM, indicating the seriousness of financier Kirk Kerkorian's increasing commitment to the company. Since that time, MGM has signed an eight-picture co-financing and distribution agreement with Miramax, as well as sold the rights to MGM's international film and home-video rights to News Corp.'s Fox Film Entertainment.

New deals

In 2000 MGM entered into a multi-picture co-financing, co-production deal with Atlas Entertainment. That same year, Kerkorian-owned MGM Grand formally acquired Mirage Resorts in a $4.4 billion deal that created one of the largest hotel-casino companies in the world. In May 2000, MGM signed a $1.4 billion deal with Showtime Networks for up to 270 first-run films, access to 1,200 library titles, and a commitment to produce three new TV series. And in the hope of capitalizing on previous successes, MGM presented plans for *Basic Instinct II* and *Hannibal*, the sequel to *Silence of the Lambs*.

On a budget

Due to a lack of major blockbusters in recent years, MGM has reduced its output and curbed the spending limit on its productions in an attempt to become more profitable. It proved to be quite the success in the case of *Legally Blonde* (starring Reese Witherspoon as an unlikely lawyer), which became one of the largest moneymakers in the history of MGM. Otherwise, MGM has primarily relied on its famed Bond-franchise to pick up the slack and *Die Another Day*, which opened in 2002, did just that when it became the largest grossing Bond opening ever.

With the purchase of a 20 percent stake in four Rainbow Media networks (including the Independent Film Channel, American Movie Classics and WE: Women's Entertainment) in 2001, MGM entered the potentially lucrative cable television industry. Failing to generate the revenue the company had expected and clearing up debt issues, MGM sold its stake back to Cablevision (Rainbow Media's parent) for about half a billion dollars in 2003.

Sony moves in

After Kerkorian's many attempts to sell off MGM (and as many repurchases), it was announced in September 2004 that Sony would acquire the company. In a race that also included Time Warner, Sony agreed to pay $4.8 billion (including about $2 billion in debt) for the slumbering lion. The $12 per share is 75 cents more than Sony's original takeover bid. Sony's equity partners in the deal include Comcast and Texas Pacific Group.

Although MGM has been quiet as of late due to budgetary restrictions (cost cuts, shrinking budgets and increased focus on cable distribution of its films), it is still a hot commodity in the film industry thanks to its massive library. In a burgeoning DVD market, the 4,000 titles are a treasure trove with films including the James Bond back catalog, the *Pink Panther* series and the *Rocky* franchise.

2004 box office

Generating more buzz off screen than on, 2004 was relatively quiet for MGM. *Walking Tall* starring action man The Rock fared well and *Barbershop 2* proved to be an established success, bringing in some $65 million domestically. Actively targeting the black market, *Soul Plane* (starring Snoop Dogg), on the other hand, failed to take flight and generated a poor $14 million in revenue. Although, the four films MGM introduced in the summer of 2004 cost less than a combined $50 million to make so there was never much at stake.

While it is not quite clear what Sony plans to do with MGM, the company has plenty of potential hits lined up for 2005. The line up includes a *Harry Potter* spoof, *Beauty Shop* (a *Barbershop* spin off), a new *Pink Panther* and *Be Cool* (the sequel to Get Shorty) starring John Travolta and Uma Thurman. Although its future is a bit cloudy

Visit Vault at **www.vault.com** for insider company profiles, expert advice, career message boards, expert resume reviews, the Vault Job Board and more.

VAULT CAREER LIBRARY   **181**

and no release date is scheduled, MGM also has the rights to *The Hobbit* which is an almost guaranteed blockbuster.

Financials

MGM has increased its revenues for four consecutive years but still failed to run a profitable business, due in part to high production costs. The company posted sales of $1.88 billion in 2003, compared to $1.65 billion the year before, but net losses still rose to almost $162 million. The company's recent remedy of cutting budgets and a possibly cash infusion from Sony should help set it back on the right path. Sony also has plans to bring MGM films to Comcast's on-demand video platform.

Third quarter revenue for 2004 was $401.3 million, compared to $457.1 million in the prior year period. The company's net loss in the third quarter was $26.7 million, or $0.11 per share. The net loss included expenses of $3.8 million, or $.02 per share, related to the pending Sony takeover.

GETTING HIRED

Hiring overview

MGM has an online resume tool available on the careers section of its web site where interested applicants can submit their resumes. There are no full-time openings listed directly on the site. An insider says, "Many people with limited prior work experience sign up with temp agencies and get their foot in the door that way." For corporate positions, the interview process is "relatively casual and friendly" but "rigorous" in the sense that there are a lot of applicants for any given position.

Internships

To qualify as an intern at MGM, an applicant should be a registered student at a college or university and eligible to earn academic credit for the internship. Internships may be either paid or unpaid. For internships that are unpaid, academic credit will be a requirement. Preference will be given to juniors and seniors in a related field of study. MGM lists all intern openings on the careers section of its web site.

National Public Radio, Inc.

635 Massachusetts Avenue NW
Washington, DC 20001-3753
Phone: (202) 513-2000
Fax: (202) 513-3329
www.npr.org

LOCATIONS

Washington, DC (HQ)
Chicago, IL
Los Angeles, CA
Miami, FL
New York, NY
San Francisco, CA

Beijing
Berlin
Jerusalem
London
Mexico City
Moscow
Nairobi
Rome
Tokyo

THE STATS

Employer Type: Private Company
Chairman: Mark Handley
CEO: Kevin Klose

KEY COMPETITORS

Jones Media Networks
Public Radio International
Westwood One

EMPLOYMENT CONTACT

www.npr.org/about/jobs

Visit Vault at **www.vault.com** for insider company profiles, expert advice,
career message boards, expert resume reviews, the Vault Job Board and more.

VAULT CAREER LIBRARY   183

THE SCOOP

"The People's Radio"

In 1967, Congress passed the Public Broadcasting Act, expanding the scope of non-commercial radio and TV nationwide. Three years later, National Public Radio (NPR) was founded as a means to broadcast timely, educational, noncommercial radio programs across the country. By May 1971, NPR unveiled its first show, *All Things Considered*. NPR was officially launched in 1972 as an alternative to commercial media with the promise of promoting "personal growth rather than corporate gain" through "many voices, many dialects." NPR's impact was felt soon thereafter as it went on to a name for itself covering the Senate's Vietnam hearings.

Chartered by Congress as "the People's Radio," the private, nonprofit radio network has managed to evade funding disasters while steadfastly maintaining its occasionally controversial programming content. From *Morning Edition* to *Fresh Air* and *Car Talk*, NPR maintains its integrity by providing consistently innovative and entertaining programming. Based in Washington, D.C., NPR beams its programming out to affiliated stations across the U.S., Puerto Rico and Guam, and in Europe through Armed Forces Radio. In 1998 NPR launched a 24-hour direct broadcast satellite channel for Europe as part of NPR Worldwide. NPR boasts 22 million listeners on 750 affiliated stations and thousands more in 50 foreign countries. Moreover, it maintains 12 foreign bureaus. An anomaly in the world of radio today, NPR has maintained much of the character of the golden days of the radio by offering hard-hitting investigative journalism, original drama and unique music programming. Seattle, San Francisco, Raleigh-Durham and Washington, D.C., continue to be among the strongest outlets of listener-ship.

For the people

Typical guests on NPR shows include "elite" sources such as current and former government officials and professional experts primarily from think tanks, academia, journalism, law and medicine. However, the last decade has also seen a steady increase of "non-elite" guests such as workers, students and members of citizen and public interest groups.

Commercialism as the cost of cuts

NPR has had to fight against serious funding cuts in the 1990s and as a result has become more business-focused. Critics have complained that because of this, commercialism has begun to insinuate itself into NPR's practices and worry that programming decisions will eventually be influenced by relationships with corporate underwriters. Some NPR fundraising plans have led people to question whether it is truly a "pure" nonprofit organization. Insiders stress the fact that the development portion of NPR is completely separate from the actual news and broadcast divisions. In 1996 NPR allowed the public to rent time in its state-of-the-art recording studio in Washington, D.C. Local commercial studios complained this was unfair competition, as NPR had acquired much of its equipment at low or no cost because of its nonprofit status. Another controversial venture was a joint effort with Dorian Records to release albums featuring alternative music. As a nonprofit organization, NPR is exempt from paying licensing fees for the music it sells, but performer rights groups argued that the radio network did not deserve that provision because it benefited at the musicians' expense. Supporters of NPR have pointed out that the radio network provides excellent publicity for these artists. (This is easily twisted, of course, into the counterargument that the radio network will benefit from increased sales by the baby-boomer audience, and so the argument could go on and on into infinity.)

NPR has also raised millions of dollars leasing space on its satellite to other groups, though this has not stirred up much controversy. In the end, cuts in NPR's government subsidy trickle down to affect all low-budget radio stations that air NPR programming. Effective October 1, 1999, NPR began charging radio stations based on the size of their audiences, rather than implementing its time-honored practice of charging based on the size of a station's operating budget.

Putting the nation back in the name

In December 1998, Kevin Klose, formerly the director of the U.S. International Broadcasting Bureau, replaced Delano Lewis as NPR president and CEO. In March 1999, NPR and Minnesota Public Radio (MPR) firmed up an agreement to create a new online network that will provide the American public with interactive news, information and arts and entertainment programming. NPR listeners are encouraged to interact online with program producers and with other listeners. In the words of one NPR trustee, this is "the type of entrepreneurship that will help secure public radio's role in the multimedia world." In 2000 the company launched its first Internet-only program, *All Songs Considered* and signed on with www.bigchalk.com

to launch an educational web resource combining NPR's content and audio with lesson plans, student activities and opportunities for classroom collaboration. Klose inspired a number of new initiatives designed to expand NPR's audience of both radio listeners and interactive participants online. Through one such plan, called the "Western Initiative," NPR included more West Coast issues in the network's programming, including discussions of immigration and population diversity. During the 2000 national elections, NPR remained on air later than the usual 10 p.m. witching hour to wait out the West Coast election returns. In March 2003, NPR and AOL teamed up to make NPR's programming available to AOL Radio Network listeners. In 2004, NPR set up a two-person bureau Miami in affiliation with local station WLRN 91.3 FM. Klose told Knight Ridder Tribune Business News that "Miami is an obvious and natural place for us to be" because the city is a "gateway to the Americas."

New dish for NPR

In June 1999, NPR announced an exclusive agreement with Sirius Radio (formerly CD Radio), the satellite-to-vehicle broadcaster, to provide programming for two of Sirius Radio's national channels. In 2002, NPR established its West Coast headquarters in Culver City, Calif., at an $8 million, 25,000-square foot facility designed to broaden network coverage. The building was purchased with the help of the James Irvine Foundation, and more than 70 people work there. When the late Joan Kroc, widow of McDonald's entrepreneur Ray Kroc, granted $200 million to NPR after her death in 2003, NPR execs were "inspired" and "humbled" – their total operating budget the previous year had been only half the size of Kroc's bequest. The network will channel $15 million in interest earned on the gift into its news division, according to an August 2004 *New York Times* article. The expansion will include more reporters and bulking up its foreign news bureaus. NPR is also currently working on a major airwave expansion, hoping to increase its public radio systems by 300 stations and help existing local stations by buying new signals, which let a station launch "a range of formats" to attract more listeners.

As previously noted, NPR listeners have a strong emotional investment in the network and don't fail to express their disappointment when the powers-that-be make decisions they disagree with. Such was the case when NPR parted ways with Bob Edwards, its popular *Morning Edition* host, in May 2004 after 25 years of service. Angry public radio devotees and partners flooded the office with e-mails and letters charging NPR with "ruining an institution." Despite the initial criticism, *Morning Edition* has remained a listener favorite. Then in November 2004, Tavis Smiley, who hosted a self-titled talk show that was the network's first program targeted specifically at a black audience, announced he was not renewing his contract. Although his show had amassed an audience of 900,000 listeners a week in just under three years, Smiley stated that he felt NPR was not doing enough to reach the black audience.

GETTING HIRED

A competitive field

National Public Radio provides detailed job descriptions on its employment web page, located at www.npr.org/about/jobs. Many of the positions require experience in radio production, but there are also openings for people with MBAs or engineering degrees. New hires typically have prior experience in either print or broadcast journalism, and NPR advises recent graduates to first gain experience at a small radio station or newspaper. "There are very few paid, full-time jobs in public radio unless you go to the big cities and then it's really competitive," an insider says. Says another source, "You have to make contacts within NPR. Basically, you have to phone up and introduce yourself."

However, neophytes can find opportunities at NPR affiliates all over the country. They may only be unpaid internships, but they are excellent ways to get experience and a surprising amount of responsibility. One former intern at the NPR affiliate in Chicago became an associate producer in a relatively short time "because the station was so short-staffed." Practical if not glorious experience will generally prove invaluable as you move forward in the radio business. Internships, which NPR offers to undergraduate and grad students and graduates who have held their degrees a year or less at the start of the program, are also an excellent way to get one's foot in the door. The network has also established the Kroc Fellowship program, which adheres to the same eligibility criteria as the internship program. Check the web site for more information on the application process.

News Corporation

1211 Avenue of the Americas
8th Floor
New York, NY 10036
Phone: (212) 852-7017
Fax: (212) 852-7145
www.newscorp.com

LOCATIONS

New York, NY (HQ)

THE SCOOP

Here, there and everywhere

If you've watched *Titanic*, read the latest Atkins Diet book or tuned into *The Simpsons*, you have firsthand knowledge of the wide-ranging influence exerted by media conglomerate, News Corporation. The $52 billion global empire includes TV, film, newspaper, publishing and other holdings, and had revenue totaling more than $20 billion in 2004. Consider this list of just a few of the company's many properties: Fox Entertainment Group, HarperCollins (the book publisher), *TV Guide*, the *London Times* and *New York Post* newspapers and the National Rugby League in Australia. News Corp.'s recent move into the satellite provider market, through its 34 percent purchase of DirecTV operator Hughes Electronics, could allow for even greater expansion, giving the company a sizable, new medium to showcase its programming.

Pulling the strings

News Corporation's story begins and ends with Rupert Murdoch. The media baron, who built News Corporation from the ground up, is one of the few chief executives of a multinational media corporation who has a controlling ownership share (the Murdoch family owns 29 percent of News Corp.) in the companies he runs.

A perennial pot-stirrer, Murdoch isn't afraid to play both sides of an issue: Turn on Fox News (News Corp. owns app. 82 percent of Fox Entertainment Group) and you might see Bill O'Reilly lamenting the demise of Americans' core values, but turn the channel to the Fox network and you could see reality-based or scripted entertainment similar to the plastic-surgery-makeover-beauty-pageant, *The Swan*.

Another thing Murdoch definitely doesn't shy away from is controversy: Sometimes it's personal (i.e., his bitter, public split from wife, Anna, in 1998, after it was revealed he'd had a long-time affair with an employee, whom he married shortly after the divorce). Other times it's business-related. (In 1986 he moved his U.K. newspaper printing operations to a new plant in Wapping, and the angry printing unions rebelled in a very public labor strike. The union ultimately capitulated, other media companies followed his lead and Murdoch's actions helped turn an unprofitable British publishing industry around.) And still other times it's financial: Murdoch was under fire in 1999 for a failing to pay net corporation tax on some 1.4 billion pounds (his corporation's complex structure allowed him to avoid the tax).

Murdoch may be a target of gossip, but he's not afraid to dish it out himself. His *New York Post* has long been home to famed gossip column, Page Six.

Critics call him an unscrupulous hypocrite; fans admire his pragmatic, hard-nosed business approach. Few would dispute his penchant for taking risks, which has generated massive wealth (in 2004 *Forbes* ranked Murdoch the 27th richest American with $6.9 billion) and also sizable losses in 1991 massive debts almost drove News Corp. to bankruptcy, and the company had to sell off properties like *New York* magazine, *Seventeen* and *Soap Opera Digest*). With sons Lachlan and James gaining more sway in the company, it looks like a Murdoch could be shaping the media for many years to come.

Early acquisitions

When Australia-born Rupert Murdoch inherited ownership of the *Adelaide News* from his influential newspaper executive father in 1952, he wasn't content to rest on the family legacy. In 1964 the ambitious 33-year-old founded *The Australian*, Australia's first and only national daily newspaper, which didn't initially have a large circulation, but quickly gained a reputation as a quality publication with an elite readership. An interesting – if unexpected – start for someone whose future media holdings wouldn't exactly be known for their, umm, highbrow appeal.

Outback expansion

Murdoch used early profits to buy floundering Australian newspapers, aggressively turning them around through radical internal shake-ups and circulation wars with competitors. Murdoch also started flexing his political muscle with his 1972 acquisition of the influential *Sydney Daily Telegraph*. (That year he used the paper to help swing the election for the Labor Party candidate, although soon after he moved away from the party, and has generally supported the Australian Liberal Party since. He has remained influential in Australian, British and U.S. politics. In 1980 Murdoch combined his many holding to form News Corp.

Murdoch's politics

Some of his publications may be racy, but Murdoch is also well known for his personally conservative beliefs. Friendly with Ronald Reagan and Margaret Thatcher, Murdoch was even credited with helping Conservative John Major, win an unexpected victory in 1992. (Murdoch's paper, *The Sun*, actively pushed Major, and later ran a headline proclaiming it "won" the race for the P.M.) His papers strongly supported George W. Bush in 2000 and 2004, and all 175 Murdoch-owned newspapers editorialized in favor of the invasion of Iraq in 2003.

Murdoch's been accused of giving positive media coverage to parties that promote policies which benefit his commercial interests. For instance, there was speculation that he stopped HarperCollins from publishing the memoirs of Chris Patten, the last British governor of Hong Kong, to gain favor with China as he was trying to launch Star TV. On the other hand, HarperCollins did publish *Stupid White Men* by vocal Bush critic, Michael Moore, in 2001.

The Dirty Digger

Murdoch, an Oxford grad, moved to Britain in the mid-1960s, establishing himself as a publishing force through the acquisition of *News of The World* and the launch of *The Sun*. However, he quickly earned a down-market reputation through allowing material of "questionable taste," such as topless girls, to make it into his publications to boost circulation. A tabloid pioneer, he used his attention-grabbing genius to shape successful tabliod. publications like *The Sun* in London, *The New York Post*, *The Herald Sun* in Melbourne and *The Daily Telegraph* in Sydney).

These methods inspired Private Eye's Aubernon Waugh to label Murdoch "The Dirty Digger"; Murdoch's 1981 purchase of the *The Times* and *The Sunday Times* in London was met with outrage from traditionalists afraid he would pollute the paper's integrity.

Outfoxing the competition

In politics, as in most other areas, perhaps Murdoch's real motivation (and genius) is that he knows what sells. In 1985 News Corp. bought a controlling interest in Twentieth Century Fox. (Around that time, Murdoch became an American citizen, allowing him to legally own TV stations in the U.S.) Renamed Fox Entertainment Group, the company expanded successfully into network TV and also launched a number of successful cable channels, many of them sports-focused. But perhaps its most lucrative move was launching a 24-hour-news-channel to compete with CNN in 1996. Catering to a right-leaning audience, the channel has gained a loyal following, largely through courting conservative viewers looking for an alternative to a perceived liberal bias in the media. In 2002 FNC overtook CNN as the No.-1 cable news station and has been gaining steadily since.

Tough pill to swallow

It's no secret that Murdoch has been grooming eldest son, Lachlan, who currently serves as deputy chief operating officer of News Corp. and publisher of the *New York Post*, to eventually take over the business. (Son, James, is no slouch either: He's the CEO of successful British Sky Broadcasting (BSkyB), a satellite broadcaster that reaches nearly 7.4 million paying customers and has grown to nearly 70 percent of the British pay-TV market.

Murdoch Sr.'s plans for his heirs were recently been put in jeopardy when Liberty Media's John Malone, Murdoch's longtime investing partner, surprised him by trying to increase his stake in the company, causing speculation that he could battle for a majority share. Murdoch quickly began crafting a poison pill (a well-known business strategy used to thwart hostile takeovers) to block any takeover intentions. Malone ultimately doubled his voting share to almost 18 percent (the Murdoch family has 29 percent). In February 2005, Murdoch confirmed that he and Malone were negotiating about Malone's interest in the company, so it looks the two media titans will ultimately resolve the conflict.

Satellite savvy

If Murdoch can fight off this threat, it looks like his empire is poised for even further growth: In late 2003 News Corp. took control of DirecTV, and has already added about 1.4 million subscribers this year (DirecTV has 13.5 million U.S. subscribers, more than all other U.S. satellite providers combined.) Murdoch has plans to launch a Fox Business Channel and Fox Reality Channel as early as mid-2005; many media analysts believe that DirecTV will be utilized as a ready-made distribution platform for these offerings. But there have definitely been some striking short-term financial costs from the acquisition.

DirecTV CEO Chase Carey has sunk $3.5 billions dollars into extending a deal with the NFL, and News Corp. will also pour roughly $894 million into retaining customers in 2004. These expenses may temporarily hurt the bottom line, but Murdoch and Co. hope they will ultimately show the same type of results as BSkyB, which had a similarly expensive launch. Only time (and subscriber numbers) will tell.

There will also be some limits to News Corp.'s programming control: The company signed an agreement the FCC that promised that any programming its units offered DirecTV had to be offered to competitors on a comparable basis. Murdoch has conceded (at least, thus far), in this situation, but he has lobbied hard to have other

FCC regulations relaxed: He has urged the FCC to increase the ownership any one media company can have in a given market (a 2004 ruling raised it from 35 percent to 39 percent) and he has also battled to topple legislation that stipulates a media company cannot own a newspaper and TV station in the same market – Murdoch has already been granted a waiver for New York, where he owns both a TV station and the *New York Post*, but the fate of the properties still remain in jeopardy due to shadowy long-term legislation on the subject.

Coming to America

In December 2004 News Corp. commenced moving its base from Australia to the U.S. (Many believe the move was a reaction to Australia's strict cross-ownership rules.) With fires to fight, 2005 looks to be another news-worthy year for Murdoch and company.

GETTING HIRED

Get Fox-y

In searching for News Corp. job openings, your best bet may be exploring job-seeking web sites like hotjobs.com, or simply going to the web sites of individual News Corp. holdings. For instance, go to harpercollins.com, and you'll find a link to a careers page, or go to nypost.com and click on the link for new job postings. To learn about jobs at the Fox Entertainment Group, go to foxcareers.com, and you can find out more about broadcast television, cable and satellite television, corporate, film, television production and sports opportunities. The site also discusses Fox's employee benefits and internships and allows job candidates to search for positions in specific locations or groups through its "job search function."

Paramount Pictures

5555 Melrose Avenue
Hollywood, CA 90038
Phone: (323) 956-5000
Fax: (323) 862-1204
www.paramount.com

LOCATIONS

Hollywood, CA (HQ)

THE SCOOP

From nickelodeon to Nickelodeon

Now a subsidiary of Viacom's entertainment group, the story of Paramount Pictures dates back to 1905, when Adolph Zukor's New York penny arcade was converted into a nickelodeon theater that screened "revolutionary" flicks. In 1912, Zukor secured American distribution rights to the Sarah Bernhart film, *Queen Elizabeth*. The film's opening on July 12, 1912, was the first full-length drama shown in the United States. It was a huge success, which inspired Zukor to found the Famous Players Film Company. Famous Players began to produce movies in New York, beginning with *The Prisoner of Zenda* and *The Count of Monte Cristo*.

The company got the Paramount name, which was first used by a film distribution company founded by William W. Hodkinson and other independent exhibitors in May of 1914, after Paramount financed and distributed films from Zukor's Famous Players, Jesse L. Lasky's Feature Play Company and other producers. Zukor and Lasky knew a good thing when they saw it, and bought controlling interest in Paramount in 1916. Zukor remained with the new company as president.

Success and acquisitions

By 1926, the company was so successful that Zukor and Lasky decided to build their offices and vast studio space on Marathon Street in Hollywood. The company continues to occupy those offices to this day. By 1927, the company was known as Paramount Famous Lasky Corporation, and in 1930 the name was changed to Paramount Publix Corporation. The firm went bankrupt in 1933, Lasky was forced out, and it was finally reorganized as Paramount Pictures, Inc. Forced to divest all its theater holdings in the 1940s, Paramount Pictures suffered in the white noise of the television age. In 1966, Paramount was purchased by Charles G. Bluhdorn's company, Gulf + Western. Through the 1970s and the 1980s, Gulf + Western successively bought and divested a great many companies and properties, though by 1989 became focused on growing out its media arms. That year, Gulf + Western sold off its Associate Investments subsidiary to Ford for $3.35 billion and reformed its remaining properties – Paramount, Simon & Schuster and Prentice-Hall – into Paramount Communications.

Story of the logo

The Paramount Pictures logo, also known to some as the "Majestic Mountain," is one of the most familiar images in Hollywood – and it's also the oldest studio logo in continuous use, predating MGM's roaring lion by almost a decade. William W. Hodkinson (the first holder of the "Paramount" name) first designed the mountain logo in 1914, and legend has it that he doodled the image of a star-crested mountain on a napkin during a meeting with Adolph Zukor. But there has been quite a bit of speculation about just where "Majestic Mountain" really is, if it exists at all. It's actually been spoofed in several Paramount films, from *Raiders of the Lost Ark* to *Geisha Boy* to *Road to Utopia*. It even served as Mount Sinai in Cecil B. DeMille's epic film version of *The Ten Commandments*. Consensus seems to be that the image most resembles that of 9,712-foot-high Ben Lomond Peak in the Wasatch Range near Ogden, Utah, close to where Hodkinson would camp as a boy.

The logo was used with only minimal cosmetic changes for over half a century. Then, in the 1970s the mountain finally fell victim to technology and the trend toward minimalism, and the original logo was replaced with a two-dimensional representation on a blue background. It was at about the same time that the simplified graphic dropped two stars, containing only 22 stars, instead of the traditional 24. Again, there's no consensus as to why this was done, but most speculate that it was probably to simplify the image and spread the stars out a little more. But the somewhat bland and decidedly un-awe-inspiring blue representational image was not to last, and in 1987 a computer-animated version was introduced featuring a "camera move" up to the mountain while the stars fly into position, which is still being used today.

Linking up online

In August 2001, www.movielink.com was formed as a joint venture among Paramount Pictures, MGM, Sony Pictures Entertainment, Universal Pictures and Warner Bros. The venture makes movies available for download to the PC through its video-on-demand Internet distribution service. Movielink was the first studio-backed service of its kind, but the project was almost scrapped several times. Delayed for almost two years as the Hollywood business community struggled with concerns about piracy and high-quality video delivery, Movielink (formerly MovieFly) finally introduced its library of about 200 films in 2002. In 2003, it expanded its film line when it signed a pact to offer Disney films on the site as well.

United, together

United International Pictures is yet another jointly owned project, backed by Paramount Pictures and Universal Pictures. Simply put, the company distributes movies, those produced by its parent companies, as well as those made by other studios, to the international marketplace. The company was formed in 1981 as successor to Cinema International Corporation, and has invested in about 36 countries, while it is represented in about 177 other countries, through a network of licensees and agents.

Paramount presence on the tube

It is ironic that Paramount, having suffered from the rise of television in the 1950s, has come to have such a strong influence over the U.S. television audience. In 1991, Paramount made its foray into television with the purchase TV-X, renaming it Paramount Stations Group. The studio's next stop on the road to TV-land was a pay-per-view venture with Capital Cities/ABC. In 1992, following these acquisitions, Paramount Communications bought a TV station from Cox broadcasting. Paramount itself was then gobbled up by Viacom just two years later. Since that time, it has exploded into the Paramount Television Group, the sixth-largest owned and operated TV network.

Paramount also runs Spelling Television, which is responsible for producing one-hour drama series, movies-for-television and miniseries created and developed under producer Aaron Spelling, responsible for past hit series such as *Melrose Place*, *Beverly Hills 90210*, *Dynasty* and *Charlie's Angels*. Another offshoot of Paramount is UPN, which was launched in January 1995 and currently reaches more than 96 percent of U.S. television homes through its affiliated stations broadcasting 10 hours of original, primetime programming each week. By late 2003, the division aired to over 125 countries, in more than 30 languages, through its six production units: Paramount Television Production, Paramount Worldwide Television Distribution, Paramount International Television, Big Ticket Television, Spelling Television and Viacom Productions. Some of the units' biggest successes are *Frasier* and *JAG*.

For your viewing pleasure

Some of Paramount's big-screen productions in 2003 included *How to Lose a Guy in 10 Days*, *The Italian Job*, *School of Rock* and *The Cradle of Life*, the sequel to *Lara Croft: Tomb Raider*. Unfortunately, the company has also experienced its share of flops in 2003, including *The Core*, *The Hunted*, *Marci X*, *Rugrats Go Wild!*, *Beyond*

Visit Vault at **www.vault.com** for insider company profiles, expert advice, career message boards, expert resume reviews, the Vault Job Board and more.

VAULT CAREER LIBRARY   **197**

Borders and *Dickie Roberts: Former Child Star*. While mainstream, big-budget films may be the company's bread and butter, Paramount's films cater to a variety of tastes and sensibilities. Paramount Classics, which was founded in 1998, is the specialty film division of Paramount Pictures. It produces and distributes smaller, more "arty" films such as *The Virgin Suicides*.

Directing: Impossible?

A few weeks before *Mission: Impossible 3* was going into production, director Joe Carnahan abandoned the film due to "creative differences." Although it meant delaying the film's release to 2006, Paramount chose to wait for *Alias* creator J.J. Abrams to become available.

Movement at the top

In June 2004, Jonathan Dolgen, longtime chairman of the Viacom Entertainment Group, announced he was stepping down, following the promotion of Les Moonves and Tom Freston to the posts of co-presidents and co-COOs at Viacom, with Freston overseeing Paramount Pictures. Even before the historically frugal Dolgen left, Sherry Lansing, president of the Paramount Motion Picture Group, had already introduced changes at the studio aimed at taking bigger financial and artistic risks. An earlier shake-up saw vice chairman and studio co-president John Goldwyn and co-president of the motion picture group Michelle Manning also depart.

But it was just a few months later, in November 2004, that Lansing announced her own plans to leave, stating that she would not seek to renew her contract that is set to expire at the end of 2005. There had been speculation within the industry as to whether Lansing would remain at her post as Freston seeks to develop films that will draw in larger audiences. Lansing, considered a female pioneer in the film industry, is often credited for commercial successes like *Mission: Impossible, Forest Gump* (Academy Award Best Picture winner in 1994) and *Titanic* (Best Picture winner in 1997). But Paramount has also produced a string of films in recent years that haven't performed as well as the company had hoped. As of November 2004, Paramount ranked as the seventh-largest film studio in the U.S. by ticket sales with sales of $427.8 million, according to Nielsen EDI. In January 2005, the company tapped manager-to-the-stars Brad Grey to fill the top spot at Paramount.

Remakes, puppets and Sponge Bob

Paramount started out 2004 slowly. Films such as *Against the Ropes*, *Twisted* and *The Perfect Score* (starring Scarlett Johansson and NBA star Darius Miles) went largely unnoticed by audiences, but the company scored a winner with *Mean Girls*. Starring teen-idol-of-the-moment Lindsay Lohan, the high school comedy grossed almost $90 million. Paramount's summer centered around two remakes of old classics. *The Stepford Wives* and *The Manchurian Candidate* both fared reasonably well among a slew of summer blockbusters. By September 2004, the two films had each grossed around $60 million.

The studio released another high-profile remake in the fall of 2004 with Jude Law updating Michael Caine's 1960s gigolo in *Alfie*. And Adam Sandler starred in a new take on Robert Aldrich's football comedy *The Longest Yard*, which hit theaters in May 2005. Of course not all the studio's productions have been updates of old favorites. Another success for the studio has been the very original and much talked about *Team America: World Police*, which opened in October 2004. The film, a *Thunderbirds* style puppet movie, is a product of the funny, but twisted minds of *South Park* creators Trey Parker and Matt Stone, and deals with terrorism and celebrity activists. Paramount also enjoyed success toward the end of 2004 with *The SpongeBob SquarePants Movie*.

GETTING HIRED

Log on to get in

Interested applicants can go to the Paramount Pictures web page at www.paramount.com/studio/jobs.htm to find a list of available positions. The company offers a full range of benefits, including health care, 401(k), life insurance and educational reimbursement.

Visit Vault at **www.vault.com** for insider company profiles, expert advice, career message boards, expert resume reviews, the Vault Job Board and more.

VAULT CAREER LIBRARY   **199**

Pearson PLC

80 Strand
London
WC2R ORL
United Kingdom
Phone: +44-20-7010-2000
Fax: +44-20-7010-6060
www.pearson.com

LOCATIONS

London, UK (HQ)
Pearson Education (54 locations worldwide)
The Financial Times Group (20 locations worldwide)
The Penguin Group (7 locations worldwide)

THE STATS

Employer Type: Public Company
Stock Symbol: PSO
Stock Exchange: NYSE
Chairman: Lord Dennis Stevenson
CEO: Marjorie M. Scardino
2003 Employees: 30,868
2003 Revenue ($mil.): $7,219.0

KEY COMPETITORS

Dow Jones
Editis
News Corp.

EMPLOYMENT CONTACT

www.pearson.com/people/developmnt.
htm

THE SCOOP

Whether it's educational books, financial info, or babes in bikinis, the London-based media company Pearson PLC is equipped with a variety of products that make the grade. Pearson's education group, bolstered by its acquisition of an educational division from Simon & Schuster, is now the world's largest educational publisher, as well as holding publisher for Penguin Group, *The Financial Times* and Pearson Television – the proud producers of the campy, but fun, *Baywatch*.

An unlikely foundation

Pearson began as a construction company during the Industrial Revolution – a far cry from what one might consider a "typical" start for one of today's largest media conglomerates. Samuel Pearson founded the company in 1844 as a construction firm in Yorkshire, England, called S. Pearson and Son. Samuel's grandson, Weetman, took over in 1880, simultaneously expanding the business while fashioning himself as one of the world's largest building contractors, with projects in Europe, Asia and Latin America. Weetman moved headquarters from Yorkshire to London, acquiring large-scale international projects for the company, from the construction of docks in Nova Scotia to digging tunnels in New York City, to laying track for railroads in Spain and China, and even building the Sennar dam in Egypt. Throughout his work, Pearson concentrated on the concept of social consciousness, providing his workers with fair wages and pensions, building hospitals and schools, and helping to provide fresh drinking water to communities. But it wasn't until after his death, that Pearson's passion for education and awareness was channeled into creating the media company that bears his name.

Moving to media

S. Pearson and Son didn't stake its claim in the media business until more than half a century after its inception, when Weetman purchased a group of U.K.-based provincial newspapers making up the Westminster Press in 1920. By then, the company had diversified and began to resemble a holding company. In 1957, Pearson purchased *The Financial Times* as "a sound, conservative investment." By the early 1970s, Pearson acquired Penguin, a popular purveyor of contemporary fiction created in the 1930s by Allen Lane, and restructured the company to incorporate a new, flexible style in its editorial, marketing and production divisions. In gaining Penguin, Pearson established a presence in the publishing world, adding the prestige of such well-known writers as Ernest Hemingway and Agatha Christie to

Visit Vault at **www.vault.com** for insider company profiles, expert advice, career message boards, expert resume reviews, the Vault Job Board and more.

VAULT CAREER LIBRARY 201

its ranks. Also in 1970, Penguin Books merged with the esteemed New York-based publisher Viking Press, adding an impressive array of authors, including John Steinbeck and Arthur Miller, and giving Pearson a stronger foothold in the American literary market. In 1985, *The Financial Times* began its first United States printing in New York City. By 1990, Pearson had acquired France's top business daily *Les Echos* and the Spanish media group Recoletos and merged the two properties into *FT*. The company also opened up printing presses in Frankfurt, Roubaix and Tokyo.

Dropping the business of business (books)

Pearson engineered two strategic sales in 1999 as part of a plan to sell unwanted reference and business publishing units. The British media company agreed to sell Jossey-Bass, a publisher of business and professional books, to John Wiley & Sons Inc., for $82 million in May. Pearson later sold its Macmillan Library Reference USA group, a publisher of books for schools and libraries, to Toronto-based media conglomerate The Thomson Corporation, in June for $86 million. Additional deals included the sale of consumer publishing units to the venture capital company Apex Partners & Co. for $236.7 million and the divestiture of Edicorp Publications S.A. in France; *Future Publishing Ltd.*, a British consumer magazine; and Futurenet, an Internet publisher.

One business publishing unit that Pearson expanded on was its technology group, which inked a three-year deal with IBM in August 2004 to print business and technology books under the IBM Press imprint, giving Pearson worldwide rights to print titles, CD-ROMs and e-books.

Education at the heart

The company began its foray into the field of educational publishing in the late 1980s, snapping up math and science publisher Addison Wesley and merging it with Longman, publisher of the first comprehensive English-language dictionary, to create Addison-Wesley Longman. In 1996, Pearson bought school and college publisher HarperCollins Educational Publishing and merged it into Addison-Wesley Longman. Pearson let go of a non-core asset when it sold off its 50 percent interest in the London-based investment bank Lazard Brothers in 1998.

Pearson Education was created in 1998 through a merger between Simon & Schuster's educational division and Pearson subsidiary Addison-Wesley Longman's educational businesses. The Simon & Schuster deal went through at $4.6 billion, Pearson's largest acquisition to date. The next year, Pearson acquired Dorling

Kindersley, a publisher of distinctive, illustrated reference books, and integrated it within Penguin to form the Penguin Group (UK), which today has more than 50 million readers across schools in 105 countries. Pearson then purchased National Computer Systems, a Minnesota-based educational testing and data management company, in a blockbuster deal worth $2.4 billion that spawned NCS Pearson, a division of the education group focused on connecting the home and school and linking curriculum, assessment, and testing. Other recent acquisitions include Dominie Press, with a catalogue of 2,300 titles targeted to the K-8 market.

The Pearson Education branch offers a variety of brands and services throughout the world in 18 languages for students of all ages, from kindergarten through college. Pearson CEO Marjorie Scardino has spent much of her seven-year tenure at the company focusing on the education business, based on her belief that testing is destined to become an increasingly integrated part of the education business. In 2003, the education division of Pearson accounted for 60 percent of its total revenue.

Textbook pricing challenge

When the school year began in August 2004, college students across the country blew through months of savings from summer jobs to purchase the latest editions of textbooks for their respective classes. One group of students, however, took a different route, spending their summer off logging multiple complaints with the U.S. House of Representatives regarding the increasing price of textbooks. In response, Pearson launched SafariX Textbooks Online that fall, a line of 300 online texts available for half the price of hardcopy editions, in addition to cheaper, soft-cover "split-edition" versions of texts that cover one semester of coursework instead of cramming in two.

Some friendly neighborhood competition

In September 2004, Pearson's Boston-based school publishing unit announced plans to move its 500 employees across town into 100,000 square feet of renovated space in the Back Bay section of the city by June 2005. The move will bring Pearson's higher education publishing operation and its Prentice Hall division for grades 6-12 closer together geographically – and a stone's throw away from rivals Houghton Mifflin, McGraw-Hill and Bedford, Freeman, & Worth. When the move is complete, Pearson will have 1,200 employees in Boston, more than any other Pearson school publishing site in the U.S.

Certainly not the weakest link in TV

Pearson Television produces more than 150 programs in over 30 countries, attracting 200 million viewers each month. Included in the lot is the popular *Baywatch* and game shows such as *The Price is Right*, *Family Feud* (also produced in Mexico) and *Let's Make a Deal*. It also broadcasts similar game shows in German, Italian and non-U.S. English speaking shows in the U.K. and South Africa. The company added the television unit in October 1997, when it purchased All American Communications Inc. for $373 million in cash and the assumption of $136 million in debt.

All the news that's fit to pink

More than two million business professionals benefit from the business news and analysis produced by The Financial Times Group. The division's flagship paper, *The Financial Times*, is amongst its publications, along with France's *Les Echos* and 50 percent of *The Economist*. In 1999, Pearson made a major investment in the group by channeling $193 million into an expansion of FT.com, the web site for *The Financial Times*. Two years later, Financial Times Information Ltd. announced a deal with Austin-based Hoover's Inc., an online business information site, to share content from FT.com in the U.S., U.K., France, Germany, Italy and Spain. In February 2002, *The Financial Times* placed a new weekly supplement in its famously pink-tinted pages aimed at the fund management industry. *FTfm*, as the supplement was known, became the world's largest circulation fund management title. The broadsheet delivered lackluster numbers in the first few years of the 2000s, as advertising fell in the second half of 2002 by 11 percent, subsequently causing profits to plummet 20 percent, compared with the prior year. However, the FT Group staged a comeback and by the summer of 2004, increasing advertising sales for the first time in three years.

Driving force

In January 2002, Pearson Education UK teamed up with the Educational Multimedia Corporation, Enl!ght Teststation and the British Computer Society, to create a unique learning package for the exploding European Computer Driving Licence (ECDL) market. This market, not quite around yet in the states, enables students to demonstrate their computer skills (in any field) online. With Pearson's partnership, ECDL need only one step to test students, as opposed to the multilevel process of computerized testing of the past.

Positive numbers

In November 2004, Pearson released its first-ever nine month trading update, highlighting a 2 percent rise in sales, a 7 percent increase in operating profits and a free cash flow "well ahead" of 2003. CEO Scardino told analysts that, although advertising remains "quite unpredictable and completely erratic," Pearson expects significant improvement for the full year. This favorable outlook comes despite problems within the Penguin publishing division, which has been plagued by chain distribution problems and a slowdown in the U.S. consumer publishing industry, which has posted a 52 percent decrease in profit for the first half of 2004. However, profits at Pearson are expected to pick up in the second half of 2004 as exchange-rate discrepancies are reduced, Penguin's nonfiction unit improves and backlist sales increase.

Pearson sold its 79 percent stake in Spanish publisher Recoletos in December 2004 for $988.6 million to Retos Cartera, an investment consortium of Spanish investors. Pearson said it would use the profits from the sale to cut down debt and invest in its businesses. CEO Scardino said Recoletos' gradual move into sport, lifestyle and general publications no longer meshed with the FT Group's focus on business and financial news.

GETTING HIRED

The Pearson web site offers little help in your employment search. Since it is a global company publishing books, educational materials, television shows and newspapers, your best bet is to research each division individually until you find who you want to work for. Once decided, contact the companies directly with your resume and letter. The Pearson web site offers contact information for the different offices and HR personnel. Visit www.pearson.com/contact/apply.htm for more information.

Penguin Group

80 Strand
London
WC2R ORL
United Kingdom
Phone: +44-2070103396
Fax: +44-2070106642
www.penguin.com

LOCATIONS

London, U.K. (Main HQ, The Penguin Group)
New York, NY (U.S. HQ, Penguin Group (USA)
Amsterdam
Athens
Auckland
Bertsham, South Africa
Dublin
Frankfurt
Madrid
Milan
New Delhi
Tokyo
Toronto
Toulouse
Victoria, Australia

THE STATS

Employer Type: Subsidiary of Pearson
Chairman & CEO: John C. Makinson

KEY COMPETITORS

HarperCollins
Random House
Simon & Schuster

EMPLOYMENT CONTACT

us.penguingroup.com/static/html/
aboutus/contactus.html#JOBS

THE SCOOP

That's one well-read bird

As one of the world's premier publishers of fiction and nonfiction, Penguin Group (USA), the American division of The Penguin Group, is one of the largest trade book publishers in the United States. In addition to paperback editions of the world's most famous works, the company's various imprints (i.e., the "brand names" under which the company publishes its books) publish hardcovers, mass-market paperbacks and film and television tie-in books. Today, Penguin annually publishes over 3,000 paperback and hardcover titles under several imprints including Viking, Dutton, Signet, Onyx, Plume and Puffin. From Lance Armstrong to W.B. Yeats, the company has mainstream and classic literature covered.

Two companies grow side by side

Penguin founder Allen Lane entered the publishing business in London in 1935. At the time, George Palmer Putnam had been busy stateside for several decades, having opened G. Putnam Broadway in New York in 1848, and spending the second half of the 19th century publishing the works of literati such as Washington Irving, Edgar Allen Poe and Nathaniel Hawthorne, in addition to military history works by a young Theodore Roosevelt. In 1936, Allen Lane formed Penguin Books Ltd., which sold more than three million books in its first year. At the same time, George Putnam's sons, in charge of G.P. Putnam after their father's death, formed an alliance with London-based Coward-McCann, enabling the publisher to reach authors and audiences on both sides of the Atlantic.

The two companies worked simultaneously throughout the next few decades, picking up imprints, authors, prestige and controversy. Putnam published Vladimir Nabakov's *Lolita* in 1958, which was banned by public libraries in American cities and officially banned by the government of France; despite (or maybe in part because of) the controversy, the book went on to become a best-seller. Penguin released the first unabridged version of *Lady Chatterly's Lover* in 1960 and was subsequently charged under Britain's Obscene Publications Act. Penguin was acquitted, and went on to sell two million copies of the book in six weeks.

Penguin went public in 1961, while Putnam acquired Berkley Books, a mass-market paperback house in 1965. After Allen Lane's death in 1970, Penguin was purchased by Pearson PLC, a British media conglomerate that also owns the *Financial Times*

Visit Vault at **www.vault.com** for insider company profiles, expert advice, career message boards, expert resume reviews, the Vault Job Board and more.

VAULT CAREER LIBRARY   207

and Madame Tussaud's wax museums. In 1975, Penguin acquired the prestigious New York-based Viking Press, whose impressive list of authors (among them John Steinbeck, Saul Bellow and Arthur Miller) gave Penguin a strong foothold in the American market. Meanwhile, MCA, Inc. acquired The Putnam Publishing Group and The Berkley Publishing Group the same year. Both companies increased their young adult and children's operations in the 1980s, collecting between them classic titles such as *Make Way for Ducklings* and the popular *Nancy Drew*, *Hardy Boys*, *Beatrix Potter*, *Madeline* and *Winnie-the-Pooh* series.

Finally, in November 1996, The Penguin Group acquired the Putnam Berkley Group for $336 million in cash and merged the two to form Penguin Putnam Inc. The new company later changed its name to Penguin Group (USA), and established itself as a publisher of affordable, quality literature.

Anti-trust lawsuit

In September 1997, Penguin paid a hefty $25 million to the American Booksellers Association, settling an antitrust lawsuit alleging that Penguin made unfair discounts to larger retailers. The settlement was one of the largest in the history of U.S. antitrust discrimination. Independent booksellers charged Penguin with giving major retailers like Barnes & Noble and Borders unfair price breaks; the bookstore chains argued that the wealth of their sales justified the discounts. Penguin cooperated fully with the ABA's investigation, though the company maintained that the discounts were unauthorized, and did not publicly agree that a consent order was violated. However, Penguin did agree to modify future consent orders to ensure equality in pricing, credit and promotional reimbursement to all booksellers, and dismissed an accountant allegedly involved in giving special discounts to the chain stores. While the case was settled, much tension still exists in the industry with independent booksellers feeling that they are being crowded out of the market by a few chains that are able to offer big discounts to customers.

Entering the entertainment ring

The Penguin Group cashed in on the entertainment business in December 1997, when Penguin U.K. signed a deal with Universal Pictures subsidiary October Films to publish between five to 10 film tie-ins, with Robert Duvall's *The Apostle* serving as the first movie. A few days later Penguin Group (USA) inked a similar agreement with DreamWorks SKG, to tout titles for films including *Small Soldiers* and *The Prince of Egypt*. Penguin Group (USA) is also responsible for Penguin Classics, a longstanding imprint of the house that includes more than 1,600 titles of classic literature with more recent scholarly introductions in the publications. Penguin Classics also has its own web site, www.penguinclassics.com, which has everything from literary quizzes to order forms.

The Oprah effect

In September 1996, talk show host Oprah Winfrey made an on-air announcement that rocked the publishing industry, in particular, Penguin Group (USA). "What we want to do is start a book club on the Oprah show," the television star said. "The first book to read is a novel called *Deep End Of the Ocean*, written by Jacquelyn Mitchard. So you all have to go out and buy it." Mitchard's book just happened to be published by Penguin Group (USA). Within one week, bookstores had ordered over half a million copies of the title, propelling the relatively unknown author to the No.-1 spot on multiple bestseller lists. When Oprah announced her next book, Toni Morrison's *Song of Soloman*, Penguin execs were thrilled: they also owned the rights to the title. Sales shot up for Morrison's 20-year-old novel, causing Cathy Hemming, an executive director at Penguin USA, to call Oprah's club, "A gift, a gift from the heavens." Oprah stopped the club in the spring of 2002 after a widely publicized clash with *The Corrections* author Jonathan Franzen, who declined to be included in the Club because he considered his work to be more high-brow than some of Oprah's selections. However, in June 2003, Oprah picked the club up again, this time with a focus on classic titles. Her first choice? *East of Eden* – owned by Penguin Group (USA). The Steinbeck classic was ranked below No. 2 million on Amazon.com's bestselling book list, but soared to No. 113 mere hours after Oprah announced it as the first title in the newly resurrected reading club. Soon, the novel – first published in 1952 – was ranked No 2, second only to the then recent *Harry Potter* novel.

Internet connections

Penguin has also had success with Internet ventures, including a September 2001 deal inked with Yahoo! to create an e-bookstore. Penguin and rivals Simon & Schuster, Random House and HarperCollins made Yahoo! Shopping one of the first online sources to offer a variety of literature from multiple publishers, including digital eBook content. Three years later, Penguin USA partnered up with netLibrary, a Boulder, Colo.-based provider of e-books. The deal provided netLibrary with electronic copies of Penguin titles for its on-line libraries. Penguin chose the company, part of the Online Computer Library Center, because of its "respect for publishing." Early in 2004, *Publishers Weekly* reported that Penguin USA had become the first American publisher to make all of its titles available for sale through its web site. In a January 2005 issue of the same publication, Penguin Group (USA) CEO David Shanks told the magazine that the company's online sales "has lived up to expectations" and that the company plans to make some minor changes to the site that will improve navigation for online buyers.

Holding onto the bestsellers

In early 2002, Penguin happily re-signed Patricia Cornwell, whose work has been published in 34 countries and 31 languages, to a contract to write another two blood-and-guts thrillers featuring sleuth forensic scientist Kay Scarpetta. Cornwell is not the only big-name at the world's No.-2 publishing house, though. Bestselling authors Judy Blume, Stephen King, Amy Tan, Al Franken, Sue Monk Kidd, Jan Karon, Nora Roberts and Ken Follett all call Penguin home. In addition, a plethora of *New York Times* bestsellers in 2004 came from Penguin, including Ron Chernow's biography of Alexander Hamilton, Lynne Truss' grammar guide *Eats, Shoots & Leaves* and Karen Joy Fowler's hit *The Jane Austen Book Club*.

GETTING HIRED

Hiring overview

Penguin Group (USA) accepts resumes e-mailed and faxed to its New York headquarters but prefers them mailed. Send resumes and cover letters to the human resources department. The company asks that candidates include a salary requirement – a bit disingenuous, considering the publishing world's notoriously paltry pay scales.

The web site offers little help for eager job seekers. The best way to get your foot in the door is through a contact person in the company. For more information, contact jobs@us.penguingroup.com and to send a resume, mail to: Penguin Putnam Inc., Human Resources Department, 375 Hudson Street New York, NY 10014. The company also frequently posts openings on Hotjobs.com.

Penguin Group (USA) also offers a coveted summer internship program to those interested in book publishing. Contact the human resources for more help on applying. Once in, you have a better shot at landing a job post-graduation.

Pixar Animation Studios

1200 Park Avenue
Emeryville, CA 94608
Phone: (510) 752-3000
Fax: (510) 752-3151
www.pixar.com

LOCATIONS

Emeryville, CA (HQ)
Boston, MA
Chicago, IL
Dallas, TX
Houston, TX
Los Angeles, CA
Memphis, TN
New York, NY
Redwood Shores, CA

THE STATS

Employer Type: Public Company
Stock Symbol: PIXR
Stock Exchange: NASDAQ
Chairman and CEO: Steven P. (Steve) Jobs
2004 Employees: 775
2004 Revenue ($mil.): $273.5

KEY COMPETITORS

Disney Studios
DreamWorks Animation
Lucasfilm

EMPLOYMENT CONTACT

www.pixar.com/companyinfo/jobs/
openings.html

Visit Vault at **www.vault.com** for insider company profiles, expert advice, career message boards, expert resume reviews, the Vault Job Board and more.

VAULT CAREER LIBRARY   211

THE SCOOP

Steve Jobs' new baby

Pixar, the creator of the mega-hits *Toy Story*, *A Bug's Life*, *Monsters, Inc.*, *Finding Nemo* and *The Incredibles* is more than just a computer animation studio. It stands poised to become one of the largest·entertainment forces of the 21st century. Born in the 1980s as the special effects division of Lucasfilm, the company was spun off in 1986 and acquired by Steve Jobs, co-founder of Apple Computer, for a cool $10 million. The new company was dubbed Pixar, after the first 3-D graphics system (the Pixar Image Computer) developed by the computer scientists and animators that worked there.

Pioneers in computer animation

Computer graphics genius Ed Catmull (now Pixar's chief technology officer) and former Disney animator John Lasseter were among the pioneers of 3-D computer animation, and set the tone that Pixar was to follow. Lasseter's *Luxo Jr.*, a short computer-animated piece about two anthropomorphic lamps, blew away the industry when it premiered at SIGGRAPH, the annual convention of the computer graphics industry. Computer animation would redefine the possibilities for the medium – in fact, it would do for the future of animation what stop-motion photography had for the first 80 years of film. After the premier of *Luxo Jr.*, Pixar focused on honing its burgeoning medium by producing animation for commercials, while Lasseter continued working on short films like *Tin Toy*, which won an Academy Award for Best Animated Short in 1988.

Enter Disney

In 1986, Pixar and Disney entered a deal for the development of CAPS (Computer Animated Production System), which uses computers to color hand-drawn images. In 1991, Disney convinced Pixar to produce three feature-length computer animated movies. Following the Disney deal, the company tinkered with its technology and produced a variety of commercials for name brands such as Listerine, Lifesavers and Pillsbury. Pixar picked up multiple honors for the animated spots, including back-to-back Gold Medal Clio awards, the Oscar of the advertising industry, in 1993 and 1994. In 1995, Pixar went public with an IPO of 6.9 million shares that raised $140 million for the burgeoning company, making its stock the highest rated IPO of the year. The same year, Pixar also released its first film with distributor Disney, and the first film of its kind, the celebrated *Toy Story*, which Lasseter directed. Originally designed to follow the adventures of the pressed-metal soldier from *Tin Toy*, *Toy Story* evolved into a completely fresh story.

Let's do lunch

Toy Story became the top-grossing movie of 1995. Audiences were wowed by the graphics, but what won the most praise (and several Oscars) was the movie's powerful story line. The Academy of Motion Picture Arts and Sciences gave a Special Achievement Award to Lasseter for his "inspired leadership of the Pixar *Toy Story* team resulting in the first feature-length, computer animated film." Box office receipts and merchandising revenue from items such as Pixar's *Toy Story* (which remains the most successful CD-ROM of all time), gave Pixar a pleasant financial boost. But with only a 13 percent cut of the profits, Pixar's situation was far from ideal. Enter CEO Steve Jobs, the business mind of the venture. Though he was busy serving as the interim CEO of Apple Computer, Jobs took time to negotiate a better deal with Disney. After a lunch meeting with Disney's Michael Eisner, Jobs walked away with a deal offering Pixar 50 percent of box office and merchandising income in addition to a four-movie deal that provided Pixar with Disney's distribution and market expertise.

It's a wonderful *Bug's Life*

A Bug's Life, Pixar's next full-length feature, was released in late 1998. It represented yet another milestone in the development of computer animation. The film had a much larger budget, and was shot in larger format, allowing for even more detailed images than those in *Toy Story*. With the help of ever-improving technologies, animators were able, for example, to make faces with more detailed expressions, and plants with softer, more organic textures. Despite the fact that DreamWorks SKG released a similarly themed feature at the same time (*ANTZ*), *A Bug's Life* was a massive success.

While Jobs still sits at the helm as CEO, he has relinquished the day-to-day management of the animation house to John Lasseter (EVP of Creative Development), Ed Catmull (CTO and co-founder) and Sarah McArthur (EVP of Production). Meanwhile, Jobs is the company's main public figure, and he plays an active role in issues surrounding corporate strategy, marketing and deal-making.

In September 1999, Ann Mather, formerly SVP of finance and administration at Walt Disney's international theatrical film division, was named CFO and EVP of Pixar

Animation Studios. The success of *Toy Story 2*, the first animated film to be entirely created, mastered and exhibited digitally, translated into box office receipts of $485 million worldwide, bringing in even larger profits for the company. *Toy Story 2* also captured the 2000 Golden Globe award for Best Picture – Musical or Comedy.

Short success

Less-known in the public sector, but still equally prominent, are Pixar's short films, which the company continues to produce alongside its blockbuster feature-length titles. Recent shorts *Geri's Game* and *For the Birds* nabbed Oscars in 1998 and 2002, respectively.

The hits just keep on coming

Monster's Inc., Pixar's next project, became the highest-grossing animated film of 2001, and the third-highest grossing animated film in history, bringing in box office revenue of $100 million in just nine days. The film went on to become 2002's top-selling DVD after a record-breaking launch. The next year, Pixar broke its own box office records with the May 2003 release of *Finding Nemo*, which became the highest-grossing animated film worldwide and the No.-1 best-selling DVD of all time. *The Incredibles*, released in November 2004, was also a critical and commercial hit, wowing audiences with its painstakingly realistic human characters, Pixar's riskiest feat yet. Next up for the animation superpower is *Cars*, a road trip movie chronicling an assortment of cars traveling across Route 66, which was recently bumped back by Jobs from a fall 2005 to Summer 2006 release.

To infinity and beyond ... with or without Disney

Pixar and Disney broke off contract negotiations in January 2004, after Disney refused to agree to a distribution only deal, in which Pixar would keep profits and pay Disney a fee to get movies into theaters. Under the current agreement, Pixar is responsible for film content, Disney supervises distribution and marketing, and both companies split the profit, with Pixar paying Disney a distribution fee. However, since Pixar's recent movies have generated such a strong cash flow, Pixar no longer needs an investment from another studio, and wants to keep revenue for itself. Analysts called the break-up a "lose-lose" situation for both parties, since Disney will lose the profitable Pixar product, which will have generated an estimated $1.9 billion for Disney by the time the contract expires, while Pixar will be forced to finance 100 percent of its projects, instead of sharing half of the cost with Disney – a potentially dangerous financial circumstance, should one of Pixar's movies tank at the box office.

In May, *The New York Times* published a report suggesting Jobs had not met with Sony, Warner Bros. or MGM – three potential suitors – sparking rumors that Pixar was not yet done dealing with Disney. Regarding the prospective partners, Jobs was quoted as saying, "We are talking, but maybe not as much as they'd like." *The Times* further speculated that Jobs would like to strike a deal with Disney, because of the company's merchandising power and family-friendly theme. In December 2004, Disney president Robert Iger announced plans to push forth with "sequels, television shows, theme park rides and other products" based on existing Pixar characters, whether a new deal was struck with Pixar or not, citing a "great desire and intention" to see sequels created from existing Disney-Pixar movies. Investors saw the announcement as a sign that the two companies would pick up negotiations in the future. Jobs hopes to announce a new distribution partner sometime during 2005.

Meanwhile, despite the Disney drama, Pixar tripled its profit in the first quarter of 2004, reporting a net income of $26.7 million, due in part to strong home video sales for *Finding Nemo*. The stock was up from $8.2 million over the previous year, when Pixar had no new films playing, furthering suggestions from analysts that Pixar's stock is "event-driven."

Trouble ahead?

The switch in the release date for *Cars* could be an outward sign of problems within Pixar. Shares for the company dropped 7 percent in December 2004 on news of the movie delay, which will no doubt hurt Pixar's earnings, as it leaves the company without a major release for 2005. Jobs claims the change in release date is simply an effort to capitalize on the abundance of kids with free time during summer vacation, and describes *Cars* as "a quintessential summer film." In addition, the delay of *Cars* could provide the animation studio with some much-needed time to figure out a new direction. Pixar plans to assess the new management structure at Disney once the House of Mouse announces its successor to CEO Michael Eisner, whose contract expires in September 2006, and who is rumored to have an "uneasy" business relationship with Jobs.

GETTING HIRED

Hiring overview

Because of Pixar's rapid growth and the lack of computer engineers skilled in Pixar's RenderMan imaging software, Pixar actively recruits new employees on its web site: www.pixar.com, where openings are listed regularly. Pixar also recruits eligible candidates from select art and film schools.

"We do check references; they count," reports one insider. "The animators have a reel, the artists have a portfolio, the technical production people can point to movies or TV shows/commercials they worked on." When potential employees are found, HR performs the initial screening and then forwards on the viable candidates" to the manager that has the opening.

Submission guidelines

For those applicants submitting samples of work, Pixar suggests applying electronically, then mailing requested materials along with a hard copy of a resume and signed submission release form. No applicants' work can be reviewed without a signed submission agreement. Also, work samples are not returned, so the company suggests sending copies, instead of originals.

Primedia

745 Fifth Avenue
New York, NY 10151
Phone: (212) 745-0100
Fax: (212) 745-0121
www.primedia.com

LOCATIONS

New York, NY (HQ)
Anaheim, CA
Atlanta, GA
Carrollton, TX
Chicago, IL
Denver, CO
Detroit, MI
Los Angeles, CA
Overland Park, KS

DEPARTMENTS

Business Information
Consumer Guides
Education
Enterprises
Enthusiast Media

THE STATS

Employer Type: Public Company
Stock Symbol: PRM
Stock Exchange: NYSE
Chairman, President and CEO: Kelly Conlin
2004 Employees: 4,500
2004 Revenue ($mil.): $1,307.1

KEY COMPETITORS

Advance Publications
Condé Nast
McGraw-Hill

EMPLOYMENT CONTACT

PRIMEDIA
745 Fifth Avenue
New York, NY 10151
Phone: (212) 745-0100
Fax: (212) 745-0121
E-mail: information@primedia.com

Check web sites of individual publications for openings.

Visit Vault at **www.vault.com** for insider company profiles, expert advice, career message boards, expert resume reviews, the Vault Job Board and more.

VAULT CAREER LIBRARY   217

THE SCOOP

Hot properties

Chances are, when you were last browsing your local supermarket magazine rack for something to read, many of the titles on display were produced by Primedia, the top special-interest magazine publisher in the U.S. The media giant publishes more than 250 titles, including consumer and trade publications, which are all produced under its Primedia Enthusiast Media and Business Information segment. A few of Primedia's better-known titles are *Soap Opera Digest* and *McCall's Quilting*. Primedia also publishes *Skateboarder*, *Snowboarder*, *Surfer*, *Stereophile*, and the photo-focused mag *Shutterbug*, as well as 10 history-themed magazines (*Civil War Times* and *Wild West*, for instance). It also publishes *Motor Trend*, *Power & Motoryacht* and more than 70 other mags related to things with wheels that go fast – cars, trucks, motorcycles, hot rods, bikes, four-wheelers, all-terrain vehicles.

Its business-to-business publishing segment, called Primedia Business Information, puts out an additional 70+ niche titles, including *Corn & Soybean Digest, Insurance Conference Planner*, *Telephony*, *Waste Age* and *Profitable Embroiderer* and the more widely known *American Demographics*.

Guides and learning tools

Primedia Consumer Guides, another business segment, publishes and distributes free guides for apartments, new homes, and autos. Its 81 *Apartment Guides*, for example, are handed out in 75 different regions of the U.S. for a combined monthly circulation of 1.6 million. Under its DistribuTech division, the company distributes not only its own guides, but also 2,000 other free publications in some 16,000 locations.

And Primedia's influence isn't limited to print; the company also has a strong web presence. Under its Enthusiast Media division, it runs About.com, the mother of all categorical "how to" web sites. The vast About.com site, combined with the sites for the various Enthusiast Media titles, account for Primedia's biggest web presence.

As if that weren't enough, Primedia also provides content to schools, governments, and corporate and public institutions through its Education and Training segment, which includes *Channel One News* – the highest-rated teen TV program – and Films Media Group-a leading source of education media products in North America. Taken together, sales from all of these magazines, guides, web sites, videos and other doodads added up to more than $1.3 billion in 2003.

Niche market mania

At the beginning of their endeavor, the company's founders set out to do one thing: venture into the farthest niches of the publishing world and amass as many properties as possible. In 1989, three executives, all of whom had left Macmillan Publishing, secured financial backing from New York investment firm Kohlberg Kravis Roberts and Co. (KKR), and a new publishing holding company was born. K-III Communications Corporation, as it was awkwardly called, embarked on a mission of strategic acquisitions of niche media properties. The company bought Intertec Publishing, which put out technical and trade magazines, and Macmillan Book Clubs, which it renamed Newbridge Communications. With that acquisition, the fledgling company also brought another 45 Macmillan staffers onboard.

In the 1990s, the company saw steady growth. With the purchase of International Thompson Transport Press in 1990, K-III moved into the realm of directory publishing. The next year, it snapped up Funk & Wagnalls, publisher of encyclopedias and other reference books, as well as the *Weekly Reader*, an informational paper that's been a staple for years in elementary schools around the country. But that same year the company made perhaps its biggest splash yet: It beat out the big boys – Condé Nast and Hearst – in its bid to buy Murdoch Magazines, which published the venerable *New York*, *Seventeen*, *Premiere*, and *Soap Opera Digest*. K-III continued in similar fashion for the rest of the decade, beefing up its educational division with video and film offerings, as well as its magazine unit with the purchase of Cahners Consumer Magazines in 1996.

New name, same old problems

Almost two years after its initial public offering, K-III changed its moniker to Primedia in 1997. But a bigger portfolio and presence as a public company weren't the only reasons for the name change. The company also had to undo damage (some of which was self-inflicted) to its bottom line. While Primedia was busy snatching up titles, it was also accumulating debt. The same year, it had to sell off a few of its non-core units, in addition to a couple of popular titles, *New Woman* and *Premiere*. It restructured, focusing on three media segments: Specialty Magazines, Education, and Information (which handles consumer and business information). Two years later, it sold off its supplemental education unit and put the proceeds toward what had by then become a $2.5 billion debt.

Visit Vault at **www.vault.com** for insider company profiles, expert advice, career message boards, expert resume reviews, the Vault Job Board and more.

VAULT CAREER LIBRARY   **219**

New chief in charge

By 1999, Primedia was ready for a change at the top. KKR, which was still the company's largest stockholder, pushed out CEO William Reilly and replaced him with Tom Rogers, a web-savvy NBC executive, to stimulate Internet business and integrate it with the company's print properties. In 2000, Rogers bought About.com- a unique network of web sites about everything under the sun, including teens, travel, home and garden, education and hundreds of other topics that are maintained by experts in those subjects. The price tag for the deal was a high one-$690 million. Next, in a complex investment scheme in January 2001, Rogers formed Media Central, a joint venture with Brill Media Holdings, publisher of (the now-defunct) *Brill's Content* magazine and Contentville.com.

Web tactic tanks

Over the summer of 2001, Rogers snapped up EMAP USA, the American arm of a British publishing company, for $515 million, making Primedia the second largest magazine publisher in the U.S. The deal added such well-known titles as *Hot Rod*, *Teen*, and *Guns & Ammo* to the stable. But ad sales – the bread and butter of magazine publishing – were tanking industry-wide. Rogers' buying frenzy coupled with the burst of the Internet bubble, spelled bad news for Primedia. And by October, *Brill's Content* had gone belly up. Owner Steven Brill agreed to sell off his share of the web site Inside.com to Primedia, ending their business relationship. Brill laid off 38 magazine employees.

Unfortunately, it wasn't just print ad sales that took a hit as the economy declined. About.com and other sites were performing more poorly than expected, forcing Primedia to implement steep staff cuts and salary and hiring freezes. About 60 percent of About.com's workforce was let go. By then, investors had become skittish over Primedia's long-term debt load, which still stood at about $2 billion, and its stock, which had been walloped by the depressed market. In the fall of 2001, the company posted net losses that were four times wider than the same time the previous year.

Try, try again

In 2002, Primedia had to part with *American Baby*, *Chicago*, and *American Bride* magazines (for $115 million, $35 million, and $50 million, respectively) to try to lessen its debt. By 2003, it had to put *Seventeen* on the block as well. But Rogers was, apparently, not cutting costs and selling off the company's hot properties fast enough. An article on Slate.com bemoaned the dilemma Rogers was facing: "For a big-shot media executive, the notion of jettisoning *New York* to focus on the likes of *Volleyball* must be humiliating. What self-respecting media tycoon wants to spend his days chatting up potential advertisers for *National Hog Farmer*?" It wasn't much of a surprise when Primedia's board ousted Rogers (or when he resigned, depending on who you ask) in April 2003. It took another six months to find his replacement, Kelly Conlin, a former newspaperman who had been named president of International Data Group in 1995 at the age of 35.

Oh New York!

The end of 2003 also saw the close of bidding on Primedia's hottest title: *New York* magazine. But the sale wasn't a straightforward affair. Whoever wanted to snap up the popular mag would likely end up losing somewhere between $1 million to $2 million a year until they could get it back on its feet again. Why? Because as it turned out, the circulation numbers were high and Primedia hadn't produced an audit for two years prior, according to a *New York Observer* article.

One of *New York*'s most prominent columnists, media commentator Michael Wolff, formed a group with several publishing heavyweights-including Mortimer Zuckerman, *Daily News* owner, Mirimax films Co-chair Harvey Weinstein, and other investors – to make a very public bid to buy *New York*. But Wall Street wheeler and dealer Bruce Wasserstein won out in the end with a $55 million bid in mid-December. In January 2004, Wolff left the magazine, bound for *Vanity Fair*.

New directions

A ton of hype was swirling around this highly public sale, and new CEO Conlin stepped in right in the middle of it. Yet most of the work he set out to do was the grittier, lower-profile work of reorganizing business segments and figuring out which magazines to spruce up. He gave Primedia the new organizational structure it uses today, with its properties divided into four categories: enthusiast media, consumer guides, education and training, and business-to-business. And he decided to strengthen and expand the company's core markets, rather than branch out in entirely uncharted directions.

Some of the titles that needed shoring up were magazines that had been neglected over the years. Conlin and company embarked on a redesign of more than a dozen publications in 2004. An insider told Min's B-To-B that Conlin, during a planning session, had essentially told under-performing magazines to shape up, fast. "Finally,

Visit Vault at **www.vault.com** for insider company profiles, expert advice, career message boards, expert resume reviews, the Vault Job Board and more.

VAULT CAREER LIBRARY   **221**

someone was talking about the product," the insider said. Improvements have been made at old standbys. *Hot Rod*, for example, got a whole new look, beginning with the July 2004 issue. It's started printing on better paper and is now perfectly bound, added 32 editorial pages, made images and photo spreads bigger, and shifted content around under the hood. As part of a stepped-up brand-extension strategy, Primedia also inked a new licensing and merchandising agreement with Alltrade Tools LLC to fire up a new line of products tied to *Hot Rod*.

New leaders for new times

The changes haven't all been cosmetic or product related. Since Conlin took helm, several Primedia titles have also added new editorial talent. *Motor Trend* and *Skateboarder* have both imported new top editors. *Motor Trend*'s Angus MacKenzie, who joined the title as editor-in-chief, has had a successful career at automotive pubs in the U.K. and Australia, while Brian Peech, who has taken over the helm at *Skateboarder*, headed up the sport's top Canadian magazine. Both came onboard in August 2004. The company has also installed new executives in key positions on the sales side who are expected to create a resurgence in revenue from retail sales.

That same month, word got out that Primedia was scaling back its interest in a couple of highly respected, but not highly profitable media-related pubs. Majority interest in *Folio*: and *Circulation Management* were acquired by publisher Red 7 Media. The new company will be responsible for producing the magazines, while Primedia will hold a minority interest. News reports had speculated that *Folio:*, *Circulation Management*, and *American Demographics* would be sold because although they produced a small profit, each relies on a small advertising base that has been eroding over the years. *American Demographics*, however, was not part of the deal with Red 7. But the future of the monthly that measures the pulse of America's tastes and attitudes remains in limbo; as of this writing, Primedia has discontinued publishing *American Demographics* and is reportedly looking for a buyer.

Stranger than fiction

Amid all the shifting, the only change at one rag was the address. *Soap Opera Digest* moved its headquarters from Manhattan's Fifth Avenue to Madison Avenue, its third location in just over a year. Why keep the non-trade, non-"enthusiast" publication when Primedia had dumped *American Baby*, *Chicago*, *New York*, and *Seventeen*? Because it's a moneymaker, even with sluggish ad sales, and loyal readers were willing to pay $0.55 more per issue on the cover price. In early 2004 Primedia even decided to bank on the successful SOD model by testing out a new title, *Reality Check*. It's a magazine all about the behind the scenes drama of, you guessed it, reality television shows. Probably even more realistic, however, is yet another new title, the soberingly named *Modern Uniforms*, devoted to the industry that clothes an estimated one in four Americans in a uniform at work.

GETTING HIRED

Think you'd be a great fit with one of Primedia's many media properties? You won't be able to start your search for your perfect position in one centralized location. The company does not have a general career page web site for all its different publications. But if you know, for example, that you would love to help educate kids by working at *Channel One*, you can look on its web site to see what positions are available – like anchor/reporter or assignment desk editor, for example. But be wary of going on a wild goose chase: some of Primedia's web sites, like the one for *Power & Motoryacht*, for example, are mostly just online stores and contain no employment information.

Visit Vault at **www.vault.com** for insider company profiles, expert advice, career message boards, expert resume reviews, the Vault Job Board and more.

VAULT CAREER LIBRARY   223

Random House, Inc.

1745 Broadway
New York, NY 10019
Phone: (212) 782-9000
Fax: (212) 302-7985
www.randhomhouse.com

LOCATIONS

New York, NY (HQ)

THE SCOOP

Free to be Random

If there's any truth to the populist saying that freedom of the press extends only to those who can afford a press, then Random House is very free indeed. Since its founding in 1925 by publishing legends Bennett Cerf and Donald Klopfer, Random House has guaranteed its imprints a high degree of editorial independence. In 1933 the company successfully defended James Joyce's *Ulysses* against obscenity charges, a significant victory for free speech rights in the U.S.

Buying and selling

The world's largest publisher of English-language books, Random House includes more than 25 imprints and publishes everything from highbrow fiction to dictionaries to movie tie-ins. Prominent imprints range from the highly prestigious Knopf and Pantheon to mass-market Random House and Ballantine. In 1965, RCA bought Random House, but then sold the subsidiary to S.I. Newhouse's Advance Publications, the nation's largest privately held newspaper conglomerate, in 1980. Under Newhouse's direction, Random House bought several more publishing houses, including Fawcett, Villard and Times Books. Outside the U.S., Random House oversees publishers such as Berlin Verlag (of which it owns 75 percent) and Plaza & Jan's.

In 1988 Random House bought Crown Books, a company whose imprints included Crown, Clarkson Potter, Harmony and the Outlet Book Company. The publisher's current line-up of authors include Nobel Prize winners such as Toni Morrison, best sellers like Anne Rice and celebrity authors, including and Colin Powell.

Interestingly enough, Random House went on to become part of another major media conglomerate and renew its old ties to RCA. In July 1998, German media giant Bertelsmann, the owner of book publisher Bantam Doubleday Dell and record labels RCA Victor and Arista, acquired Random House from its parent company, Advance Publications, for $1.3 billion. Peter Olson succeeded Alberto Vitale as CEO of Random House, which absorbed Bertelsmann's Bantam-Doubleday-Dell (BDD) publishing group. The deal made Bertelsmann the world's largest English-language trade publisher, with combined sales of about $2 billion. As of 2004, the company is publishing about 8,000 books a year and has a backlist catalog of some 50,000 titles, employing about 5,300 people worldwide.

Visit Vault at **www.vault.com** for insider company profiles, expert advice,
career message boards, expert resume reviews, the Vault Job Board and more.
V/\ULT CAREER LIBRARY   **225**

Management changes

In November 1997, former Publisher and President Harold Evans resigned amid rumors of a power struggle with his successor, President and Editor-in-Chief Ann Godoff. Reportedly, then-CEO Alberto Vitale had attempted to move Evans, who was known as a tireless promoter associated with celebrity books, to a new position. But in January 2003, after five years as president of Random House, Godoff herself was dismissed by President and Chief Executive Peter Olson, as part of a major shake-up at the publisher.

Apparently, Godoff had spent too much on acquisitions in 2002 – in one instance paying $3 million for a two-book deal to the authors of *The Nanny Diaries*, based on viewing three sample chapters. In a memo to staffers, Olson announced his fiscal displeasure with Random House: "They have been the only Random House Inc. publishing division to consistently fall short of their annual profitability targets," he said. While at Random House, Godoff published best sellers like *Midnight in the Garden of Good and Evil, The Alienist, White Teeth* and *A Short Guide to a Happy* Life. The change in leadership occurred just as the entire company was moving into its new headquarters at 1745 Broadway in Manhattan.

Following Godoff's departure, the operations of Random House and Ballantine were combined and veteran publisher Gina Centrello (who was president of Ballantine at the time) was tapped to be publisher of the new group. Writers and other publishing industry insiders were initially concerned about the change in leadership, particularly because Godoff's editorial instincts are near-legendary, while Centrello is known as a bottom-line kind of manager. Centrello quelled some of the fears, however, by naming long-time editor Daniel Menaker as the division's editor-in-chief of Random House. In 2004, another editor, Jonathan Karp, took over the editor-in-chief duties as Menaker broadened his responsibilities.

Hello, goodbye

In January 2002, Peter Olson boasted of a corporate triumph when he hired his good friend Phyllis Grann, the former chief executive of the rival publisher Penguin Putnam as a consultant. Grann is a legend in the publishing industry, having turned Penguin into a hit factory consistently turning out blockbuster books. Hiring Grann, Olson said at the time, was like deciding to "hire Michael Jordan to come back and play on any team in any position." Well, just as Michael Jordan left the Bulls, so too did Grann exit Random House, bolting a mere six months into her tenure. Grann cited "boredom" as the reason for her hasty departure. Part of the problem was

Random House's management structure. The company operates with a highly decentralized structure of editorially independent and internally competitive publishing divisions like Knopf, Bantam Dell and Doubleday Broadway. Grann had no clear territory within the company's many rival fiefdoms, and she complained that the company's many publishers seldom sought her advice.

Electronic ventures

In April 2000, Random House announced it was buying a 49 percent minority stake in publishing services company Xlibris, a pioneer in the field of print-on-demand since 1997. The Philadelphia-based Xlibris allows authors direct and personal access to publication in hardcover, trade paperback and e-book formats.

A deal in 2000 with the company Audible resulted in Random House Audible, which distributes digital audio books online. The digital books cost 20 percent less than cassettes and are downloadable to hand held devices. Sample chapters of new books are available online before each book's print release. The acquisition of Listening Library Inc. brought the audio version of J.K. Rowling's immensely popular *Harry Potter and the Sorcerer's Stone* to the Random House collection. Similarly, an agreement with Disney made Random House the publisher of activity and story books based on characters from *Toy Story 2* and *The Lion King*, as well as Disney staples like Mickey and Minnie Mouse. By the end of 2003, Audible had proven itself a profitable venture, with yearly revenue of $18.5 million, a 69 percent increase over 2002.

Classic literature, electronically

In an effort to jump on the e-everything bandwagon so prevalent before the dot-com shakeout of 2001, the company announced the launch of AtRandom, a unit for electronic books in July 2000. After a lukewarm initial reception that fell well short of expectations and lack of public excitement for e-books in general, Random House announced that it was folding the imprint in November 2001. That didn't spell the end of e-books for Random, though, as the company said it will continue to publish titles simultaneously in paper and electronic formats under each imprint's moniker.

e-legal wrangling

Starting in 2000 and going on into the beginning of 2001, a publisher called Rosetta Books contracted with several authors to publish their books in digital format over the Internet. Titles that were signed for the venture include *The Confessions of Nat*

Visit Vault at **www.vault.com** for insider company profiles, expert advice,
career message boards, expert resume reviews, the Vault Job Board and more.

VAULT CAREER LIBRARY   227

Turner and *Sophie's Choice* by William Styron; *Slaughterhouse-Five*, *Breakfast of Champions*, *The Sirens of Titan*, *Cat's Cradle* and *Player Piano* by Kurt Vonnegut; and *Promised Land* by Robert B. Parker. In February 2001, Rosetta Books officially launched its e-book business, offering those titles and others for sale in digital format. The next day, Random House filed a complaint accusing Rosetta Books of committing copyright infringement and interfering with the contracts Random House had with Parker, Styron and Vonnegut by selling its e-books. It simultaneously moved for a preliminary injunction prohibiting Rosetta from infringing copyrights.

Sounds pretty cut and dry, right? Well, in the wild and yet-to-be fully regulated world of e-publishing, not quite. Essentially, Random House argued that e-books really are just another form of paper books. Random House asserted that when authors granted it the exclusive right to publish, print and sell their copyrighted works "in book form," this implicitly included books in electronic form. On July 11, 2001 a court ruled in favor of Rosetta, and when Random House appealed in March 2002, the Court of Appeals for the 2nd Circuit again rendered a unanimous decision in favor of Rosetta Books, denying Random House's request to overturn the July 2001 ruling. In so doing, the court handed Rosetta Books its second victory in this landmark litigation, proving that (so far) authors control electronic rights to their works.

In handing down its ruling, the 2nd Circuit did note that "there is some appeal to [Random House's] argument that an 'e–book'-a digital book that can be read on a computer screen or electronic device ... is simply a 'form' of a book, and therefore within the coverage of [Random House's] licenses." But, under the governing law of New York, there is a "restrictive view of the kinds of 'new uses' to which an exclusive license may apply when the contracting parties do not expressly provide for coverage of such future forms."

Resolution

Finally, in December 2002 Random House settled the lawsuit. Under terms of the deal, Rosetta Books will continue publishing the disputed works and will collaborate with Random House on additional books. With rights to countless old titles at stake, the publishing industry has closely followed the case. Simon & Schuster and Penguin Putnam were among those backing Random House, while the Authors Guild and the Association of Authors' Representatives supported Rosetta Books; the settlement leaves the issue unresolved. The two sides essentially agreed it was better to work together than to fight. Under the agreement, Random House will grant Rosetta exclusive e-book rights to "mutually agreed-upon titles," both old and recently published.

A falloff; then an upturn

In June 2002, Random House's German parent company, Bertelsmann, disclosed that Random House recorded an operating loss of $14.2 million in the second half of 2001, the first loss in at least four years at Bertelsmann's book division. Although all major publishers felt a decline in demand for books because of the lingering recession and the aftermath of the September 11 terrorist attacks, no other major publisher that publicly reports results suffered as much as Random House did financially. The company did rebound somewhat in 2002, as its sales increased from $1.7 billion in 2001 to $2 billion. This trend continued into 2003. According to *Publishers Weekly*, a Random House spokesperson reported, "a tremendous fourth quarter and a very strong finish [for the] fiscal year."

Code red

Nearly two years after it was released, Dan Brown's runaway bestseller *The Da Vinci Code*, published under the Random House imprint of Doubleday, struck an unforgiving chord with members of the Vatican. The novel, which first appeared on bookstore shelves in March 2003 and has since sold 29 million copies in 44 different languages, details the work of a symbolism expert and cryptologist trying to uncover the meaning of a code intrinsically linked to the works of Leonardo Da Vinci and the Priory of Sion, an actual secret society whose members included, among others, Isaac Newton, Victor Hugo and Da Vinci. Cardinal Tarcisio Bertone pushed for a boycott of the novel in March 2005, claiming Brown's work deceived Catholics, distorted Christianity and "offended millions of believers" with its suggestion that Jesus Christ married Mary Magdalene and produced descendants, and its unflattering portrayal of the conservative Catholic organization Opus Dei. Doubleday defended the novel as a work of fiction, while Brown suggested the story was merely meant to entertain and "promote spiritual discussion and debate."

Big books from big names

Random House chose Mark Winegardner, an author and creative writing professor, to pen the sequel to Mario Puzo's *The Godfather* in February 2003. Though Winegardner, of German-Irish ancestry, lacked the Italian blood so often shed by the Corleone family and others in the book, *The Godfather Returns*, published in November 2004, was a critical and commercial success. This followed on the heels of the successful release of former President Bill Clinton's personal memoir, *My Life*. Clinton's tome set a one-day non-fiction sales record in June 2004 with first-day sales exceeding 400,000 copies. In other biography news, Random House is rumored to be in the bidding for Martha Stewart's

Visit Vault at **www.vault.com** for insider company profiles, expert advice, career message boards, expert resume reviews, the Vault Job Board and more.

VAULT CAREER LIBRARY   **229**

"prison diary" based on her experience at the federal women's prison in Alderson, W.V., in a deal that could be worth more than $5 million. Overall in 2004, Random House put together an impressive literary portfolio, with three of the publisher's novels (Alice Munro's *Runaway*, Orhan Pamuk's *Snow* and Ha Jin's *War Trash*) landing on *The New York Times'* Book Review's prestigious Top 10 of 2004 list.

On the slate for 2005 is a new Hannibal Lector novel, *Behind the Mask*, by *Silence of the Lambs* author Thomas Harris, as well as two books for young readers penned by Illinois Senator Barack Obama. And for the millions of fans waiting for Anakin Skywalker to eschew his chosen status for the helmeted confines of Darth Vader, there are eight (yes, eight) new *Star Wars* titles related to George Lucas' final film in the space-age franchise, *Star Wars Episode III: Revenge of the Sith*.

GETTING HIRED

Hiring process

Random House lists open positions on its web site at www.randomhouse.com/careers. Prospective employees can also learn more about the publisher's departments, read employee profiles and submit an online application. There is also information on college internships and the company's associates program, which is designed for college graduates as an entry-level gateway to a career in book publishing.

Each summer, members of the company's intern class participate in the creation of a book consisting of essays describing their respective experiences at Random House. The company offers internships at its headquarters in New York and in its operations center near Baltimore. The internship program, which is geared to students between their junior and senior years in college, consists of a 10-week session, which runs from mid-June to mid-August. Once a week, interns get together for lunch to hear key executives speak about their roles and how their divisions operate. Interns also travel to the operations center in Baltimore for a tour of the facilities and to hear from key executives there. The annualdeadline for application to the summer internship program is March 1st.

Once in the door, say insiders, "you should never get bored. Rather than moving from company to company, you can move from department to department." Another contact agrees, saying, "Publishing isn't static, if you do a good job, you can bet that it will be noticed and you'll move through the ranks. The market is a bit tight right now though, so advancement has slowed a bit over the last few years, but it can be done."

Reed Elsevier

Reed Elsevier PLC
1-3 Strand
London
WC2N 5JR, United Kingdom
Phone: +44-20-7930-7077
Fax: +44-20-7166 5799
www.reedelsevier.com

Reed Elsevier NV
Raderweg 29
1043 NX Amsterdam
The Netherlands
Phone: +31 20 485 2222
Fax: +31 20 618 0325

LOCATIONS

Amsterdam (HQ)
New York, NY
London
(Offices in Europe, U.S. and around
the globe)

THE STATS

Employer Type: Public Company
Stock Symbols: RUK [ADR] and ENL
[ADR] / REN
Stock Exchange: NYSE/Euronext
Amsterdam
Chairman: Jan Hommen
CEO: Crispin Davis
2004 Employees: 35,600
2004 Revenue (Euro bil.): 7

KEY COMPETITORS

McGraw-Hill
Pearson
Reuters
Thomson Corporation
VNU
Wolters Kluwer

EMPLOYMENT CONTACT

www.reedelsevier.com/index.cfm?
articleid = 67

Visit Vault at **www.vault.com** for insider company profiles, expert advice,
career message boards, expert resume reviews, the Vault Job Board and more.

VAULT CAREER LIBRARY   231

THE SCOOP

Merger

The 1993 merger between London-based Reed International and Amsterdam-based Elsevier quickly deemed joint-venture Reed Elsevier a media giant, producing more than 1,200 academic and science journals that are published mainly in Europe and the U.S. Reed Elsevier PLC, based in London, and Reed Elsevier NV, based in Amsterdam, share parent duties for the company, and are joint owners in their combined entities. PLC owns the publishing and information businesses, while NV is in charge of financial activities. Since merging, the company has experienced some unsteady times.

The publisher divides its output into four groups: business, education, law, and science and medicine. In addition to its academic and science journals, Reed Elsevier publishes thousands of legal and business titles, and, through subsidiary Reed Exhibitions, organizes exhibitions around the globe. The company also owns the world's largest provider of full-text online information LEXIS-NEXIS, which provides legal, news, public records and business information, including tax and regulatory publications in print or online. Harcourt, the educational publishing part of the business, provides materials, testing services and professional development tools. Elsevier publishes scientific, technical and medical information.

The great divide

One component of the business segment organizes more than 335 events in 24 countries, attracting more than 110,000 participants and 5.5 million buyers annually. Reed Exhibition Companies' events concentrate mainly in marketing and business services, publishing, IT/communications, manufacturing, aerospace, leisure, electronics, hospitality, travel, entertainment and retail. The business segment also includes Cahners Business Information in the U.S. (with 110 magazines), Elsevier Business Information in Continental Europe (publishing 10 news tabloids) and Reed Business Information in the U.K. (holding 100 magazines, directories, and online services). Combined, the three subsections control all business magazines and information activities, including Cahners' *Variety* and *Publishers Weekly*. Through print, online and CD-ROM versions, the scientific division supplies a wide range of research to scientists and research libraries primarily by subscription, releasing more than 1,200 journals worldwide.

Reed Elsevier's professional segment contains a large group or companies, which incorporated publish legal, tax, educational and reference materials. Encompassed in this group is LEXIS-NEXIS, a leader in providing legal and professional information. LEXIS-NEXIS online information service, LEXIS-NEXIS Europe and LEXIS Law Publishing provide extensive information to the legal, corporate and government markets. LEXIS-NEXIS is losing market share on its legal services, as competition continues to surface on the Web.

Reed and Robbers

The roots in the combined company reside in Europe near the end of the 19th century. Jacobus George Robbers started a company of his own in Rotterdam in 1880, to publish literary classics and an encyclopedia. Robbers' venture was called NV Uitgeversmaatschappij Elsevier (North Holland Elsevier Publishing Company), and derived the name "Elsevier" from a 16th century Dutch family of booksellers and printers. Across the North Sea, Albert E. Reed first established his newsprint manufacture, Albert E. Reed & Co., in Kent, England, in 1894; the company later went public in 1903.

During the 1930s, Elsevier entered the scientific publishing realm, establishing Excerpta Medica, a medical communications agency, by 1946. Elsevier opened a New York branch through a joint venture with Nordesmann Publishing in 1937, a printing press in Texas in 1951, and later established The Elsevier Publishing Company in the U.S. and U.K. in 1962. Reed was equally busy, opening a paper production manufacturer in New Zealand, its first overseas outing, in 1955, and an Anglo-Canadian pulp mill in Quebec, Canada five years later. Reed acquired Spicers Ltd., a paper merchant, in 1963, and Wall Paper Manufacturers Ltd., the then-largest decorating products organization world wide, and Polycell, an originator of do-it-yourself products, in 1965.

Simultaneous growth

Reed formed Reed Consolidated Industries Ltd. in Australia the following year, and went on to acquire International Publishing Corporation (IPC), including The Mirror Group of newspapers, in 1970, and changed its name to Reed Group Ltd. A year later, Robbers' company merged with Excerpta Media to form Associated Scientific Publishers, which was later renamed Elsevier Scientific Publishers in 1979. Reed established Reed Paper Ltd. in Canada in 1972, and split its publishing activities into two groups two years later: Mirror Group Newspapers and IPC. Elsevier and Edicom

Visit Vault at **www.vault.com** for insider company profiles, expert advice, career message boards, expert resume reviews, the Vault Job Board and more.

VAULT CAREER LIBRARY   **233**

merged in 1975 to form Elsevier Nederland. The same year, Elsevier published the first Elsevier *Trends Journal*.

Throughout the 1980s, Reed and Elsevier underwent a number of acquisitions, gaining between them twelve magazine titles, including *Mac World*, *PC Magazine* and *Variety*, while divesting Mirror Group Newspapers. The acquisitions spree continued into the 1990s, as the two picked up a variety of companies in the law, exhibition, science and business arenas. On January 1, 1993, Reed-Elsevier was officially born. Afterwards, Reed-Elsevier picked right back up where it had left off, continuing to grow through strategic purchases – most notably LEXIS-NEXIS in 1994, the U.S. legal publications of Stamford, Conn.-based Thomson Corp. in 1997, and Chestnut Hill, Mass.-based Harcourt, the world's largest publisher of English-language textbooks, in a $5.65 billion, 2001 deal that received heavy scrutiny from the British government concerned with anti-competition. Recently, LEXIS-NEXIS and Harcourt have done their share of acquiring, enhancing Reed-Elsevier's stake in both legal and educational publishing.

New look for the new century

In the late 1990s, Reed Elsevier channeled spending into the electronic publishing market, a move which caused second-half profit in the fiscal year 1998 to drop 11 percent. Weaker sales in scientific and business publications further hampered growth in 1999, prompting the company to hire Crispin Davis as CEO and Morris Tabaksblat that summer. News of the hiring lifted shares in London and Amsterdam, and Davis was hailed as an ideal fix-it man to lead the company in the burgeoning businesses of Internet and electronic publishing.

One of Davis' first ventures was to cut costs. A plan announced in February 2000 sought to cut 1,500 jobs, mainly in the U.S., while spending $1.2 billion to put publications on the Internet for wider distribution, a move expected to save $272 million annually. Reed also said it would spin off some non-core businesses, including OAG Worldwide, the global leader in airline directories, and create a stand-alone Internet unit. At the end of the fiscal year 2003, the company topped analysts' expectations, reporting a net profit of $630 million, an 85 percent increase over the year prior, though Reed warned the fiscal year 2004 would most likely not include such high gains due to a decline in U.S. textbook sales. In July 2004, Reed purchased Seisint Inc., a provider of online access and analysis of public records to aid government and law firms in tasks such as pre-employment screening and debt recovery, for $775 million in cash as part of an effort to expand in the U.S. risk management market.

Tops in business publishing

Reed Business Information, the largest business-to-business publisher in the U.S., is the American arm of the larger business division of Reed Elsevier. Through its connection to Reed Elsevier, RBI offers information through more than 130 industry-focused and business-to-business publications, over 115 web sites and web portals, and directories for the media, printing, construction, retail, hospitality, manufacturing and electronics industries. In addition, the company conducts research, creates business lists, offers training programs and performs custom publishing services. RBI boasts seven million subscribers and a total circulation of more than 21 million.

GETTING HIRED

Where the jobs are

Reed Elsevier has operations in the United States, Europe, Asia Pacific, Latin America and Africa. The company's corporate web site lists HR contacts for specific jobs within its different divisions and locations. Corporate jobs are available in London; Amsterdam; New York City; Singapore; and Chatswood, Australia. Science and medical jobs are available in Amsterdam; Oxford, England; New York City; and Orlando, Florida. Legal services are located in Miamisburg, Ohio; London; and Paris. The education division operates in Orlando; Austin; San Antonio and Oxford. The business division is located in New York City; Sutton, Surrey, U.K.; Amsterdam; and Richmond, Surrey, U.K.

Visit Vault at **www.vault.com** for insider company profiles, expert advice, career message boards, expert resume reviews, the Vault Job Board and more.

VAULT CAREER LIBRARY   235

Reuters Group PLC

85 Fleet Street
London
EC4P 4AJ, United Kingdom
Phone: +44-20-7250-1122
Fax: +44-20-7542-4064
www.reuters.com

LOCATIONS

London (HQ)
New York, NY
(Offices worldwide)

THE STATS

Employer Type: Public Company
Stock Symbol: RTRSY
Stock Exchange: NASDAQ
CEO: Thomas H. Glocer
2003 Employees: 16,744
2003 Revenue ($mil.): $5,702.0

KEY COMPETITORS

Associated Press
Bloomberg
Dow Jones

EMPLOYMENT CONTACT

about.reuters.com/careers

THE SCOOP

Informing the world

Reuters certainly has come a long way since founder Paul Julius Reuter started using pigeons to fly stock market quotes between Aachen and Brussels; just two years later, he opened his first office in London in 1851. Now supported by 2,300 journalists, photographers and camera operators, it comes as no surprise that the company is the world's largest international news agency. Reuters serves over 130 countries in more than 19 languages with 197 bureaus. Still based in London, Reuters runs its main operations from two outlets: Reuters Information and Reuters Trading Systems.

Serving and the company's primary product, the information division publishes about 600 stories daily through various media outlets such as TV, print and radio. Coupled with its staff and a reputation for integrity, speed and accuracy, Reuters fits easily into its premier position as a global news and information group. Financial data is provided on 40,000 companies, along with more than 940,000 stocks, bonds and other financial instruments. Keeping up with new technologies, Reuters renders news and information to almost 250 Internet sites, generating about 150 million page views each month, not including other media outlets.

The trading systems division designs and installs information and risk management systems for the financial markets and provides equity and foreign exchange transaction systems.

Taking the world by storm

In 1998, Reuters expanded its business to South America, creating a real-time financial news and information service called Reuters Focus for Brazilian investors. Focus joined Reuters' already strong presence in the region, with 13 offices in 10 countries, including Argentina, Chile and Mexico. Reuters joined forces in July 2000 with Verlagsgruppe Handelsblatt, a German media group and major provider of financial information, to launch a personal finance web site for the company's private investors. A year later, Reuters inked a deal with TIM, an Italian mobile operator, to supply news, linked pictures and graphics to TIM via Reuters Flash SMS products. Also in 2001, Reuters signed a deal with Multex.com to launch a financial portal for Japan's retail investor market.

Visit Vault at **www.vault.com** for insider company profiles, expert advice, career message boards, expert resume reviews, the Vault Job Board and more.

VAULT CAREER LIBRARY   **237**

The growth of the newswire

In 1999, Reuters signed a deal with Dow Jones to supply newswires through Reuters' worldwide services. The combined service was called Factiva. The two companies further combined their online databases, creating one of the largest financial newswires in the world. The partnership between Dow Jones Interactive and Reuters Business Briefing provided customers with 8,000 sources in 118 countries, including over 270 newswires and 1,000 newspapers.

A company divided

Reuters announced in February 2000 that it planned to invest $800 million in its Internet services, while splitting into two distinct units. Its Information Division would merge with its Trading Solutions Division to create a new unit, Reuters Financial, which would generate company cash flow and dividends. The other unit, Reuterspace, would house new media ventures and other operations and focus on accelerating growth and new technologies.

A 150 year anniversary party!

The year 2001 held special meaning for Reuters, for the British based company turned 150 years old (or young, depending on your outlook). And Reuters certainly celebrated in style: It opened offices in San Francisco, Canada and New York City. The Times Square location, a $360 million 30-story office tower, houses the company's U.S. headquarters and utilizes a variety of advanced technological innovations and environmentally sound building practices, as well as full-scale LED signage. That same year, in July 2001, Tom Glocer was appointed as the new CEO of Reuters. He had served as CEO of Reuters Latin America and vice president of Reuters America.

Tragedy abroad

During the U.S. attacks on Afghanistan, several Reuters journalists rushed to the scene to cover the stories for readers around the world. In Novemeber 2001, several members of the media, including two Reuters' employees, Azizullah Haidari and Harry Burton, were killed in an ambush. The killer was tried and convicted in Afghanistan and given the death penalty in November 2004.

Wired for the future

In 1998, Reuters unveiled its Reuters Plus product, folding Quotron, its provider of real-time news and equities information, into the new Reuters Plus, which delivers information to customers via the Internet. Reuters launched Reuters Inform, its first real-time news and information service delivered over the Internet, in October 1999. Reuters Inform was the first in a series of real-time financial services products Reuters released through a public Internet, e-commerce format. In May 2000, Reuters purchased Yankee Group Research, a division of Primark, for $72.5 million. The Yankee Group is an international technology research and advisory firm providing consulting services to e-businesses.

Later that year, Reuters announced plans to launch more online products aimed at professionals, including its Reuters Credit, an online credit information service. Reuters Credit, a subscription-based service, combines credit news from Reuter's proprietary database with the credit data of its partners, including Standard & Poors and JP Morgan. In October 2001, Reuters implemented the first phase of its new local area network (LAN) technology, installing wireless LANs in its offices in the U.K. and Nordic region. In early 2002, Reuters and Citywire, an online source for business reports, launched New Online Reportsuters, a global information, news and technology group. The two companies combined their financial content to attract investors to their online sites. The new report focuses on funds, stocks, shares, and personal finance tips focused on the needs and interests of retail investors in the U.K.

Message: loud and clear

In October 2002, Reuters and Microsoft inked a deal to link their instant messaging computer services, enabling 100 million Microsoft MSN network users to correspond with another instant messenger service's users for the first time ever. Reuters also signed deals with America Online (which added 60 million active instant messaging accounts), and IBM's Lotus Instant Messaging, with the possibility of adding Yahoo! Instant Messenger in the future. Reuters' interest in the instant messaging phenomenon is rooted in its quest to find a secure tool with which financial professionals can communicate with clients in real time without the use of a standard telephone. Reuters also contracted IMLogic Inc. to deploy its IM Manager platform to manage connectivity between its IM service and MSN Messenger. Reuters Messaging is created with Microsoft's Greenwich enterprise instant messaging technology.

Journalism rivalry

In 2004, Reuters and long-time rival Bloomberg engaged in a nasty dispute: Reuters claimed Bloomberg staff were rewriting and attaching their bylines to stories originally written by Reuters staff on the beat in the Middle East. Reuters employs 40 correspondents in Iraq; Bloomberg pulled its staff from the war-torn country after President Bush declared victory in 2003. Reuters' writers were particularly insulted, saying they were risking their lives in the streets of Iraq for the stories that Bloomberg writers lifted from newswires in the comforts of corporate offices. Bloomberg admitted to using Reuters for research and acknowledging its reports as a source when necessary, and suggested companies like Reuters should thank Bloomberg for promoting "trench-warfare journalism." Although legal action against Bloomberg remained unlikely, Reuters brought the issue to the public to expose what the company considers to be Bloomberg's "unethical" journalism practices.

Financial woes

In February 2003, Reuters announced a pretax loss for the first time since going public in 1984, signaling a reduction in staff by 19 percent, affecting 3,000 employees. For Reuters, the cuts came after a two-decade long rollercoaster ride of successes and mishaps that left the company's future in peril.

Reuters overzealous expansion in the 1980s and 1990s, during which it increased its staff from 2,400 to 19,000 was ultimately the cause of its trouble. Peter Job took the helm in 1991, and compiled a string of bad business moves, including not creating a 24-hour news channel (later successfully created by MSNBC), and rejecting a chance to buy the international business credit information supplier Dun and Bradstreet. Job also failed to take the Internet seriously, passing up a chance to buy 10 percent of America Online in 1994. Reporters, harboring long-term resentment toward management for what they considered poor compensation, were laid off in the mid-1990s. In Reuters' worst performing year, 2002, new CEO Glocer and other top execs received bonuses totaling over $2 million pounds sterling. Glocer spent half of the bonus to buy Reuters' stock in a show of support for the ailing company. Shareholders voiced disgust for Glocer's salary at a time when their own shares were rapidly diminishing.

Persistent financial troubles caused Reuters to pare down its product line, which contained 1,300 products in 2000, to a mere 50 in 2003. Reuters made the cuts after consumers complained they were overwhelmed by all the new financial services the company was offering. Reuters announced in July 2001 that it would cut 1,340 jobs over the course of the next two years, the largest cutback in the company's history. As profits decreased in 2002, Reuters announced the termination of 1,800 jobs in February, and an additional 300 jobs in April. Glocer cut a total of 2,100 jobs over all in his first two years as CEO. Reuters returned to profitability in the first half of 2003, but conceded an overall decline in revenue at the year's end. That February, Reuters announced plans to trim its workforce by 10 percent, vowing to cut 3,000 jobs by 2006.

Some good news

Reuters scored huge in January 2003 when it won an exclusive contract to provide news and data to Switzerland's Credit Suisse, stealing business away from rival Bloomberg. That August, Reuters signed a contract with Goldman Sachs, the financial services giant, which allowed for the streamlining of select Reuters products across the firms, such as Reuters 3000 Xtra and the Reuters BridgeStation Plus. Reuters again beat out Bloomberg to secure the deal. Reuters is hoping to find success in the future through its fledgling instant messenger services, as well as through its big-name contracts.

Further cuts

In an effort to reduce costs and boost efficiency, Reuters announced in November 2004 that it would transfer some London and D.C.-based editorial positions to Singapore and outsource some graphics-related positions in Miami. The plan is expected to affect about 50 positions and reduce the editorial department's headcount by about 10. *The Guardian* reported that additional jobs, perhaps as many as 250, were being cut in the U.K. The company is also exploring the sale of its 62 percent stake in the Instinet stock trading business.

GETTING HIRED

For more information on working for Reuters, visit the career page of the company's web site at about.reuters.com/careers. There is a comprehensive listing and description of each division and subsidiary of the company. Before you apply, research each division and location so that you know what you are interested in before you contact the HR department. Reuters recommends reading the profiles listed on the career page before submitting a resume.

Visit Vault at **www.vault.com** for insider company profiles, expert advice, career message boards, expert resume reviews, the Vault Job Board and more.

VAULT CAREER LIBRARY   241

Scholastic Corporation

557 Broadway
New York, NY 10012
Phone: (212) 343-6100
Fax: (212) 343-6934
www.scholasticinc.com

LOCATIONS

New York, NY (HQ)

THE SCOOP

A classroom staple

Scholastic sold over 50 million of its own children's books in 2004 and distributed another 350 million – most notably through the Scholastic Book Club. Founded in 1920 as *The Scholastic*, the nation's first classroom magazine for high school students, the company's materials are now used in 90 percent of American classrooms and saw $2.23 billion in profits in 2004, a number that had been remained stagnant at around $1.9 billion from 2001 through 2003. As of 2004, Scholastic has about 10,800 employees worldwide, who produce curriculum software, television shows, videos, magazines, books and toys. The company's lineup also includes some three dozen classroom magazines and a graphic novel imprint. In addition to publishing, Scholastic also sponsors book fairs, the nation's largest and oldest scholastic writing and art contest, and the National Teacher of the Year Program.

Mo' money, mo' Potter

By 2004, the first five *Harry Potter* books have sold more than 250 million copies worldwide, and have been sold in more than 200 countries and translated into 60 languages – giving Scholastic a cash cow. The fifth book in the series, *Harry Potter and the Order of the Phoenix*, enjoyed unprecedented sales. The series author, J.K. Rowling, just finished the sixth – and second to last, *Harry Potter* book. The series is credited for generating renewed interest in reading for young people.

In mid-2004, the company also announced the launch of a new graphic novel imprint, called Graphix, with the publication of author Jeff Smith's award-winning series, *Charlie Bone*. Graphix is scheduled to debut in January 2005. The company is backing the imprint with a six-figure marketing campaign, which includes national advertising and publicity. As if that weren't enough, Scholastic also signed a deal with the LEGO toy company in June 2004 to develop products in a wide range of formats based on LEGO-owned properties throughout the world.

Slumps and cutbacks

In the late 1990s, Scholastic experienced a downturn caused primarily by a slump in the sales of the *Goosebumps* books, its best-selling product. Scholastic's stock price was nearly halved, forcing the company to slash 400 jobs (about 7 percent of its work force), fold its magazines *Agenda*, *Superscience Red* and *Math Power*, sell the

Visit Vault at **www.vault.com** for insider company profiles, expert advice, career message boards, expert resume reviews, the Vault Job Board and more.

VAULT CAREER LIBRARY   **243**

profitable *Home Office Computing* and *Small Business Computing*, and streamline its Jefferson, Mo., distribution center. Through these moves, Scholastic managed to squeak by with a profit of $361,000 for the fiscal year 1997. Scholastic learned its lesson – it no longer puts too many eggs in one basket. But the company's financial woes continued because of the slumping retail and book market. In 2003, Scholastic laid off another 400 employees as sales decreased across the board.

Scholastic's recovery

By 1998 the company had successfully implemented a turnaround program that brought it back to a satisfactory profit level. By branching out into electronic products such as CD-ROMs (made in partnership with Microsoft) and an online service (produced with America Online), Scholastic regained even more strength. Scholastic returned to the instructional curriculum business, which it initially entered in the 1970s, when school enrollments were slumping. It had left the business in the early 1980s, just as the birthrate was rising again.

In 1999 the company signed an agreement with book publisher HarperCollins to manage Scholastic's customer service, billing and credit functions beginning in July 2000. Also in 1999, Scholastic launched its revamped scholastic.com web site. In May 2000 the company signed an agreement with Yahoo! to provide "Newswire for Kids" on the Yahooligans! web guide.

Brand-name strength

Through thick and thin, generations of teachers still know and love Scholastic and await its new products. The company placed importance on the book series called *Animorphs*, released in 2001 about kids who can turn into animals, and *Dear America*, a historical fiction collection of stories started in 1996. The company also counted on the Scholastic Productions division, which has already produced films based on the Scholastic book series, *The Baby Sitters Club*.

Scholastic has since stepped up the marketing of its popular, science-oriented *The Magic School Bus* books, which have become a TV cartoon series. The Census Bureau recognized Scholastic's comeback in the late 1990s, selecting the company to conduct its "Census in the Schools" program, meant to increase response to the 2000 Census. The company's *Teen Magazine* Network has also posted a strong rebound – with more than eight million readers, it had the highest overall teen readership by the end of the 20th century. For most of 1999 the company had the top seven books in

Barnes & Noble's juvenile bestseller list. Boosted by the success of the *Harry Potter* books, the company reported record revenues and improved earnings for fiscal 1999.

Grolier acquisition

In June 2000 Scholastic announced it had completed its acquisition of Grolier from French publishing giant Lagardere for $400 million. The acquisition strengthened Scholastic's position as the world's largest publisher and distributor of children's books. Grolier specializes in direct-to-home children's book distribution as well as children's reference products (including *Encyclopedia Americana*) sold primarily to U.S. school libraries. The company publishes Orchard Books, Children's Press and Franklin Watts imprints.

Scholastic has also been banking on international expansion as a means of securing its place as a leader in educational products. The company has operations in Canada, the United Kingdom, Australia, New Zealand, Mexico, Hong Kong, Argentina, Indonesia, Ireland, Malaysia, the Philippines, Singapore, Taiwan and Thailand. In India, the company has also set up its own publishing facility, claiming that the country India has become the company's fastest-growing foreign market, especially since it is "a market where education is really valued." Moreover, Grolier has a large commission sales force in Asia that Scholastic is making use of.

2001: a scholastic odyssey

The year 2001 brought an influx of praise, financial gain and prestige. The *Harry Potter* phenomenon increased Scholastic revenue. In the last few weeks of the year, Scholastic acquired Tom Snyder Productions from the Canadian publisher, Torstar Corporation for $9 million. Tom Snyder is a leading developer and publisher of interactive educational software. The acquisition included *Soup2Nuts*, the animated television production arm of the Massachusetts-based company. Together, they cover the K-12 demographic with television and books.

That same year, the company opened its first retail store in New York's Soho district which carries Scholastic books, videos, CD-roms, as well as sets of books for parents and teachers.

New acquisitions and alliances

In December 2002, the publisher forged an alliance with DreamWorks, making Scholastic the primary publishing licensee for DreamWorks' animated films. The

Visit Vault at **www.vault.com** for insider company profiles, expert advice,
career message boards, expert resume reviews, the Vault Job Board and more.

VAULT CAREER LIBRARY   245

deal gave Scholastic the rights to publish all coloring and activity books for DreamWorks' next five animated features, including *Shrek 2*. The company also acquired children's publisher Klutz that same year.

The acquisition of Grolier two years earlier proved to be a costly one as the company made a public debt offering of around $300 million in 2002. The money helped fill the financial holes related to the Grolier deal. Not scared of continued international expansion, Scholastic purchased a stake in British book distributor The Book People. The U.K. remains the company's main market outside the U.S. In 2003, Scholastic announced *The Misadventures of Maya & Miguel*, an animated series which debuted on PBS in the fall of 2004. The series sees the company reaching out to the growing Hispanic population.

GETTING HIRED

The way in

Scholastic's job hotline lists job openings in several employment categories. Most employees work in the company's New York headquarters, although many accounting and finance employees work in Lyndurst, N.J. Scholastic's distribution center is located in Jefferson City, Mo. The company's production units and warehouses are scattered throughout the U.S., Europe and Mexico. Scholastic also hires freelance writers, editors and artists for specific projects. Visit the career page of the web site at www.scholastic.com/aboutscholastic/job/index.htm for more information about joining the company, or send a resume in to jobs@scholastic.com. Scholastic has consistently ranked among the top companies for executive women, according to *Working Woman*'s annual ranking, sponsored by the National Association of Female Executives which is the largest women's professional association in the country.

Scholastic offers a summer internship program. Information for the 2006 summer internship program will be posted in December 2005.

Simon & Schuster, Inc.

1230 Avenue of the Americas
New York, NY 10020
Phone: (212) 698-7000
Fax: (212) 698-7099
www.simonsays.com

LOCATIONS

New York, NY (HQ)

THE STATS

Employer Type: Subsidiary of Viacom
President and CEO: Jack Romanos

KEY COMPETITORS

Harper Collins
Random House
Time Warner Book Group

EMPLOYMENT CONTACT

www.simonsays.com/content/
   consumer.cfm?sid = 33&app =
   employment

THE SCOOP

A publishing giant

The publishing arm of media conglomerate Viacom, Inc., Simon & Schuster is a
staple in the lives of school children, reference-seekers and professionals in over 150
countries. The company regularly claims some 60 *New York Times* bestsellers each
year through its dozens of recognizable labels, including Scribner, The Free Press,
Pocket Books, Archway Paperbacks and Macmillan. S&S also boasts an Internet
"super site" featuring a subscription-based service with a full text of books,
downloadable software and the option to order books online. S&S successes include
Pearl Buck's *The Good Earth*, Dr. Benjamin Spock's *Baby and Child Care*, and
Frank McCourt's *Angela's Ashes*.

S&S also created an imprint with *The Wall Street Journal* in December 1999 that
produces a dozen titles a year by writers and editors of the *WSJ*. Wall Street Journal
Books is designed to extend to the world of nonfiction books with the same high
standards of writing and reporting that are featured in *The Wall Street Journal*.

A history of firsts

Dick Simon and Max Schuster first began their careers in publishing in 1924, with a
crossword puzzle book that had a first printing of 3,600 copies (a great success at the
time), retailed for $1.35 each and included an attached pencil. A year later, the
company began the practice of allowing booksellers the option of returning unsold
copies of books for credit – an offer previously unheard of in the book publishing
business. Simon & Schuster would go on to claim a number of other industry firsts,
including being the first to apply mass market production and distribution techniques
to books, the first to publish an "instant book" in 1945 (a memorial to Franklin D.
Roosevelt released six days after his death), and the first publisher to offer an original
work by a major author exclusively in electronic form (Stephen King's eBook
"*Riding the Bullet*," released in 2000).

The Three S's

In 1930, the duo linked up with Leon Shimkin, dubbed the "third S" at S&S. Pocket
Books was launched in 1939, publishing pocket-sized paperback reprints of classics
and bestsellers such as Emily Bronte's *Wuthering Heights*. Off the success of Pocket
Books, the three S's launched a new subsidiary aimed at children, Little Golden

Books, in 1943. By the end of its first year of publication, 2.7 million Golden Books had been shipped, with two million on back order. Simon & Schuster and Pocket Books were sold to Marshall Field, the Chicago merchandising whiz, in 1944, but bought back in 1957 after Field's death. Simon retired that same year, making Schuster and Shimkin equal partners. The company then sold its share in Golden Books to Western Publishing, while acquiring Washington Square Press for the Pocket Books division, which went public in 1961. By 1966, Simon had died and Schuster had retired, leaving Shimkin in charge. Shimkin sold the company to Gulf + Western in 1975, and retired from the book business.

Within a decade of the sale, Simon & Schuster had acquired over 60 companies, including Prentice-Hall and Silver, Burdett, and posted revenue of over $200 million. In 1989, Gulf + Western became Paramount Communications, and was picked up five years later by Viacom, just as Simon & Schuster was acquiring Macmillan Publishing Company. Simon & Schuster Online was launched in 1996; a year later, the company raked in revenue of over $2 billion.

S&S in transition

In one of the largest publishing deals in history, Pearson plc, the largest publisher in Britain, bought the majority of S&S's operations from Viacom in the summer of 1998 for $4.6 billion in cash. (What they actually acquired was the education division for $3.6 billion. A leveraged buyout firm, Hicks, Muse, Tate & Furst, Inc., bought the reference, business and professional divisions for $1 billion, but that deal fell through, and Pearson announced its intention to keep those divisions.) Pearson already owns the Penguin Group, Scott Foresman (another educational publisher bought in 1996), *The Financial Times*, and Madame Tussaud's Wax Museum. Viacom maintains the consumer trade division, which publishes authors like Frank McCourt, Mary Higgins Clark and Stephen King. Hicks, Muse will control the portion of the company that publishes *Webster's Dictionary*, *Betty Crocker* cookbooks and the ubiquitous *Idiot's Guide* series. In 2000 S&S completed the consolidation of its sales force, which had previously been split into three separate units.

Oops

S&S has been in the news for other reasons as well. In 1997 the publisher recalled more than 4,000 copies of a children's book on religion after critics charged that it portrayed the prophet Mohammed in a negative light. Members of a Muslim

Visit Vault at **www.vault.com** for insider company profiles, expert advice,
career message boards, expert resume reviews, the Vault Job Board and more.

VAULT CAREER LIBRARY   **249**

organization sent a letter to the publisher claiming that the portrayal of Mohammed was disrespectful and did not belong in a publication directed at young readers. After pulling the book from the shelves, the company invited the Islamic group to collaborate on a revision of the chapter for a new edition.

Stephen King online

In March 2000 Simon & Schuster made headlines for releasing a Stephen King short story, "Riding the Bullet," but not offering it in bookstores. The 16,000 word story was only made available online. The story comes out encrypted on the computer, making it impossible to print out. At the time of the release, King commented, "I'm curious to see what sort of response there is and whether or not this is the future." S&S seems to think so, for in May 2000 the company partnered with Microsoft, helping the software giant secure exclusive rights to put some books in its Microsoft Reader format, including Michael Crichton's *Timeline*.

Award winning actress Shirley Maclaine also went to S&S in 2000 to launch her book, *The Camino*, online. She wanted the web to be its first audience. Live interviews and web casts soon followed the online publication via the Internet.

Parting with Viacom?

In early 2000, *The Sunday Telegraph* reported that Viacom had put Simon & Schuster up for sale. The newspaper said that Viacom had come very close to closing a deal with W.H. Smith Group, the U.K.'s largest bookseller, for as much as $735 million. Industry observers pointed to Viacom's merger with CBS as a reason why it would be keen on selling S&S. As of 2005, though, Viacom is still the proud owner of S&S.

New imprints

In April 2000, Simon & Schuster partnered with PBS to create PBS KIDS Books, a new line of children's books based on the animated television series *Sagwa, The Chinese Siamese Cat*, written by best-selling author Amy Tan. Futher partnerhips with the Public Broadcasting Station include the relaunch of PBS KIDS Online (pbskids.org), PBS KIDS Home Video and the PBS KIDS Channel.

In July 2001, SimonSays.com, the online portion of Simon & Schuster, launched Blackbookscentral.com, an online community of readers and writers showcasing the talents of African-American authors from Simon & Schuster. The site is a forum for discussion in addition to an information source for author appearances, book releases and tours.

Reading, not wrasslin'

The fromer WWF (now WWE) joined forces with Simon & Schuster to create the imprint World Wrestling Federation Books launched in the fall of 2002. Under this program, Simon & Schuster will publish multiple titles yearly, based on the personalities, programming, storylines and other topics of interest to World Wrestling Entertainment and its fans.

Mafia mess

Simon & Schuster sued Michael Pellegrino in February 2002 over a book contract worth $500,000, which Pellegrino was granted on the claim that he was the illegitimate grandson of the late Mafia boss Carlo Gambino. Pellegrino wrote *The Honored Society*, published in November 2001 under Simon & Schuster's Pocket Books imprint, which publicized Pellegrino as "the highest-ranking mob member ever to record the innermost workings" of the Mafia. However, after publication, questions regarding Pellegrino, his ties to the Mafia and the authenticity of his claims emerged. A spokesperson for the company said, "Neither Pellegrino nor his agent were able to provide us with satisfactory proof of bona fides." The book was withdrawn after publication, and Simon & Schuster sued both Pellegrino and the agency representing him, Los Angeles-based Artists Management Group. Pellegrino countersued, claiming he had not been paid the final $100,000 of his book advance. Pellegrino's lawyer suggested his client had fulfilled his contract by writing the book he promised, and said the contract had no relation to Pellegrino's biographical claims. The two sides reached a settlement, in which terms were undisclosed, in February 2004. Pellegrino was said to be "very happy" with the settlement, and went on to sell the controversial story to New Line Cinema for a future movie.

Killer scoops

Other authors with Simon & Schuster have also had their share of controversy recently – and success. The company beat out a number of rivals for the rights to former First Lady-turned-New York Senator Hillary Rodham Clinton's memoirs with an offer of $8 million in advance – a sum many in the industry thought CEO Jack Romanos was crazy for putting up. The immediate success of the resulting book, *Living History*, deftly silenced Romanos' critics. Published in June 2003, *Living*

Visit Vault at **www.vault.com** for insider company profiles, expert advice, career message boards, expert resume reviews, the Vault Job Board and more.

VAULT CAREER LIBRARY   **251**

History sold 600,000 copies just one week off the press, landing Simon & Schuster in the black despite the big money advance it paid, a remarkable feat for any publisher to achieve. Clinton's tome also beat the Barnes & Noble record for non-fiction sales by selling 40,000 copies in the first 24 hours of its release.

In February 2005, Simon & Schuster published *Disney War* by James B. Stewart, a chronicle the corporate meltdown at the Walt Disney Company under the direction of CEO Michael Eisner, including never-before-seen memos, letters and transcripts. Although it was rumored in *The New York Times* that Disney might sue Simon & Schuster for the explosive "inside" scoop at the House of Mouse, Disney claimed the controversy surrounding the book was "over nothing."

Spotlight on Entertainment

Simon & Schuster began a new imprint, Simon Spotlight Entertainment, in the fall of 2004, with a dedicated focus on the world of entertainment and pop culture geared toward teens and young adults. Romanos called the imprint "an important and logical step" in the company's "successful history of incorporating crossover from other media into our publishing efforts." SSE's first title, *He's Just Not That Into You*, a dating guide written by former *Sex and the City* staffers, was a runaway bestseller. Equally well-received were comedian Lewis Black's *Nothing's Sacred* and *Poker: the Real Deal* by Phil Gordon, host of the television series *Celebrity Poker Showdown*.

Simon Spotlight was first established in 1997 within the company's children's publishing division to handle media tie-in publishing, and is one of the fastest growing imprints in children's book history. Expect the new SSE branch to rely heavily on the benefit of Viacom's vast source of media connections as well as Simon & Schuster's already popular series of television show media tie-ins for small-screen hits like *Alias*, *Buffy the Vampire Slayer*, *American Dreams*, *Everwood* and *Charmed*, and the company's existing MTV Books division, which publishes "innovative fiction" and "cutting-edge authors" in addition to the popular *Real World* series.

Driving SSE online is an addition to the company's web site, called SimonSaysTHESPOT, which helps web surfers find Simon & Schuster's latest books in a variety of "hip" categories, from entertaining to home décor to sex and dating. In addition, SSE recently teamed up with *Good Morning America* for the Story Of My Life contest, in which one lucky winner, determined by a panel of publishing professionals and a nationwide vote, will get his or her life story published and sold across the country.

GETTING HIRED

Hiring overview

Simon & Schuster doesn't have a lot of openings – those that do appear on one of the company's automated job listings are quickly snatched up. Applicants must write in response to a posted listing. Simon & Schuster also posts jobs on its web site, www.simonsays.com. Resumes can be sent by regular mail to the following address:

Attn: Human Resources
Simon & Schuster
1230 Avenue of the Americas
New York, NY 10020

All submissions will be kept on file for several months and forwarded to Simon & Schuster's various publishing branches. One recent hire describes her interview process: "Of all my interviews, those I had with Simon & Schuster were the most pleasant. The human resources department is generally frank and friendly."

SourceMedia

One State Street Plaza
27th Floor
New York, NY 10004
Phone: (212) 803.8200
www.sourcemedia.com

LOCATIONS

New York, NY (HQ)

THE STATS

Employer Type: Subsidiary of Investcorp
President and CEO: James Malkin
2003 Employees: 1,200

EMPLOYMENT CONTACT

www.sourcemedia.com/careerzone.html

THE SCOOP

Financial news you can bank on

Chances are, if you work in the vast financial industry, you've stumbled upon one of SourceMedia's publications or worked with one of the company's databases or other information products. Formerly Thomson Media, SourceMedia targets more than 75,000 clients, but is actually part of a global investment firm Investcorp, which acquired it from the Thomson Corporation in October 2004 for $350 million. The company changed its name in February 2005.

SourceMedia produces a number of publications for the financial industry related to banking, capital markets, credit, investment management and technology. Titles of magazines and newsletters include *American Banker*, *U.S. Banker*, *Financial Planning*, *National Mortgage News*, *The Bond Buyer*, *Securities Industry News*, *Bank Loan Report*, *High Yield Report*, *Investment Dealers' Digest*, DM Review and Private Placement Letter. SourceMedia offers National Regulatory Services (NRS), products and solutions for investment advisers, broker dealers and insurance employees. TFP, the official routing-number registrar for the American Bankers Association since 1911, is yet another division of SourceMedia, providing data and software solutions for both financial and corporate institutions. TFP's solutions facilitate the automated exchange of operational data among financial institutions, with the aim of avoiding illegitimate business practices like fraud and money laundering.

The big sale

Investcorp acquired Thomson Media from the Thomson Corporation in October 2004, picking it up for $350 million. Investcorp agreed to keep Thomson Media's management team in place – a concession that separated Investcorp from a pack of similarly priced bids. The transaction placed Thomson Media (now SourceMedia) 40 percent higher than the company was valued in 2001.

SourceMedia changed its name from Thomson Media in February of 2005, owing to its new owners, Investcorp. The firm says that SourceMedia's name change is reflective of its role as the source of comprehensive business-critical information, data and market solutions that aim to optimize clients' business.

Visit Vault at **www.vault.com** for insider company profiles, expert advice, career message boards, expert resume reviews, the Vault Job Board and more.

VAULT CAREER LIBRARY   **255**

GETTING HIRED

On the Web

When visiting the company's web site, www.sourcemedia.com, you can access current job offerings by clicking on the Careers link. Jobs are listed by each location. E-mail addresses for human resource contacts in Texas, Chicago, Skokie, Ill., Georgia and other locations are provided to easily forward a resume.

Time Warner

1 Time Warner Center
New York, NY 10019
Phone: (212) 484-8000
Fax: (212) 489-6183
www.timewarner.com

LOCATIONS

New York, NY (HQ)
Atlanta, GA
Baltimore, MD
Burbank, CA
Indianapolis, IN
Terre Haute, IN
Washington, DC
West Hollywood, CA

Sydney

THE STATS

Employer Type: Public Company
Stock Symbol: TWX
Stock Exchange: NYSE
Chairman and CEO: Richard D. (Dick) Parsons
2004 Employees: 84,000
2004 Revenue ($mil.): $42,089.0

KEY COMPETITORS

Viacom
Walt Disney
Yahoo!

EMPLOYMENT CONTACT

www.timewarner.com/corp/careers
   index.html

Visit Vault at **www.vault.com** for insider company profiles, expert advice,
career message boards, expert resume reviews, the Vault Job Board and more.

VAULT CAREER LIBRARY   257

THE SCOOP

Media giant on a rocky course

Formed by the January 2001 marriage of America Online (AOL) and the properties of Time Warner, which was itself the result of the 1989 merger of Time Inc. and Warner Communications, (previously AOL Time Warner) is today one of the largest and most prominent entertainment/media conglomerates in the world. Its holdings include the Warner Bros. movie studio, Internet sites, interactive videos, cable television networks and systems, and myriad magazines and book operations.

The $154 billion Time Warner merger with America Online ushered in a new era for a quintessentially old-media company. But despite the early buzz, the conglomerate suffered punishing losses of revenue in 2002. In 2003, it was plagued by allegations of improper accounting practices, shareholder lawsuits and shakeups among top management. In an ironic turn of events, America Online asked the corporate entity in August 2003 to drop "AOL" from its name to create some distance from a spate of negative publicity. And it didn't take CEO Richard Parsons and the members of the board long to decide that scaling down the company's name might be a healthy move.

The promise ...

When the merger between these stalwarts of media and online content was announced in January 2000, the possibilities seemed endless. In any other decade, Time Warner would have been the acquiring company; but in the Internet Age, it was the acquired party. Banking on Time Warner's huge stable of magazines, movies, news outlets and books, AOL eagerly anticipated joining with Time Warner to create a media footprint few other companies could hope to match. AOL executives claimed the deal would spread "Internet DNA" through Time Warner's operations. Through the 1990s, AOL had committed itself to bringing different forms of media content (from ads to movies) online. Time Warner, for its part, had tried and failed to bring itself into the digital age with Pathfinder, a web site devoted to its magazines. But Pathfinder, which proved hard to navigate and slow to download onto users' screens, lost money and was shuttered in 1999. Upon consummation of the deal between AOL and Time Warner, the new company hoped to capitalize on a bonanza of cross-promotional opportunities.

... and the reality

It didn't quite turn out that way. Just a few months after the merger became reality, management had to lower some of its ambitious growth targets in September 2001. The company, which had been forecasting annual earnings growth in the double-digit range, now cut that projection down to the mid-to-high single digits. At AOL, once-healthy revenue slipped as subscriber growth slowed and advertising dollars dropped. The dot-coms that had flocked to AOL to cut deals and raise their visibility (and status) were folding at an alarming rate. By the first quarter of 2002, it seemed the synergies promised by the merger were out of reach. AOL logged relatively flat growth in its services division, with sales up 8 percent to $2.3 billion from the previous year. New subscribers during the period tallied 1.4 million, down from 1.9 million in 2001. In contrast, at Time Warner, sales were up 19 percent to $2 billion. It had become clear that the "new media" operations had lost some luster.

Some crown jewels

Despite its troubles, there were still some gems to be found in the huge stable of Time Warner's media properties. The company's movie operations, which include Warner Bros., New Line Cinema and Castle Rock Entertainment, hit box office gold in 2001 with offerings like the first installment of *The Lord of the Rings* trilogy and *Harry Potter and the Sorcerer's Stone*. With its films grossing $1.8 billion, the company was the leading movie producer for that year, and it continued to make good on its success in 2002 with blockbuster sequels like *The Lord of the Rings: The Two Towers* and *Austin Powers in Goldmember*. In 2003 another cash cow for the company, *The Matrix Reloaded*, brought in over $42 million on its opening day, capturing the record for the biggest one-day opening in movie history in the process.

Time Warner also owns cable networks operations that include Home Box Office (HBO), which boasts wildly popular series such as *The Sopranos*, *Six Feet Under* and *Sex and the City*, which concluded a successful run in 2004. The company dominates the cable world with other properties, including several channels founded by Ted Turner (CNN, TNT and TBS) which Time Warner acquired when it bought Turner Communications in 1996. In May 2003, media rival Viacom completed its acquisition of the company's 50 percent stake in the Comedy Central cable channel, which Time Warner sold to help relieve its lingering debt. Generating $1.225 billion in cash for Time Warner, the transaction gave Viacom full ownership of the cable channel, home to hit shows like "*South Park*" and "*The Daily Show*." Also in May 2003, board member Turner sold 60 million of his shares in the company to Goldman Sachs Group, Inc. This reduced his stake in the company by over half.

Visit Vault at **www.vault.com** for insider company profiles, expert advice, career message boards, expert resume reviews, the Vault Job Board and more.

VAULT CAREER LIBRARY   **259**

A strategy launched in April 2003 to increase subscriptions to Time Inc.'s magazines and provide AOL subscribers with premium content, has done well. The company ended free online access to articles in 13 of the companies' magazines in that month, limiting access to only those who subscribe to the magazine, purchase them on the newsstand or subscribe to AOL. Since the move, the company has seen an increase in subscriptions purchased online for several of its titles. In addition, the company has received some glowing reviews of the latest release of its online service, AOL 9.0, which was released in the fall of 2003, and has signed up about 300,000 subscribers for its high-speed AOL for Broadband service, which was introduced in March 2003. The ultimate success of the broadband service is yet to be determined – many of the subscribers joined through promotions for free trials, and it remains to be seen if they will stay on as paying customers.

Bertelsmann enters the picture ... then leaves

AOL's book-publishing unit was also on the auction block for a brief period in the spring of 2003. Consisting primarily of Warner Books, Little, Brown & Co. and a distribution arm, the book division was expected to fetch less than the $400 million target price. The company was said to be negotiating with Perseus Books Group for about $320 million. But when German media titan Bertelsmann AG stepped up to the plate, the sale was widely anticipated to be a done deal, even rating mention in a scathing July 2003 *New York Times Magazine* profile of Peter Olson, chairman and CEO of Bertelsmann-owned Random House. But Time Warner took its book division off the market in the summer of 2003, stating that the prices offered for its imprints were far too low.

Interactive media

In January 2002, AOL joined forces with AT&T to make e-mail and AOL Instant Messenger (AIM) service available to AT&T Wireless Web users. AOL built on this success in July 2003 by hooking up with Sprint to provide AIM and AOL e-mail services on PCS Vision Phones across the country.

In 2003 Time Warner reached an agreement with Microsoft to work together on long-term strategies to expedite consumer use and enjoyment of digital content. The partnership resolved an antitrust lawsuit filed against Microsoft by America Online in January 2002 on behalf of its subsidiary, Netscape Communications. Besides paying $750 million to Time Warner, Microsoft agreed to provide AOL with a new distribution channel for its software to designated PC users around the world. A seven-year license, sans royalties, of Microsoft's browser technology was also forged between the two companies, along with other measures to help their products work more effectively with each other and step up AOL subscriber experiences on Microsoft operating systems.

A new leader and a management shakeup

When AOL merged with Time Warner, America Online CEO Steve Case became chairman, while Time Warner CEO Gerald Levin stepped into the role of the first AOL Time Warner chief. Levin stepped down in May 2002 and was succeeded by Richard Parsons as CEO.

The company shook up its management structure yet again just a few months later. A slumping stock price and friction between the "old" and "new" media businesses tarnished the company's reputation on Wall Street. In July 2002, Chief Operating Officer Robert Pittman, who had ascended to the company's No.-2 spot after taking control of the online business in the spring of 2002, resigned.

Old media again?

In tandem with Pittman's resignation, AOL Time Warner reorganized its assorted businesses into two new groups. Don Logan, formerly the chief of Time Inc., became chief of the media and communications group, which oversees AOL. HBO head Jeff Bewkes became chairman of the entertainment and networks group, a division that includes HBO, New Line Cinema and Warner Bros. Both executives report directly to Parsons. On the heels of the shakeup, industry observers suggested that the promotions of the Time Warner executives signaled that the "old media" part of AOL Time Warner would drive the company's future.

Accounting issues

July 2002 brought new issues surrounding AOL to light. The Securities and Exchange Commission (SEC) opened an investigation into the company after articles in *The Washington Post* suggested AOL might have reported inflated revenue figures in previous years. According to the *Post*, AOL might have reported fees from advertisers paid to end contracts, but may not have disclosed that those fees would not be recurring. And AOL, the paper reported, may have recognized advertising sales it made for other companies, including eBay, as its own revenue. The SEC probe hit like a ton of bricks, partly because of increasing scrutiny due to recent accounting revelations by other companies. By the end of July, AOL shares were trading in the single digit range – the lowest they've traded at in several years.

Things got worse before they got better. At the end of the first quarter of 2002, AOL Time Warner shed $54.24 billion, or $12.25 a share, on revenue of $9.41 billion. This was largely attributed to a $54 billion write-down which was related to the AOL division. Company losses eventually plummeted to a record low of $99 billion for the year. Drastic measures were put into place, including corporate restructuring, employee layoffs and sales of stakes in company holdings. For a while, the strategy seemed to be working, with a surge in profitability in 2003 and a sunnier economic outlook for the conglomerate. First-quarter profits rose in 2003 to $396 million, or nine cents a share, on revenue of $10 billion, prompting top brass to suggest that the company was back on track to achieve its earnings goals for the rest of the year.

Two California pension funds sued AOL and Time Warner in July 2003, alleging that the company's accounting irregularities added up to almost $500 million in investment losses. The University of California had filed a separate suit that April, alleging that AOL "materially misrepresented its revenues and number of subscribers," thus "misstating its financial condition" and inflating shares. At the time of the merger, UC owned 11.3 million shares of common stock in Time Warner work roughly $800 million. Ohio's five pension funds and Bureau of Workers Compensation later accused Time Warner of violating federal securities and state laws resulting in a loss of over $100 million.

Phantom subscribers?

More problems were just around the corner. In July 2003, the SEC asked America Online to hand over documents about its little-known bulk-subscription program. Launched in 2000, the program was reported to have generated at least 830,000 subscribers to the online service during 2001 and 2002. That figure accounted for almost 17 percent of AOL's total subscriber growth of about five million for the period. The numbers, however, turned out to be misleading. The subscription program worked by striking deals with AOL marketing partners like Target, Sears, Roebuck & Company and J.C. Penney, offering limited-usage online accounts for rates as low as $1 to $3 a month. The companies, in turn, could offer AOL service to their employees at a discount. But the so-called new subscribers may never have gone on to accept or activate their accounts, and with no rules in place to monitor the reporting of these figures, the probe raised questions about inflated numbers and past business practices at AOL.

In November 2004, Time Warner announced plans to set aside $500 million to cover costs relating to federal inquiries of AOL's booking keeping and accounting procedures, and said it would reinstate earnings from 2000 and 2001 to include losses from AOL Europe. The reinstatement could potentially increase Time Warner's reported loss from $4.2 billion in 2001 by as much as $855 million, and reduce a reported net income of $1.2 billion by as much as $308 million.

Losing their Case

Investor irritation with disappointing merger results took their toll on the company's leadership in January 2003, when Steve Case stepped down as AOL chairman. Case's resignation took effect in May 2003, although he remained at the company as a director. Dick Parsons was named as the new chairman, in addition to his position as CEO.

Put the blame on the name

Amid ongoing SEC investigations of accounting practices at Time Warner, largely in the AOL division, AOL CEO Jonathan Miller expressed concerns in an August 2003 e-mail to staff that the reputation of the online service was becoming tainted by association. And so, AOL asked Parsons to remove "AOL" from the conglomerate's name. Executives from the Time Warner side were reportedly just as eager for the symbolic separation. In September 2003, Parsons announced that the company would in fact drop "AOL" from its corporate name, citing the need to eliminate "confusion between our corporate name and the America Online brand name." The company wasted little time in implementing the strategy. When making the announcement in September, Parsons noted that the change – including switching its stock ticker to TWX from AOL and changing signage on its buildings – would be complete within a few weeks.

Making sweet music

Time Warner Inc. sold off its Warner Music Group to a group of investors led by Edgar Bronfman Jr. for $2.6 billion in November 2003; the sale created one of the world's largest independent music companies. The company has retained the name Warner Music Group and houses the Atlantic and Elektra record labels, as well as Warner/Chappell Music publishing services. Billionaire Haim Saban, once interested in the Warner music division, backed out of the deal at the last minute. Time Warner chose Bronfman over EMI, which had tried to woo Time Warner with an offer of $1

Visit Vault at **www.vault.com** for insider company profiles, expert advice, career message boards, expert resume reviews, the Vault Job Board and more.

V∧ULT CAREER LIBRARY   **263**

billion for a majority stake. In September 2004, the Warner Music Group mulled options for an initial public offering to arrive on the stock market by the spring of 2005. The company is valued at up to $5 billion.

The same month, Time Warner Cable San Antonio donated $50,000 worth of musical instruments to help restore under-funded music programs at two San Antonio elementary schools in conjunction with VH1's Save the Music Foundation. Since Time Warner joined with VH1 in 1999, the two have donated $385,000 worth of new musical instruments to 15 music programs in the San Antonio area.

Developing interest in foreign films

Warner Bros. Pictures made international headlines in October 2004 when it partnered with the China Film Group and the Hengdian Group to create Warner China Film HG Corporation, the first Chinese-foreign joint venture filmed-entertainment company in the history of the People's Republic of China. The resulting Warner China Film combines the entertainment leadership of Warner Bros., China's leading state-run filmed entertainment conglomerate, China Film and China's largest privately owned film and television business, Hengdian. The company will develop, produce, market and distribute Chinese-language feature films, telefilms and animation.

A new look for AOL

AOL's CEO Jonathan Miller announced a broad corporate restructuring in November 2004 that effectively split the company into four divisions: content and advertising, Internet access, free-service expansion and fee-based services. In addition, Miller announced the company was releasing 700 people, roughly 5 percent of its workforce, after posting flat sales and a loss in subscribers. That same month, America Online became the first national Internet service provider to offer customers virus-protection programs for free as part of basic membership. McAfee VirusScan Online was automatically included in the AOL 9.0 Security Edition, released in November 2004.

A summer of success

The success of its feature film version of *Harry Potter and the Prisoner of Azkaban* in the summer of 2004 helped Time Warner improve upon the previous year's financial performance. In fact, the company showed gains across all units. Its major networks, Turner Broadcasting, HBO and WB, earned $602 million; the magazine publishing sector brought in $288 million a 75 percent gain; the two television and film studios, Warner Bros. and New Line Cinema, raked in $339 million; its cable-operator division increased revenue by 10 percent to $443 million; and America Online saw overall growth for an income of $276 million, the first time in two years it witnessed a growth in advertising revenue.

Time Warner expanded its brand name into the sporting realm, securing the naming rights to the University of Dayton baseball stadium in August 2004. The new stadium, the Time Warner Cable Stadium, is part of the Arena Sports Complex near Dayton, Ohio. The completed stadium will be ready for the 2005 baseball season.

Bringing technological advancement to the box office

Warner Bros. took a huge financial risk in 2004 with the release of *The Polar Express*, a film that utilizes spectacular advancements in computer-generated animation and digital cinema. The production costs added up to roughly $170 million by the time the movie was finished, a bill many major studios were too afraid to foot. Studio rival Universal backed out of a co-production deal citing concern with the untried, expensive technology. For the film to break even, it would have to gross $500 million, a hefty weight to carry home from the box office. On the upside, the film had the potential to become an evergreen holiday classic that would do well in DVD sales even if it didn't perform well at the box office. Warner Bros. president Alan Horn was confident the movie – featuring the award-winning team of director Robert Zemeckis and actor Tom Hanks – would be a success, despite posting disappointing opening-weekend ticket sales of $23.5 million.

GETTING HIRED

The job connection

Time Warner lists career opportunities on its web site, with links to both the AOL and Time Warner sides of the business. These opportunities can be found on the career page of the AOL Time Warner web site at www.timewarner.com. Applicants must create an online account with the company, submitting an e-mail address and password and then submitting a resume online to the AOL Time Warner database. The process must be completed for resumes to be accepted, though jobseekers have the option of applying either for specific openings or to the company

Visit Vault at **www.vault.com** for insider company profiles, expert advice, career message boards, expert resume reviews, the Vault Job Board and more.

V/\ULT CAREER LIBRARY   **265**

Tribune company

435 North Michigan Avenue
Chicago, IL 60611
Phone: (312) 222-9100
Fax: (212) 489-1573
www.tribune.com

LOCATIONS

Chicago, (IL) (HQ)
Allentown, PA
Baltimore, MD
Chatsworth, CA
Costa Mesa, CA
Deerfield Beach, FL
Fort Lauderdale, FL
Glens Falls, NY
Hartford, CT
Houston, TX
Irwindale, CA
Los Angeles, CA
Melville, NY
New York, NY
Oak Brook, IL
Saint Louis, MO
Santa Monica, CA
Seattle, WA
Stamford, CT

THE STATS

Employer Type: Public Company
Stock Symbol: TRB
Stock Exchange: NYSE
Chairman, President & CEO:
Dennis J. FitzSimons
2004 Employees: Over 21,000
2004 Revenue ($bil.): $5.7

KEY COMPETITORS

Gannett
New York Times
Dow Jones
Viacom

EMPLOYMENT CONTACT

www.tribune.com/employment/index.
  html

THE SCOOP

The world's greatest

Chicago's popular WGN-TV owes its distinctive call letters to Col. Robert McCormick's proclamation of his *Chicago Tribune* as the "World's Greatest Newspaper." Today, the Chicago-based Tribune Company is not only responsible for heading up the third-largest newspaper concern in the country due to its $8 billion merger with the L.A.-based Times Mirror Company (publisher of the *L.A. Times*), but it also publishes the seventh-largest daily newspaper in the U.S. (the *Chicago Tribune*), owns and operates 13 daily newspapers, 26 television stations, a radio station (and manages the web sites of Tribune's daily newspapers and television stations), Major League Baseball's Chicago Cubs, and a television production company. In addition, Tribune has developed an educational book publishing division, online services such as the Orlando Sentinel Online, and a growing television network–the WB Network–through a joint venture with Time Warner. With such a rapidly expanding media empire, the only thing missing is a World Series ring.

As of early 2004, Tribune has 4,500 journalists (and 21,000 employees) working in offices around the world. The company's media holdings reach more than 80 percent of U.S. households and it is the only media organization with television stations, newspapers and web sites in the nation's top three markets

History

Tribune's media empire was built on the back of the *Chicago Tribune*, founded in 1847 and led for most of its first 50 years by Joseph Medill. The company began to expand its operations into other media in the 20th century, launching its first radio venture in 1924 and entering television in 1948. Today, Tribune has a television station in nearly every major market. On the print side, its newspapers include the *Chicago Tribune*, *L.A. Times*, *Baltimore Sun*, *The Hartford Courant* and New York's *Newsday*. Magazines acquired though the Times Mirror merger include *Golf Magazine*, *Field & Stream* and *Popular Science*.

The multimedia empire

With the 1996 purchase of TV station conglomerate Renaissance Communications for $1.1 billion, Tribune's broadcasting business became nearly as large as its

Visit Vault at **www.vault.com** for insider company profiles, expert advice, career message boards, expert resume reviews, the Vault Job Board and more.

VAULT CAREER LIBRARY   267

newspaper business. Despite a court order to sell either the South Florida-based *Sun-Sentinel* or WBZL-TV in Miami, Tribune has continued to challenge the federal ban on same-market cross-media ownership. The FCC has indicated that it may loosen regulations regarding cross-media ownership. If it does not, Tribune will have to sell either newspapers or television stations acquired in 2000 that are present in the same markets. In 1997 the company poured more than $30 million into its highly regarded *Chicago Tribune* web site and other interactive services. The following year saw the creation of an in-house multimedia newsroom for its newspaper, cable TV and online journalists. In May 1999, Tribune Interactive was started, which combined the interactive departments of Tribune's newspapers, TV stations and other products like BlackVoices.com and Go2Orlando.com. Through its Tribune Ventures division, the company has invested in online supermarket service Peapod, the Excite web portal, America Online, local service provider Digital City, online entertainment network Pseudo Programs and iVillage.com, to name a few. Tribune also owns a partial interest in job search service CareerPath, a consortium of classifieds from the country's leading newspapers; and in Classified Ventures, a partnership with seven other media companies that provide online classifieds for jobs, cars, and real estate.

In early 1998, Tribune, which currently owns 25 percent of the WB Television Network, cut back Cubs game broadcasts to accommodate shows with national appeal, including *Buffy the Vampire Slayer* and *Xena, Warrior Princess.* That same year, a rookie pitcher named Kerry Woods and Dominican slugger Sammy Sosa brought hope to Cubs fans everywhere. As the season progressed, the network added more games to its WGN-TV prime-time schedule. In July 2000 Knight Ridder teamed up with Tribune Co. to acquire and combine job sites CareerBuilder Inc. and CareerPath Inc. CareerBuilder cost the publishing companies $300 million; details of the CareerPath transaction were not released.

Awards

In April 2004, Trib newspaper *The Los Angeles Times* won five Pulitzer Prizes, including citations for breaking-news reporting for its coverage of the massive wildfires that afflicted Southern California in 2003. *The Times* also received the Pulitzer in national reporting for its examination of how Wal-Mart has become the largest company in the world.

Web gems

In January 2004, Tribune Interactive inked a content agreement with Yahoo! to provide national and local headlines and news stories to Yahoo! News. The companies already had a local news content agreement that stretches back to 2001, but this renewed agreement adds daily national headlines and news stories from the *Chicago Tribune* and *Los Angeles Times*, as well as local headlines and news stories from nine of Tribune's newspaper websites. Other Tribune websites supplying local news include newsday.com, sunspot.net (*The Baltimore Sun*), sun-sentinel.com (*South Florida Sun-Sentinel*), orlandosentinel.com, ctnow.com (*The Hartford Courant*), mcall.com (The Morning Call) and dailypress.com (the online version of the Hampton Roads (Va.)-based *Daily Press*). A year earlier, in January 2003, chicagotribune.com and latimes.com were awarded 2003 Digital Edge Awards at the Newspaper Association of America Connections Conference. Both sites won Digital Edge Awards for Most Innovative Use of Digital Media.

A good year

For the year 2003, revenue at the company increased to $5.6 billion, up from $5.4 billion in 2002. Similarly, profit grew to $1.4 billion, from $1.3 billion in the previous year. There were gains across the board at the company, with the publishing division seeing revenue of $4.0 billion, up from $3.9 billion in 2002. Broadcasting and entertainment revenue hit $1.6 billion, up from $1.4 billion in 2002 and television revenue increased to $1.3 billion, up from $1.2 billion in 2002. Finally, radio/entertainment's full year 2003 revenue increased to $235 million, up from $222 million in 2002.

Also in 2003, the company reached an agreement with cable provider Comcast to launch a new regional (the Chicago area) sports network in September 2004. The network will receive rights fees for the 72 Cubs games that will air on the channel, plus a percentage of the network's profits. Trib also sold its 8.6 interest in The Golf Channel to Comcast for $100 million. In March, Tribune completed its acquisition of KPLR-TV in St. Louis, and KWBP-TV in Portland, Ore., from ACME Communications for $275 million. And on a possibly very lucrative note, in September, Tribune Broadcasting announced that it had acquired the off-net syndication rights to the award-winning HBO series *Sex and the City*. The series premiered on Tribune Broadcasting stations in September 2005 six days a week.

Visit Vault at **www.vault.com** for insider company profiles, expert advice, career message boards, expert resume reviews, the Vault Job Board and more.

VAULT CAREER LIBRARY 269

GETTING HIRED

The company offers a career site at www.tribune.com/employment/index.html , and allows prospective job seekers to look for jobs, and apply, online; and the same goes for internships. The company also outlines its benefits package on the site.

USA Network, Inc.

152 West 57th Street
New York, New York 10019
Phone: (212) 314-7300
Fax: (212) 314-7309
www.usanetwork.com

LOCATIONS

New York, NY (HQ)

EMPLOYMENT CONTACT

nbcuni.com/About_NBC_Universal/
Careers

THE SCOOP

All together now

It's a brave new world in the television game, kicked off by the May 2004 blockbuster deal that merged NBC and Vivendi Universal Entertainment, creating NBC Universal, a global media and entertainment enterprise. How does USA Network fit into the equation, you ask? Well, other than owning television networks NBC, Telemundo, Sci-Fi Channel, Bravo, Trio, CNBC and MSNBC; film studio Universal Pictures; television production studios Universal Television and NBC Studios and interests in five theme parks including Universal Studios Hollywood and Universal Orlando, NBC Universal also owns USA. But since NBC Universal is itself owned by GE (an 80 percent share, with Vivendi controlling the remaining 20 percent) it is quite a corporate stew.

USA's slice of the pie

USA stands as cable television's leading provider of original series and feature movies, sports and theatrical films. The network is available in about 90 million U.S. households, and for the first quarter of 2004, it was the most-watched and fastest-growing basic cable network in overall total viewers. Some of the network's biggest original series include *Monk* (the highest-rated scripted series in basic cable history), *Touching Evil*, *The Dead Zone* and *The 4400*. USA also operates cable TV's eponymous station, USA Network, as well as the Sci-Fi Channel and the Home Shopping Network. The company also produces TV shows and made-for-TV movies through its Studios USA division and owns 13 TV stations through USA Broadcasting. The media titan also owns Ticketmaster and 60 percent of its Internet sibling, Ticketmaster Online-City Search.

Crime and punishment and sports

The network, which has achieved success airing a slate of crime dramas, plans to continue with that formula for the 2004-2005 season. Seven series and five movies have debuted or are in development, most of which have a crime or mystery theme. And aside from the returning (and very popular) *Monk* and *The Dead Zone*, USA airs repeats of the NBC viewer favorite *Law & Order: SVU* (how's that for synergy?) and is expected to run repeats of the parent network's *Law & Order: Criminal Intent* when they become available.

Industry insiders are predicting that because of USA's ability to reach so many American households, new parent NBC will be anxious to also air major professional sporting events on the network. And, indeed, the peacock appears to be testing the waters by airing coverage of the Olympic trials and Athens summer games on USA. A May 2004 article in *Broadcasting & Cable* magazine speculated that NBC would put in a bid for rights to broadcast NFL games or NASCAR races when they become available in 2006.

The Diller deal

Former USA Network Chairman Barry Diller is not the typical college dropout. As a UCLA student, distracted by the bright lights of Hollywood, Diller dropped out of school in 1958, opting to get his education in being a mail boy for the William Morris Agency. He quickly moved up the ranks and became an agent for a time before entering into the executive suites of ABC television. He is credited with having conceptualized the miniseries and the made-for-TV movie. In 1974, after a highly successful stint as the VP of ABC programming, Diller stepped up to the big screen and was named the chairman of Paramount Pictures. After a decade in the biggest lot in Hollywood, Diller ventured back to TV land and transformed Fox, a fledgling network at the time, into a network superstar. Insiders say that this was a career high for Diller, albeit a brief one, cut short by personality frictions between himself and Fox head Rupert Murdoch. After the falling out, Diller decided to go into business for himself. In 1998, after acquiring the Home Shopping Network and Ticketmaster, Diller's enterprise purchased all operations of USA Network from Seagram for $4.1 billion. The USA Network thrived under Diller's direction, and Diller later purchased October Films, Gramercy Pictures and part of the PolyGram film business from Seagram Co. in 1999.

Bouncing around

USA has seen its share of mergers, going back further than its newest slot as part of the NBC Universal super conglomerate. In December 2001, Diller sold USA back to Vivendi (which owns Seagram, the company from which Diller bought USA in 1997), for $10 billion. Vivendi already owned 44 percent of USA, and the deal was simply for the rest of its assets. But the good times only lasted about a year, as by the end of 2002 Vivendi began its now legendary flameout. Massive losses led the company to begin shedding its U.S. assets as fast as it could unload them. In October 2002, for example, it announced the sale of its European and Latin American publishing units to Hachette for $1.2 billion while shopping its other English-language publishing interests. Finally, in October 2003, Vivendi announced its deal with NBC, completing it in May 2004.

Visit Vault at **www.vault.com** for insider company profiles, expert advice, career message boards, expert resume reviews, the Vault Job Board and more.

VAULT CAREER LIBRARY   273

It's Hammer time

After the merger was completed, veteran cable executive Bonnie Hammer was named president of USA Network. Prior to being elevated to the head of USA, Hammer was president of the Sci-Fi Channel, a position that she continues to hold. Hammer knows USA well, though; she's worked in programming at the basic cable network for years. And Hammer has enthusiastically taken on her new role. In speaking with *Variety* in June 2004, shortly after her appointment, Hammer said she is anxious to "find the pulse of USA." Hammer went on to discuss broadening the network's reach even further, telling the trade publication that "while our shows are reaching lots of eyeballs, I'm wondering if we shouldn't seek programming that's hipper and younger, that displays a little more diversity. Maybe a little less meat and potatoes and a little more sushi and salsa?"

Loss equals gain

USA began airing The Biggest Loser in 2004. The show, hosted by Caroline Rhea from *Sabrina the Teenage Witch*, is a "weight-loss drama" in which two celebrity fitness trainers join with health experts to help 12 overweight contestants transform their bodies. In true *Survivor* style, the contestants are divided into two teams, alliances are struck and one person is voted off every week. The winner, and *Biggest Loser*, walks away with a grand prize of $250,000.

USA became a bigger winner when it premiered *The 4400*, a dramatic miniseries about a group of people who had been abducted by aliens and later returned to Earth. About five million households tuned in, making *The 4400* the highest-rated show to ever premier on a basic cable network. Pleased by the success of the miniseries, USA decided to bring the show back as a regular series in June 2005.

GETTING HIRED

USA's employment page is located at nbcuni.com/About_NBC_Universal/Careers, as the network is part of the Universal group of NBC Universal. Job postings are searchable by function, group and location, and you can apply for open positions online. Internships are for students who are currently registered at an accredited undergraduate or graduate institution. The network offers both paid and unpaid internships, and its internship cycles run through the fall, spring and summer sessions.

Viacom Inc.

1515 Broadway
New York, NY 10036
Phone: (212) 258-6000
Fax: (212) 258-6464
www.viacom.com

LOCATIONS

New York, NY (HQ)

THE STATS

Employer Type: Public Company
Stock Symbol: VIA
Stock Exchange: NYSE
Chairman and CEO: Sumner M. Redstone
2004 Employees: 38,350
2004 Revenue ($mil.): $22,525.9

KEY COMPETITORS

News Corp.
Time Warner
Walt Disney

EMPLOYMENT CONTACT

https://jobhuntweb.viacom.com

Visit Vault at **www.vault.com** for insider company profiles, expert advice,
career message boards, expert resume reviews, the Vault Job Board and more.

VAULT CAREER LIBRARY   275

THE SCOOP

Media mogul

Viacom is one of the world's largest media companies, with holdings that span the cable, broadcasting, publishing, Internet and video industries. The diversified entertainment company has operations in five segments: networks, entertainment, parks, publishing and online. It operates almost 20 cable television outlets, including MTV, VH1, Showtime, Nickelodeon, BET, the Sundance Channel and Comedy Central, along with broadcast stations like CBS and UPN. The company also owns Viacom Television Station Group, which itself owns and operates some 40 TV stations in the U.S., and also has its hand in the movie business, having Paramount Pictures in its stable, and radio, though Infinity Radio (which accounts for 185 radio stations across the country). Paramount Parks and Simon & Schuster are also members of the Viacom family. The company reported $26.6 billion in revenue in 2003 and employs over 122,000 people.

CBS offspring

CBS created Viacom in 1970 in response to an FCC ruling, which stated that TV networks could not own cable stations and TV stations within the same market. The newly formed Viacom took control of CBS' program syndication division and launched Showtime, a pay cable station, in 1978. In 1987, CEO Sumner Redstone purchased 83 percent of Viacom's stock for $3.4 billion. Six years later, Redstone made a deal to acquire Paramount Communications for $10 billion. The high-profile wheeling and dealing continued the next year when Viacom bought Blockbuster Entertainment Corp. for $8.4 billion. Soon after the purchase, Viacom hit a rough patch. A badly slumping Blockbuster, depressed ratings at MTV and poor box office numbers at Paramount, along with a host of other problems, pressured Viacom's stock despite the booming market.

Rebounding

However, since 1998, the media conglomerate showed signs of rebounding. That year, Viacom announced the sale of its educational publishing operations to U.K. media conglomerate Pearson for $4.6 billion. Viacom kept Simon & Schuster's trade publishing division, a cash cow that produces serious literature, like Frank McCourt's memoir *Angela's Ashes*, as well less-literary fare, including novels based on characters from the various *Star Trek* series. The sale made a dent in Viacom's debt load, estimated to be between $8 billion and $9 billion at the time, and cleared the way for the company to focus on its entertainment divisions.

Blockbuster battle

The company also revamped Blockbuster, boosting the number of hot-ticket recent releases available for rental and giving a dollar off rentals returned early. As part of its strategy with Blockbuster, Viacom crafted a revenue-sharing deal with film companies, which enabled the chain to triple the volume of popular titles in stock. While it certainly seemed to be a shrewd move, Viacom ran into legal issues regarding its agreements with the film studios. CEO Redstone appeared on the stand in a Texas courtroom in June 2002, defending his company against charges that Viacom conspired with movie studios to keep independent video retailers from entering into revenue-sharing deals similar to the one enjoyed by Blockbuster. The suit was filed in 1999 in Texas and California by about 250 independent retailers against Viacom, Blockbuster and eight movie studios, and alleged that Redstone sought favored treatment for Blockbuster during negotiations with the studios. Redstone testified that he had done nothing wrong in aggressively competing against other players in the rental business. A Federal Court in Texas struck down the lawsuit in 2002 and the case was finally resolved in February 2003 when the Los Angeles County Superior Court ruled in favor of Blockbuster Inc.

Blockbuster has experienced other setbacks. For one, it experienced a drop in sales because Wal-Mart and other retailers offered lower prices on DVDs for sale. Blockbuster also suffered from a bloated inventory and competition from mail order rental companies such as Netflix. In October 2004, Viacom finalized the sale of its majority interest in Blockbuster, which Viacom had always struggled to fully integrate into its operations.

Together again

In May 2000, Viacom and CBS finalized a merger that created the world's second-largest media conglomerate behind AOL Time Warner (now known as Time Warner). The $34.8 billion deal was announced about a month after the FCC loosened its regulations concerning television station ownership. Talks began shortly after the regulatory sea change, which allowed companies to own more than one station in the same city. Viacom CEO Redstone remained at the helm of the organization, while CBS CEO Mel Karmazin became president and chief operating officer.

BETting on a new network

Viacom gained instant access to a fast growing market in November 2000 when it paid $2.3 billion to acquire BET Holdings II Inc., the parent company of Black Entertainment Television (BET). Viacom purchased nearly all of BET's assets, including its cable network, a jazz network, the Action Pay Per View service, publishing company BET books and web portal BET.com. The deal made BET's founder Robert Johnson the second-largest shareholder of Viacom stock. Johnson is set to retire from the company when his contract expires in 2006.

California dreamin'

In February 2002, Viacom purchased KCAL Channel 9, the last independent major broadcast station in the Los Angeles market. Viacom operates two local stations (KCAL and KCBS) in a duopoly, giving the corporation its eighth media duopoly in the U.S. The company purchased another station in 2004, this time in Sacramento, Calif. The deal, which was announced in December 2004, will see the conglomerate take acquire Sinclair Broadcasting's CBS affiliate for $285 million. Although the station is one of its top performers, Sinclair is selling it because of FCC regulations that restrict companies' ability to own more than one station in a given market.

Big Bond - and big comedy

In April 2002, Viacom's television networks, TNN, CBS and UPN, along with MGM Worldwide Television Distribution (a unit of Metro-Goldwyn-Mayer Inc. MGM) announced a multi-million-dollar licensing agreement under which the networks licensed the exclusive U.S. television rights to 15 classic titles from MGM's *James Bond* franchise from October 2002 through most of 2004. TNN began telecasting the *Bond* titles in October after the films completed their run on ABC.

A year later, in April 2003, Viacom announced that it had reached a deal with Time Warner, Inc., in which Time Warner sold its half ownership in Comedy Central to Viacom, the cable channel's other owner, for a total of $1.2 billion. The purchase was followed by the announcement that Comedy Central was cutting 20 percent of its staff. The layoffs affected about 80 employees in its sales, legal, finance and human resources departments.

A fine line

In November 2004, the company reached an agreement with the Federal Communications Commission over an investigation regarding complaints that some material aired on Viacom's radio and TV networks was offensive. The conglomerate agreed to pay a $3.5 million fine to the agency and also said it would put some safeguards in place to prevent future incidents, including instituting transmission delays for live programs and training its on-air talent about indecency laws. The settlement did not cover a $550,000 fine that had been imposed on Viacom as a result of the 2004 Superbowl incident in which singer Janet Jackson's breast was exposed. The company believes that the incident was not something it could have predicted and has continued to fight that fine.

Executive shake ups

Mel Karmazin, Viacom president and COO, abruptly resigned in June 2004 after rumors of internal strife with Chairman and CEO Sumner Redstone had surfaced. Karmazin was replaced by two division heads; CBS chief Les Moonves and Tom Freston, former MTV head honcho. (In November 2004, satellite radio provider Sirius announced that Karmazin would join the company as CEO.) It's been believed that one (or possibly both) of them will replace Redstone, who turned 81 in 2004. The change-over had been expected to take place in 2007, but in March 2005, Redstone stated that the board may decide to split the company into two separately traded entities, with Freston running MTV and Paramount Pictures and Moonves commanding CBS and the company's other television properties. According to a report published by Knight Ridder Tribune Business News in April 2005, the split could take place as soon as the first quarter of 2006.

The dual appointment of Moonves and Freston was not the only high-profile leadership change the company experienced. In November 2004, Sherry Lansing, president of the Paramount Motion Picture Group, announced she planned to leave, stating that she would not seek to renew her contract, which is set to expire at the end of 2005. There had been speculation within the industry as to whether Lansing would remain at her post as Freston seeks to develop films that will draw in larger audiences. In January 2005, the company tapped manager-to-the-stars Brad Grey to fill the top spot at Paramount.

In other major personnel news, longtime news anchor Dan Rather announced in November 2004 that he would step down from his role as anchor and managing editor of the *CBS Evening News* in March 2005; he was replaced by Bob Schieffer. Rather, who has continued working for the network as a correspondent on *60 Minutes*, had been criticized regarding details in a September 2004 report on that show about President George W. Bush's service in the National Guard. Shortly after the report aired, questions surfaced as to the legitimacy of documents used to

Visit Vault at **www.vault.com** for insider company profiles, expert advice, career message boards, expert resume reviews, the Vault Job Board and more.

VAULT CAREER LIBRARY   **279**

substantiate the report. While the timing of Rather's exit as it relates that incident isn't particularly fortuitous, it also shouldn't come as a surprise. At the time of Rather's announcement, Tom Brokaw, another seasoned anchor, had already announced his departure from NBC, and it had been speculated that the 73-year-old Rather might soon leave the anchor desk, as well.

Gaining momentum

After a rocky 12 months, Viacom seemed to be regaining its footing somewhat. For the second quarter of 2004, the company reported operating income of $1.4 billion, an increase of 10 percent from $1.3 billion for the same period in 2003. For the second quarter, the company brought in revenue of $6.8 billion, an increase of 7 percent from the same period in 2003. In the third quarter of 2004, the company reported revenue of $5.8 billion, which was a 4 percent improvement over the previous year. Although the company posted a net loss of $487.6 million for the quarter because of a write-down related to Blockbuster, Viacom raised its dividend and announced a stock buy-back program. However, the company did not close out the year on a good note. For the fourth quarter, Viacom reported a loss of more than $18 billion due to a write-off related to the company's radio assets. This resulted in a net loss of $17.46 billion for the entire year of 2004, according to a February 2005 *Chicago Tribune* article. Excluding the write-off and a one-time tax benefit, Viacom's revenue would have been $714 million.

In a move related to Viacom's potential split into two companies, executives revealed in April 2005 that cable operators may have to start paying a fee to carry CBS. Up until now, the broadcast networks have allowed cable operators to broadcast their signals for free, but as Viacom reexamines its business model, traditional agreements with cable operators could be subject to negotiation.

Going against industry trends, Viacom plans to spend more money on movies (up to $150 million for some) and is introducing a host of new cable channels, including a much talked about gay network.

GETTING HIRED

Hiring overview

A highly diversified conglomerate, Viacom's hiring and recruiting process is decentralized. Applicants should contact the human resources department of the specific company at which they want to work. The parent company's employment web page, located at https://jobhuntweb.viacom.com, lists some job openings and internships for which resumes can be e-mailed or sent to the provided addresses.

Paramount Pictures maintains a separate recruiting web page at www.paramount.com/homecareer.shtml. Positions at the Macmillan Publishing division of Simon and Schuster are listed on its own web page at www.simonandschuster.com/jobview.cfm. "They hire young," particularly, "a lot of people straight out of school – it's not uncommon," an insider says. "They don't drug test, if that's a concern." Sources add that "Viacom also hires a lot of freelancers, so if you just want to test the waters or get your foot in the door, it is something to ask about."

Vivendi Universal

42 avenue de Friedland
75380 Paris Cedex 08
France
Phone: +33-1-71-71-10-00
Fax: +33-1-71-71-10-01
www.vivendiuniversal.com

LOCATIONS

Paris (HQ)

THE STATS

Employer Type: Public Company
Stock Symbol: V
Stock Exchange: NYSE
Chairman and CEO: Jean-Rene Fourtou
2003 Employees: 55,451
2003 Revenue ($mil.): $32,036.0

KEY COMPETITORS

Bertlesmann
France Telecom
Virgin Group

EMPLOYMENT CONTACT

www.vivendiuniversal.com/vu/en/
careers/index.cfm?idR=12

THE SCOOP

Still kicking

Vivendi Universal has seen better times. The once feared French conglomerate that evolved from a water utility into the world's No.-2 media company has had its Hollywood and big media dreams dashed. After a two-year, $100 billion acquisition spree, the Paris-based company has reverted to shedding all the major assets it can, with finalization in October 2003 of a deal that transfered its U.S. film, theme park and cable television interests to a joint venture with NBC owner General Electric. In 2002, the company still employed 61,800 people worldwide, and realized $61 billion in sales, compared to $51 billion for 2001. The numbers, combined with the cash generated through all of its recent divestures, mean that things may finally be looking up for this beleaguered company. In fact, in October 2003, company officials said that they hoped to be debt free (their debt stood at €13 billion at the time) by the end of 2004.

Making sense of it all

How did a company that went from being a large French water and media company to international monolith with its hand in the film, television, Internet, alcohol and beverage, publishing and theme park businesses fall flat on its face, you ask? Indeed, it's been a winding road the company has traveled to get to this point. Even tracing Vivendi's origins can get a bit complicated. The company's roots go back to 1832, when Charles-Louis Havas established a foreign newspaper translation agency and bookshop in France. But it also has links to Compagnie Générale des Eaux (CGE), which was founded in 1853 and began by supplying water to Paris, Lyons, Venice and Constantinople. Both companies did well, and grew throughout the 19th and 20th centuries. By the late 1990s, CGE was operating in over 90 countries with a workforce of 235,000 people. Its portfolio covered waste management, transport, energy, construction, property development and management, and communications. The two firms would eventually merge in 1983, when they joined to establish the Canal+ pay television group in France. By 1998, the companies had decided to change the name of the parent company from CGE Group to Vivendi, and soon thereafter, set out on a course to make the company into a global media powerhouse–a path that would lead the company into financial disaster by 2002, and force it to shed most of the gains it had made in the previous two years.

Visit Vault at **www.vault.com** for insider company profiles, expert advice, career message boards, expert resume reviews, the Vault Job Board and more.

V/\ULT CAREER LIBRARY   **283**

It all began with Seagram

In 2000 Vivendi announced its $34 billion takeover of Seagram, the American beverages giant controlled by one wing of Canada's Bronfman family. But Seagram is much more than a beverages company. The company had earlier purchased Universal (parks, TV and film production and distribution, cable TV, book and music publishing) from Japan's Matsushita – and in 1998 acquired the EU Polygram music recording empire.

When Vivendi bought the company in 2000, the new conglomerate included the world's largest music company, second-largest film library, a major film production studio, second-largest theme park company, major book publishing interests and strategic investments in groups such as U.K. broadcaster BskyB. When it purchased Barry Diller's USA Networks in 2002 for $10.3 billion, Vivendi acquired a group that included Expedia.com, Hotels.com and Ticketmaster.

The rise ...

After the Seagram acquisition, the company changed its name from Vivendi to Vivendi Universal. Seagram was a corporate behemoth in itself, which bought a 14.5 percent stake in Time Warner in 1994, and in 1995 sold its 24 percent stake in chemical company DuPont, (which it acquired in 1980) to help pay for its $5.7 billion acquisition of MCA from Matsushita–renaming it Universal Studios. In the same year, Vivendi bought the 51 percent of European TV provider Canal+ that it didn't already own. In addition to this, the firm also owns 70 percent of telecom provider Cegetel and 20 percent of Veolia Environment, the world's No.-1 water distributor. In the midst of all this buying and selling, it also bought the entertainment assets of InterActiveCorp, which it combined with Universal Studios into the 86 percent-owned Vivendi Universal Entertainment. In 2001, Vivendi bought U.S. publisher Houghton Mifflin for $1.7 billion. In the same year Vivendi bought MP3.com for $372 million.

... and fall

But the good times soon ended, and by 2002–a mere two years after this whole shopping spree began–massive losses led the company to begin shedding its U.S. assets as fast as it could unload them. The upshot of this process is likely to reduce it to a significant but much smaller French film, television, publishing and telecommunications operator–probably minus the "Universal" part of the corporate name following sale of its U.S. assets.

In October 2002, for example, it announced the sale of its European and Latin American publishing units to Hachette for $1.2 billion and was poised to sell its English-language publishing interests. In November it sold a further 20 percent of the Vivendi Environnement division (renamed Veolia Environnement in 2003) to Eléctricité de France and other investors for €1.8 billion. In December 2002 it increased its stake in French telco Cegetel to 70 percent by paying €2.5 billion for BT's 26 percent holding, a move considered by some to be a precursor to sale of its film and music interests. Also in 2002, the company shed its health care and business publishing units for €1.2bn, sold Groupe Express-Expansion (inc l'Express), Groupe l'Etudiant) and Comareg to Hersant's Socpresse for €330 million, sold its 50 percent share of the Vizzavi Internet company for €142 million and sold 89 percent of its stake in Canal+ Technologies to Thomson Multimedia for €190 million.

The NBC deal

But the biggest fire sale came in October 2003, when NBC, a unit of General Electric, won Vivendi Universal's show business auction with a multi-billion dollar merger to create a new entertainment industry giant. The NBC deal brings together assets including Vivendi's Universal Pictures and cable television network USA, with NBC's broadcast network and cable channels CNBC and Bravo. According to terms of the agreement, GE owns 80 percent of the merged company while Vivendi holds 20 percent. As part of the deal, Vivendi said shareholders of Vivendi Universal Entertainment would receive $3.8 billion of "cash consideration" against a commitment by GE to issue its stock as well as a $1.6 billion debt reduction.

The deal brought to an end a long summer of negotiations with a whole host of suitors throwing huge numbers on the table in hopes of scoring Vivendi's sizeable assets. NBC beat several other potential buyers for the Universal entertainment businesses, including Viacom, Liberty Media Corp., Metro-Goldwyn-Mayer Inc. and Comcast Corp. The new company will include the NBC television network; its cable channels CNBC, MSNBC and Bravo; and Spanish-language broadcaster Telemundo, as well as Vivendi's Universal movie and TV studios. Not only that, the USA, Sci-Fi and Trio cable channels and several theme parks will be part of the mix. The newly created company will have about $13 billion in annual revenue, making it a sizable competitor in the media field but still smaller than Time Warner's $41 billion in revenues last year or Disney's revenue of $25 billion.

The deal went a long way in helping fix what ails Vivendi. The company will have the chance to begin selling its 20 percent stake in the new company starting in 2006. The companies estimated the combined media and entertainment business would be worth $43 billion, meaning a 20 percent stake would be worth about $8.6 billion. In addition, NBC will take on $1.7 billion of Vivendi's debt. Finally, the merger allows Vivendi to reduce debt to $5 billion and be a profitable company by the end of 2004, according to Vivendi officials.

Messier mess

In 1996, after successful stints in the French Finance Ministry and Lazard Freres & Co., Jean-Marie Messier was tapped to head conglomerate Compagnie Generale des Eaux, and he promptly turned that troubled company into Vivendi by engaging in the new millennium spending spree. Things looked great until early 2002, when the company's stock plummeted 70 percent (and took a non-cash loss of $11.8 billion) on the heels of some of the more ill-advised acquisitions. By July of that year, Messier was forced out of the company due to mounting debt and unwieldy subsidiaries, although he walked away with a $23 million compensation package as well as use of a New York apartment until the end of the year, worth an estimated $17.5 million.

Sounds like a good deal, but in October 2003, things continued to deteriorate for Messier. Although he conceded that he had made mistakes during his tenure and said that he was prepared to use mediation to end a lawsuit brought by Vivendi over his $23 million severance pay, that didn't stop the U.S. Securities and Exchange Commission from investigating dealings during Messier's tenure, and asking a U.S. Federal Court in New York City to freeze the funds. The request was granted in September, only days after a state court ordered Vivendi to pay Messier.

EU troubles

In October 2003, the European Union opened an investigation into Lagardere Groupe's $1.4 billion takeover of Vivendi's publishing assets, demanding more information on the deal. The purchase would combine the two largest publishers of French-language books, including houses such as Grasset, Fayard, Hachette and dictionary publishers Larousse and Nathan. European antitrust officials expressed "serious doubts" about the deal last June because of concerns over publishing rights, book distribution and sales. The Commission has until January 13, 2004, to decide to block or clear the deal. Lagardere has said it wants to keep two of Vivendi's publishing houses, including Spanish publisher Anaya and Larousse. French booksellers and smaller publishers have fiercely opposed the consolidation, fearing it would give the new entity a near-monopoly in many areas of book publishing and distribution. They insist any solution approved by regulators will have to leave two major French publishing companies intact. Consumer groups have also spoken out against the merger, arguing the tie-up would leave Lagardere in control of half the French-language book publishing market in Europe.

GETTING HIRED

Being a French company, Vivendi doesn't keep much of a presence in the United States, but its Universal Music, Vivendi Universal Games and Vivendi Universal Entertainment subsidiaries do have offices spread out over the United States. Interested applicants can log on the corporate web site: www.vivendiuniversal.com to peruse job openings at the various locations.

Walt Disney Company, The

500 S. Buena Vista Street
Burbank, CA 91521-9722
Phone: (818) 560-1000
Fax: (818) 560-1930
www.disney.go.com

LOCATIONS

Burbank, CA (HQ)

KEY COMPETITORS

NBC Universal
Time Warner
Viacom

EMPLOYMENT CONTACTS

corporate.disney.go.com/careers/index.
html

www.wdwcollegeprogram.com

THE SCOOP

The house the mouse built

Walt Disney dreamed of creating an entertainment company that provided something for the entire family. Although he accomplished a great deal during his lifetime, at the time of his death in 1966, some of his plans had not come to fruition. For instance, he enthusiastically planned, but did not live to see his "Florida project," (today's EPCOT and Walt Disney World) come to life.

Now fast-forward a couple of decades to the start of the Michael Eisner era. Eisner may not have been the fairy godmother some Disney supporters had hoped for, but the simple fact remains that under Eisner, the company has grown maybe even beyond the dreams of its famous founder. Currently Disney operates feature and short animated film companies, production studios for more serious and adult-oriented films, several publications, its own cable television network and several other niche networks and various online properties. Disney's historic 1996 acquisition of Capital Cities/ABC put the company in an even stronger position to play a major role in the entertainment industry well into this century. The combination of its world-famous theme parks, countless memorable characters and other properties have made Disney one of the most recognizable brands in the world. After a long, drawn-out battle with Disney higher-ups that itself seemed straight out of a Hollywood blockbuster, Eisner was ousted in 2004, replaced by Robert Iger in October 2005.

A portrait of Mickey as a young mouse

Walt and Roy Disney founded Disney Brothers Studios in Hollywood in 1923. In 1928, Mickey Mouse was introduced to the world in a cartoon entitled "Plane Crazy." Nine years later, Disney released its first full-length animated feature, the perennial children's favorite, *Snow White and the Seven Dwarfs*. Walt Disney Productions, as the company was then known, went public in 1940. In 1955, Disneyland opened the gates to its Magic Kingdom theme park for the first time. When Walt Disney died of lung cancer in 1966, his brother Roy took over as chairman of the company. Disney World in Florida opened in 1971; that same year Roy Disney also passed away. With both patriarchs gone, Roy's son, Roy E. Disney, was left as the primary individual shareholder of Disney stock. In 1984, he allied himself with the wealthy Bass family to purchase a controlling interest in the company. Disney and the Basses appointed two executives from rival studios, Michael Eisner from Paramount and Frank Wells

Visit Vault at **www.vault.com** for insider company profiles, expert advice, career message boards, expert resume reviews, the Vault Job Board and more.

VAULT CAREER LIBRARY   **289**

from Warner Brothers, to run the company, ushering in a new phase in the company's history.

Eisner comes aboard

When Michael Eisner joined the Walt Disney Company in 1984, the company was in the midst of a troubled period. That year, it had a flagging film division that produced few hits. Eisner, then a chief at Paramount Pictures, seemed a natural to take control of this area. Having helped restore Paramount to its former glory, he had already cemented his status as a legend in the industry.

Eisner spurred growth by engaging in what would have previously been considered some very un-Disney-like activities. With a wealth of more "grownup" entertainment acquisitions such as the Miramax and Touchstone film companies, as well as a new corporate strategy that sought to aggressively grow the company and its holdings worldwide, Eisner guided Disney back into the big leagues. The new CEO helped prove that Disney could be far more successful by expanding beyond its cute and cuddly corporate stance – the company has been very successful at maintaining the kid-friendly identity of its various Walt Disney-branded properties, while also producing adult-themed fare.

The 1990s, however, saw the end of Eisner's honeymoon. Disney president Frank Wells, Eisner's close friend and right hand man, died in a helicopter crash in 1994. That tragedy foreshadowed a rash of corporate shakeups. Just after Wells' death, Jeffery Katzenberg left the film unit he helped to revitalize in a huff after not being promoted to Wells' former position. Passed over for Mike Ovitz, Katzenberg struck out on his own and founded the DreamWorks film studio with Steven Spielberg and David Geffen. Ovitz, Eisner's longtime friend and co-founder of the Creative Artists Agency, entered the company riding high on a reputation as "the most powerful talent agent in Hollywood." However, Ovitz, never got a chance to get comfortable in his new role. In December 1996, he too packed his bags after just 16 months on the job. Allegedly, Ovitz's departure was caused largely by personality clashes between Eisner and his new lieutenant. As a result, Eisner took on more and more duties himself.

Mickey in Paris

The 1990s were a wilder roller coaster ride for Disney than any of its theme parks could possibly hope to offer. Euro Disney opened Disneyland Paris to heavy criticism from the French in 1992 and was immediately written off by critics as a massive – and costly – failure. For a few months, many major publications in the U.S. served up scathing articles with photos of the near-empty theme park. But by 2002, the park was drawing more than 12 million visitors a year to its five "lands" which feature about 40 rides and attractions, restaurants, shops and live entertainment. Euro Disney also runs hotels, convention centers and the Disney Village entertainment complex that links the park to the on-site hotels. Euro Disney pays royalty and management fees to Walt Disney, which owns 39 percent of the operation.

But since that flush period, European travel and tourism has begun slowing down, and the park has fallen deep into red. Still, Euro Disney continues to survive. The company, which looked to be headed toward bankruptcy, convinced banks and large investors to back its debt reorganization plan in September 2004.

Lands, worlds and other Disney territories

Disney has organized all its various ventures into four main business groups: parks and resorts, media networks, studio entertainment and consumer products.

Disney's parks and resorts group includes not only the company's theme parks, but also its cruise lines and sports teams. The theme parks division has traditionally been a reliable source of income for the corporation, taking in a cool $7 billion from its hotels, resorts and amusement parks in 2003. Disney's theme parks include Walt Disney World, Disneyland, Disneyland Paris and Tokyo Disneyland (Disney doesn't actually own Tokyo Disneyland, but does earn hefty royalties from it). Other attractions include the Magic Kingdom, EPCOT, Disney-MGM Studios Theme Park and Disney's Animal Kingdom (all located within Orlando's Walt Disney World Resort). The Florida park also features the Downtown Disney Marketplace, where the company also operates a 16,000-square-foot toy store in partnership with Hasbro. During the summer of 2002, Disney also built a 65-foot-tall Tinker Toy tower which includes an interactive play area with Buzz Lightyear, Mr. Potato Head, Lincoln Logs and Tinker Toys.

There's always something new in the Disney parks, it seems. The summer of 2002 saw the opening of Disney's Beach Club Villas in Florida, consisting of 208 units spread over five "wings." The villas are "inspired" by mid-Atlantic seaside homes built in the early 20th century. Each of the studio's one- and two-bedroom villas has either a pool or garden view.

In February 2001, Disney's California Adventure, along with the entertainment district Downtown Disney and Disney's Grand Californian Hotel, debuted at the

Visit Vault at **www.vault.com** for insider company profiles, expert advice, career message boards, expert resume reviews, the Vault Job Board and more.

VAULT CAREER LIBRARY   291

Disneyland Resort in Anaheim, home to the original Disneyland theme park. Following this, in September 2001, Disney unveiled Japan's second Disney theme park when Tokyo DisneySea – a park inspired by the myths and legends of the sea – opened its gates adjacent to Tokyo Disneyland. In March 2002, the company expanded its holdings in Europe with the opening of the Walt Disney Studios at Disneyland Paris. Located next to the Disneyland Paris theme park, Disney Studios is a real production studio where guests can go behind the scenes to learn how movies, television and animation are made. Attractions include special effects shows such as *Armageddon*, *Catastrophe Canyon* and *Rock 'n' Roller Coaster Starring Aerosmith*.

The Magic (expanding) Kingdom

The parks and resorts group was hurt badly by the recession and decrease in travel that followed the September 2001 terrorist attacks. During the first quarter of 2002, Walt Disney World attendance was down about 25 percent compared to the first quarter of 2001. For the year, revenue was down more than $500 million, about 8 percent, and the group's earnings decreased by 26 percent compared to 2001. Disney officials reported gradual improvement in the unit's performance during 2003 and into 2004, but the company's tourism business has yet to fully recover.

The Mouse has deep pockets, though, and Disney is not a company that is easily intimidated by a few bad quarters. The company continues to aggressively expand its resort operations, with the highlight being the brand new theme park in Hong Kong that opened in 2005. The 309-acre resort, which overlooks the water at Penny's Bay on Lantau Island, was built with the full cooperation of the Hong Kong and Chinese governments. Further down the road is the opening of Expedition Everest, a high-speed thrill ride currently under construction in the Animal Kingdom theme park. Expedition Everest will debut in January 2006. In the meantime, the Mouse must have been pleased with the list of top U.S. theme parks released by *Consumer Reports* in 2003. Disney swept the top three spots, with Orlando's EPCOT Center, Disney-MGM Studios and the Magic Kingdom placing 1-2-3.

The Mission: Space ride was launched at EPCOT in 2003. Developed in consultation with NASA and former astronauts, the interactive adventure takes guests on a simulated flight into outer space, including creating sensations of weightlessness and a series of sustained G-forces. Not everyone is thrilled about the opening of Mission: Space, however. Environmental Tectonics Corporation (ETC), a maker of flight training devices hired by Disney to develop the centrifuge technology used in the ride, filed a breach of contract lawsuit against the company in August 2003. ETC alleged that it was not paid in full for the work it performed for Disney. The suit seeks damages of more that $15 million, the right to participate in the ride's safety testing and the right to retain ownership over the technology developed for Mission: Space. Later that year, Disney countersued and the case is still pending.

Saturating the spectrum

Disney's media networks group is a far-flung collection of media properties that includes several Disney-owned local television stations, the ABC broadcast network and 230 affiliated television stations, ABC radio networks and 2,900 affiliated radio stations, a stable of cable channels, television production studios and Disney's various Internet properties. Plagued by low ratings and slumping advertising, ABC fell from its position as the top-rated network to the third spot during the 2001-2002 television season and the 2003-2004 season saw ABC drop to fourth, behind FOX. Things have looked up for the mouse network in terms of its 2004-2005 season, though. It has bona fide hits on its hands in the form of *Desperate Housewives*, a campy soap about the lives of suburban housewives, and *Extreme Makeover: Home Edition*. The network has also received critical acclaim for the drama, *Lost*, which also debuted in the fall of 2004, and in 2005 debuted promising new shows *Jake in Progress* and *Eyes*. (Radio Disney, a venture aimed at children, has also stepped up its radio presence, operating 70 U.S. stations at the end of 2003, putting it in more than half of American demographic marketing areas.)

When Disney purchased ABC, a major selling point for the deal was the acquisition of majority ownership in ABC's crown jewel, all-sports cable network ESPN. The channel is one of cable's top rated operations, has two spin-off networks (ESPN2 and ESPNews), and is providing Disney with the opportunity to take on main rival Time Warner on a new front. ESPN's success is especially relevant considering the low to which ABC has sunk. In 1997, *ESPN Magazine* was launched. The magazine, though, has yet to garner the level of popularity as the network on which it's based. *ESPN Magazine* is currently still a pretender to the throne of Time's *Sports Illustrated*.

Disney's 2003 media networks revenue topped $10 billion. Over the last several years, Disney has purchased partial ownership stakes in networks such as A&E, The History Channel, Soapnet, E! Networks and Lifetime Television. In October 2001, the company acquired Fox Family Worldwide for $5.2 billion, and renamed it ABC Family. The company also operates a dozen worldwide networks, which reach more than 15 million subscribers in Europe, Latin America and Asia Pacific. In 2004, the

Visit Vault at **www.vault.com** for insider company profiles, expert advice,
career message boards, expert resume reviews, the Vault Job Board and more.

VAULT CAREER LIBRARY   **293**

Mouse's house strengthened its children's programming when it bought the rights to the Muppets and other Jim Henson characters.

Whistle while you work

In music, Disney's Hollywood Records relies mostly on the sales from the soundtracks to Disney movies for income but has finally produced a starlet of its own, in the form of teen star Hillary Duff. Other artists on the roster include such rock 'n' roll mainstays as Queen and Los Lobos, along with alternative Texan hippies Polyphonic Spree and legendary talk and game show host Regis Philbin.

Angels out, Ducks in (for now)

Disney also owns Anaheim Sports Inc., which controls the National Hockey League's Mighty Ducks of Anaheim (which explains their laughingstock cartoon logo) and, formerly, Major League Baseball's Anaheim Angels. In April 2003, Disney sold the Angels to Arturo Moreno for $180 million. The sale came just months after the Angels defeated the San Francisco Giants to win their first World Series championship. With the purchase, Moreno became the first Mexican-American to own a major U.S. sports franchise. Disney acquired the Angels in 1996, but had struggled with the team since then. According to Major League Baseball, the club lost $99.8 million from 1995 through 2001. The Mighty Ducks also had a successful 2002-2003 campaign, reaching the Stanley Cup finals before falling to the New Jersey Devils. Nevertheless, Disney continues to seek a buyer for its hockey team as well, and a group headed by Howard Baldwin (former owner of the Pittsburgh Penguins) has emerged as the leading candidate. The group is believed to have offered $50 million for the Ducks, the same amount Disney paid for the team back in 1992. Both sports clubs, despite their recent successes, have long been a financial drain on Disney.

At the movies

For most of its early years, the film division was Disney's most successful. In the years following Walt and Roy's deaths, the importance of the company's film activities dropped off in favor of the theme parks. Much of this change was a result of fading creativity in the film division. That trend continued well into the 1980s, when film revenue accounted for a mere 5 percent of the company's annual take. After taking the helm, Michael Eisner immediately set to work to pump up the film division. The much-heralded *The Little Mermaid*, released in 1989, marked a Disney animation renaissance. But it wasn't just animated features the stirred the popular imagination. Disney subsidiary Miramax scored commercial and critical successes, putting out movies like *Life is Beautiful*, *Shakespeare in Love*, *Amelie*, *Chicago*, *Gangs of New York* and *The Hours* – while being rewarded with several Oscars in the process. Disney's movie road was a little bumpy in 2003-2004, including hits such as *Signs* and *Pirates of the Caribbean* and disappointments like *The Alamo* and *Treasure Planet*.

Current and recent Disney execs like Eisner, and particularly Katzenberg, breathed new life into Disney's film productions; the movie and home video arms of the company now account for a sizable percentage of the company's business. The company's acquisition of Miramax Films, the studio responsible for such critically acclaimed films as *Pulp Fiction*, *The Crying Game*, *Good Will Hunting* and Oscar-winner *Chicago*, was successful in establishing Disney in the mainstream film industry. Disney markets and produces films from a number of recognizable studios. Theatrical releases are handled through the company's Hollywood Pictures, Touchstone and Walt Disney Theatrical divisions.

However, Miramax and its parent had a falling out when Disney refused to distribute Michael Moore's much-talked-about documentary *Fahrenheit 9/11*. Miramax took matters in its own hands and bought the rights to the film from Disney, distributing it through third parties such as Lion's Gate. The *Fahrenheit* feud was one of the last straws in the tumultuous, 12-year history between the outspoken Weinstein brothers, founders of Miramax, and the more conservative Disney. The two sides came to terms regarding a separation in March 2005. Disney retained Miramax's name, and library of 550 films, while the Weinsteins gained $130 million to start a new film company, as well as the rights to the Dimension Films label, which has gained success with the horror-themed franchises *Scream* and *Scary Movie*. A search is currently being conducted for a new executive to run the Miramax division after the Weinsteins' contract expires in July 2005.

Invading Broadway

Disney discovered an unexpected venue for its film creations in the early 1990s with the successful Broadway launch of *Beauty and The Beast*. The musical met with massive popular acclaim, though many critics decried the production as all style and no substance. So, when Disney prepared *The Lion King* for a similar Broadway rendition, skeptics everywhere braced themselves for outlandish costumes, sets and production costs masking a thin story line. Instead, Disney surprised everyone by hiring cutting-edge talent to oversee the production, and the musical picked up six

Visit Vault at **www.vault.com** for insider company profiles, expert advice,
career message boards, expert resume reviews, the Vault Job Board and more.

VAULT CAREER LIBRARY   **295**

1998 Tony Awards (including Best Musical). The company built on that success with the production of *Aida*, another hit.

Flying off the shelves

Despite these successes, the company has continued to look for ways to tighten its belt. In 2001, The Walt Disney Studios cut its annual investment in live-action films by $600 million, in part by eliminating unproductive talent deals and streamlining the script development process. The division continues to grow, however, due in no small part to the revenue generated by the DVD and VHS sales of *Toy Story II*, *Monsters, Inc.* and *Snow White and the Seven Dwarfs*. The DVD and cassette sales of these animated features have been so successful, in fact, that they're shattering records. In September 2002, *Monsters, Inc.* sold 5 million DVD and videocassettes in one day, topping the industry one-day sales record of 4.5 million units. A record set, incidentally, in 1995 by another Disney release – *The Lion King*. Even more astounding is that in just one week of sales, *Monsters, Inc.* sold 11 million DVD and videocassette units in the United States and Canada, shattering every DVD-era home entertainment industry sales record in the process.

From paint to pixels

In 1991, Disney entered into a partnership with Pixar Animation Studios, led by Steve Jobs of Apple Computer fame, to co-produce high-tech, computer-animated feature films. The deal has resulted in some of Disney's hottest properties in recent times, including *A Bug's Life*, *Toy Story*, *Toy Story II* and *Monsters, Inc.* Another recent Disney/Pixar feature, Finding Nemo, has also scored a home run for Disney. The film took in $70.3 million in its first weekend in release in June 2003. That total broke the record for weekend box office revenue by an animated feature. *Nemo* went on to pass the $300 million mark in ticket sales during the summer of 2003, making it the highest grossing animated film of all time. However, the success story seems to have come to an end; Pixar has announced it will look for a new distribution partner in 2006 – though Jobs has recently suggested his company would be willing to re-open negotiations following the departure of Eisner, whom he has repeatedly – and publicly – fought with over the years. Industry analysts put the odds of a new Disney-Pixar deal at "less than 50-50."

Multimedia Mouse

Already operator of popular web sites such as Disney.com and Family.com, Disney bought a 42 percent interest in Internet search engine Infoseek for $70 million, in 1998. The two launched the Go Network (www.go.com) in January 1999, and Disney later bought the rest of the company. Although Disney combined all of its Internet holdings – including sites run by ABC, ESPN and Disney's film production companies – under the auspices of the Go Network, the going was rough. In 2001, Disney's Internet properties underwent a massive overhaul, including a name change (Go Network is now the Walt Disney Internet Group), and several rounds of layoffs. Since Disney laid off Go.com's entire 400-person staff in January 2001, the company has put the web divisions of its most popular media brands, such as ABC and ESPN, back under the control of their respective parents. As a result, Disney's web efforts have become offshoots of traditional businesses rather than standalone units. Disney also officially shut down the struggling MrShowbiz.com in November 2001.

Despite the halting of Go, Disney.com remains a formidable online presence, receiving the No.-1 children's entertainment site ranking from ComScore Media Metrix in March 2003. Recent innovations introduced on the site include Toontown Online and Magic Artist. Toontown Online, introduced in May 2003, is the first massively multiplayer 3D online game for kids. Magic Artist, meanwhile, is an online tool that allows visitors to print out coloring-book pages, greeting cards, calendars and play sets featuring Disney characters.

Everything Mickey

While the rest of the world may get sick of plush Lion Kings, talking Hercules dolls and the ever popular "mouse ears," two groups of people are guaranteed to never tire of Disney merchandising – children and Disney executives. Disney's consumer products group consists of the company's various merchandising tie-ins as well as the chain of Disney Stores and the company's publishing holdings. Disney Interactive, a developer of "edutainment" software, is also a part of the consumer products group.

In 2001, Disney entered into an alliance with the Minute Maid division of the Coca-Cola Company to develop juices and juice drinks for kids. As a result, Disney Xtreme! Coolers and Disney Hundred Acre Wood 100 percent Juice hit the stores that year. The company is also developed milk- and water-based drinks that hit the market in 2003. The Kellogg Company is another Disney consumer products partner. Disney hooked up with the cereal maker in 2001, striking a deal that will give Disney a larger presence in grocery store aisles worldwide. The first co-branded products,

Visit Vault at **www.vault.com** for insider company profiles, expert advice, career message boards, expert resume reviews, the Vault Job Board and more.

V/\ULT CAREER LIBRARY   **297**

ready-to-eat breakfast cereals, hit the market in 2002. Additional items such as Pop-Tart toaster pastries and Eggo waffles came later. In a shrewd move, Disney inked a deal with the Gillette Company in 2001 to offer a line of oral care products for children. Disney-branded toothbrushes hit store shelves in the fall of 2001, ensuring that after eating a sugary Pop Tart or waffle, children will scrub the cavities away with another Disney product. In June 2003, the company announced a deal with Wal-Mart to cash in on its latest hot property, the Disney Channel's *Kim Possible* show. The *Kim Possible* line of products will include lunchboxes, clothes, stationary, books, DVDs and dolls, available exclusively through Wal-Mart.

Retail in a rut

The Disney Store began as a wildly popular outlet for everything from T-shirts to Disney stationary to DVDs to Goofy keychains. At one point the company operated over 700 of these stores worldwide, but as the economy started to slide, so did the venture's profit margin. By the end of 2001 the company had closed 51 Disney Stores, with plans to close about 50 more during 2002. Following the closures and some in-store remodeling at remaining locations, sales began to pick up in 2002. In 2003, however, retail performance has once again been a disappointment. By June 2003, there were 380 Disney stores remaining in the U.S. and 160 more abroad. In May 2003, the head of Disney's retail division resigned. A month later, 140 staff members at the Disney Store's headquarters in Glendale, Calif., were laid off.

Company officials are reportedly contemplating a sale of the entire Disney Store business. In a deal that could close as soon as in the summer of 2005, clothing and toy retailer The Children's Place has signed a letter of intent to acquire the 310 Disney stores throughout the nation. If the deal goes through, Disney becomes the last movie studio to pull the plug on its retail operations. The move would not be unprecedented. In 2001, Disney sold its Japanese stores to the Oriental Land Company in return for annual royalty payments, and, that same year, rival studio AOL Time Warner sold off its entire Warner Brothers Studio Stores operation.

Disney in print

Disney also has a full line-up of publishing properties under its control. Through its Disney Press, Hyperion Press, Hyperion Books for Children, Mouse Works, Disney Hachette Editions and Disney Hachette Press imprints, the company publishes a variety of books – from children's stories about Mickey Mouse and Winnie the Pooh to companion books for movies like *Toy Story* and *Mulan* to sports books on the careers of Shaquille O'Neal and Jimmy Johnson. Its magazine arm, Diversified Publishing Group, produces magazines like *Family Fun* and *Disney Adventures*. Mickey Mouse had a standout year in 2003, when Disney Publishing reintroduced Mickey and Donald Duck comic books. As part of the 1996 acquisition of ABC, Disney acquired magazine publisher Fairchild Publications. Fairchild, however, struggled with profitability, and Disney sold the company in 2001. Adding to this publishing diversity, the company even has a newspaper division, Cap Cities ABC Publishing. In February 2002, Disney bought a 50 percent interest in Wenner Media's popular *US Weekly* magazine. In March 2005, Disney sold its science magazine, *Discover*, to concentrate on its other titles.

Boardroom breakdown

Another Michael infamous within the walls of the Magic Kingdom – Michael Ovitz – took center stage in October 2004, when the long-awaited trial regarding his severance package finally hit the Delaware courtroom scene. The Disney board initially came under attack for a severance deal issued to Ovitz in 1996 after his departure from the company, worth roughly $38 million in cash and $100 million in stock. Shareholders, furious at the hefty amount allowed to Ovitz, promptly filed suit in 1997, though lawyers defending the Michaels claim their clients did not break any laws, since no laws exist restricting CEO compensation.

The case finally made it to trial in October 2004, a rarity in the realm of corporate law, where most cases are typically settled or thrown out. Ovitz, Eisner and a slew of Disney directors took the stand in a battle that exploited inner tensions within the Disney board (on which only two members present in 1996 currently sit). Shareholders are demanding repayment of Ovitz's exit package. Litigation is ongoing as of April 2005.

Repairing the public image

At the beginning of Disney's annual shareholder meeting held in February 2005, Thomas Skaggs, the company's chief financial officer, joked, "It's been just short of a year since our last meeting here, and, well, pretty much nothing has happened since then." Skaggs revealed that despite stock hitting a 52-week low in August 2004, Disney posted solid gains from its theme park businesses, ESPN sports cable network and movie studio benefiting from positive home video sales of *Finding Nemo* and *Pirates of the Caribbean*, and the success of the Disney-Pixar blockbuster *The*

Incredibles. Net income increased 5 percent to $723 million, while sales inched up 1 percent to $8.7 billion.

Just as the company was trying to put a positive spin on its public image, Viacom-owned publisher Simon & Schuster released a scathing book from James B. Stewart entitled *Disney War: Battle for the Magic Kingdom.* Disney was rumored to have both attempted to block the book's publication, and, alternately, to have dismissed Stewart's tome as "much ado about nothing." Regardless, the book's March 2005 publication granted the public insight through "thousands of pages of never-before-seen letters, memos, transcripts, and other documents" that, according to its publishers, detailed "mysteries that enveloped Disney for years," including Eisner's multiple falling outs with Katzenberg, Ovitz, Jobs and Roy Disney.

Now it's time to say good-bye ...

After a board fracas in 2004, which saw two long-standing directors resign (including the only remaining Disney family member, Roy E.), and the rejection of a $47 billion takeover bid by Comcast, almost half of Disney's shareholders voted against Eisner's re-election. This prompted Eisner to announce that he would retire at the end of 2006, sparking a frenzy of rumors as to who would emerge as his successor. Disney announced, in September 2004, that it had hired an executive search firm and sought to find a replacement by June 2005, ending Eisner's reign somewhat prematurely. Bob Iger, Eisner's right-hand man, and former Disney president, was announced as Eisner's successor in February 2005, and is set to take the helm in October. Iger's promotion came as little surprise to industry insiders, who had named Iger as Eisner's likely replacement from the beginning. Not everyone was pleased with Iger's nomination, though – former board members Roy E. Disney and Stanley P. Gold wrote a biting piece in the *Los Angeles Times* in March 2005 that called the search for a new CEO "nothing short of disgraceful," accused chairman George Mitchell of refusing to look outside of Disney for a replacement, and admonished the board for allowing Eisner to influence the selection process through his personal campaigning for Iger.

It remains to be seen whether Iger, long viewed as Eisner's lackey, can stand up in his own right and put his personal stamp on the company. One of Iger's first moves as incoming CEO was to disassemble Disney's strategic planning division, and return more authority to individual units, including theme parks, media networks, movie studio and consumer products. A small corporate group, headed by Skaggs, remained intact to develop a five-year plan, and identify new business opportunities. Peter Murphy, who was formerly in charge of the planning unit, stepped down to become a senior advisor to Iger. Two main areas of interest in the near future for Iger are new technology and international expansion.

GETTING HIRED

It takes all types

Disney is looking for everything from accountants to marketing analysts. The company's hiring is generally decentralized, with different geographic areas handling their own staffing. Regardless, Walt Disney's job hotline, which can be reached at either (818) 558-2222 or (407) 828-1000, is a good ticket into the Magic Kingdom. The hotline gives information on the requirements and responsibilities of available jobs in all of the company's business units, including its theme parks, retail business, and creative studios. Each unit has an individual address and fax number, which are available on the hotline.

Disneyland openings are also listed at Disney.com. Resumes can be submitted by fax or regular mail, and applicants should not be afraid to submit them frequently. "Cold resumes do not end up in the right pile," warns one Disney corporate worker, so applicants are advised to keep up to date on the job postings. Disney employees have stressed the importance of temporary work in landing that permanent job at the Magic Kingdom.

The role of a lifetime

College students might want to check out www.wdwcollegeprogram.com, which provides details on internships at Disney World in Florida. Far from the dreary cubicle-world, Disney World interns have the opportunity to join the theme park's "cast" in roles such as costuming assistant, vacation planner, lifeguard, cook or even character performer. Fair warning though: Students who wish to spend their summer as Goofy must first audition for the role during one of the casting calls in Orlando. For those lucky enough to land the gig, typical job responsibilities for character performers include signing autographs, posing for photos, appearing in parades and "creating everlasting memories." Now that's hard work.

Candidates with MBAs tend to get hired into consumer products or operations planning. Most work in finance positions, such as operations finance in one of the theme parks or in marketing and sales finance. Some go into financial reporting

Visit Vault at **www.vault.com** for insider company profiles, expert advice, career message boards, expert resume reviews, the Vault Job Board and more.

VAULT CAREER LIBRARY   **301**

(basically an accounting group), although in that field, "most come from regional MBA programs like Rollins."

Presentation counts

For creatives, the application process is complicated. Portfolios should be submitted with resumes and a cover letter detailing areas of interest. Portfolios should measure 24 x 30 inches or smaller and shouldn't exceed 25 "pages" in length. A "page" can consist of individual drawings, several smaller drawings, a sketchbook or short videotape. Work should either be behind plastic or mounted on sturdy paper. Chalk, charcoal or pastel drawings must be mounted behind plastic. Slides or photocopies will be accepted, though are not preferred. VHS tapes or reels of no more than four minutes in length are OK as well. What doesn't pass muster, though, are rolled submissions, stretched or framed work, or portfolio pages not bearing the artist's name or initials.

Qualifications

The qualifications necessary to land a job at Disney vary vastly throughout the company. For example, the creative departments – animation in particular – have rigid requirements, including several years of formal art training, preferably with animation experience; and natural drawing skills. Good classes to take include life drawing, perspective and quick sketching or their equivalents. Computer animation skills are a definite plus, what with the changing nature of feature animation. Schools offering programs that meet Disney's requirements include, but are not limited to, the Academy of Art College, Cal Arts, New York School of Visual Arts, MIT, the University of California at Berkeley and Brown University.

Other departments don't have any set requirements, though the company frequently favors candidates with business school degrees. Requirements include a bachelor's degree in accounting, finance or the equivalent; three years of work experience; proficiency in Microsoft Excel or equivalent; self-motivation; and strong communications skills. For MBAs, Disney prefers "entertainment experience or corporate finance experience," although "they don't penalize you if you don't have an entertainment background." Either way, in inimitable Disney fashion, "they want happy, happy, happy people. The more you smile, the better off you are."

Interview format

Disney's hiring procedures are as varied as the divisions of the company. For candidates seeking positions on the business side however, there are some basic characteristics of the process. The most basic is that it is almost always long and drawn out. Comments one interview survivor, "What a pain!" As a result of the length of the hiring process (which can reportedly be as long as three months), Disney "comes on campus very early" compared to other companies. The 25-minute, first-round interview with business school students is "conducted by a functional line manager or a finance manager" and is "more of a behavioral assessment. They are not probing deep." There is also one other gatekeeper, the "greeter from human resources you meet first. She is supposed to be there just to answer questions, but is really judging you just as much as the interviewer. They are looking for enthusiasm, your interest in the company and if you show passion."

After the first round, Disney will "discard the mean people, and put the remaining resumes in a big pile." These are then sent out to different departments to try to find an appropriate match. "Just because you 'make it through' the first round, you're not guaranteed a second-round interview," warns one former interviewee. Among the lucky ones, "for the top 15 business schools, they take the top candidates and fly them in around mid-November." They are then subjected to "a full day of interviews, usually on a Friday." Interviews are about "50 minutes each" and the day entails meeting "seven people in seven hours" from different areas. Fortunately, these generally are "easy interviews, with not a lot of detailed questions." Remarks one cast member who went through the process, "Disney is a pretty easy place to interview. You have a lot of amateurs [conducting interviews], so you've got to take control to have a great one." In the course of the seven meetings, candidates can expect "one case study question." At the end of the day, the pressure is off and it is time to have fun, Disney-style. "That weekend, they comp everything – free park admission, admission to Pleasure Island and free beer." Such wooing tactics are effective: By the end of the process, "people get stars in their eyes." Further extending the process, the winners "find out about a month a half later."

For candidates in MBA programs not on Disney's recruiting schedule, as well as those seeking summer employment, "the burden is on you to find out where there are opportunities." Disney is less than forthcoming in this area. "You must put in an effort to call and call to find out where the opportunities are and when someone will get back to you. You must build a familiarity with them." The company does seem to keep track of who has shown the most effort and interest in this regard, and looks more favorably upon determined candidates, insiders say. Second-round interviews

Visit Vault at **www.vault.com** for insider company profiles, expert advice, career message boards, expert resume reviews, the Vault Job Board and more.

VAULT CAREER LIBRARY   **303**

for summer interns in the corporate divisions are conducted over the phone with just one person. They last for about an hour and are "both behavioral and resume-based." At this point "most of the screening has [already] been done," so applicants usually get a phone call with an offer within a week.

Career path

According to employees, the Disney career path is convoluted. "They have a history of not promoting from within," says one. If you want to advance "you have to grab for it, prove yourself – maybe even elsewhere – and then, maybe, the job is yours." According to employees, this policy holds true across the board, even in the creative departments. "When you change jobs, you do it on your own," says an insider. There is not much hands-on help, and no career counseling or career track. Some people want a structured career track, but I haven't seen it." The entire process from new hire to division VP can be anywhere from five to seven years for an MBA, but it rarely works out that way. Says one finance guru, "Movement has been more lateral [in this group]. It's kind of disappointing." Before even being in a position to make a move, "you must manage your relationships carefully, which is tricky." One employee advises that the best course of action is "be very proactive throughout your career. If you see something you want to participate in, show your interest and see that it happens." For many Disney employees, particularly MBAs who might otherwise go into professions with a regular schedule of progression, having to schmooze in order to advance is "kind of a pain in the ass." Among other factors, this helps to explain why in the corporate offices, "they have troubling retaining everybody."

W.W. Norton & Company

500 Fifth Avenue
New York, NY 10110
Phone: (212) 354-5500
Fax: (212) 869-0856
www.wwnorton.com

LOCATIONS

New York, NY (HQ)

THE STATS

Employer Type: Private Company
Chairman: W. Drake McFeely

KEY COMPETITORS

Harcourt Education
McGraw-Hill
Random House

EMPLOYMENT CONTACT

www.wwnorton.com/area4/
jobs.htm

Visit Vault at **www.vault.com** for insider company profiles, expert advice,
career message boards, expert resume reviews, the Vault Job Board and more.

VAULT CAREER LIBRARY   305

THE SCOOP

Books for the years

W.W. Norton & Company is the oldest and largest publishing house wholly owned by its employees. The company publishes fiction, nonfiction, college textbooks, art books and professional books under the slogan, "publish books not for a single season, but for the years." William Warder Norton founded the company with his wife, Mary D. Herter Norton, in New York City in 1923, when they began publishing lectures delivered at the People's Institute, the adult education division of the New York City college Cooper Union. The couple soon moved onto acquiring manuscripts by celebrated academics from the U.S. and abroad. W.W. Norton became well known as a distinguished publisher of both trade and college textbooks covering the fields of philosophy, music and psychology. Some of the authors published by the company in its early years included famous thinkers such as Bertrand Russel and Sigmund Freud. Currently, the company publishes roughly 400 books annually, both in hardcover and paperback.

Expanding into new horizons

The company expanded its history textbook publishing division in the 1940s with the acquisition of Edward McNall Burns's *Western Civilizations*, which is currently in its 14th edition, and added to its literature base with the now-famous *Norton Anthology* series, which have sold over 20 million copies. In the 1960s, Norton added poetry to its repertoire; Norton has published Pulitzer Prize and National Book Critics Circle Award winners to its ranks since then, including Rita Dove, Stephen Dunn, Stanley Kunitz and Adrienne Rich. In addition, the company published Seamus Heaney's best-selling, Whitbread Award-winning translation of the epic poem *Beowulf* in 2001.

Publishing the best

Norton has developed an eclectic list of literary luminaries and best sellers in the past few years, including Sebastian Junger' *The Perfect Storm*, Jared Diamond's Pulitzer Prize-winning best-seller *Guns, Germs, and Steel*, and Patrick O'Brian's acclaimed naval adventure series. The work of economists, paleontologists, physicists and historians all find a home at Norton, mixing with leading titles in the company's college department, to create a scholarly force to be reckoned with. The 1985 introduction of the Norton Professional Books series expanded the company's cache in psychotherapy and neuroscience genres, as well as in architecture and design. In addition, Norton acquired the Vermont-based Countryman Press in 1996, adding nature, history and outdoor recreation titles.

New business ventures

In 1999, Norton took to updating Countryman, repackaging its *Explorer* and *Backcountry* guidebooks to generate interest in the press' backlist. The two guidebooks series have sold well, registering over 750,000 copies to date between them by 1999. The same year, Norton announced it would publish a new line of books in conjunction with *Outside* magazine through a new imprint called Outside Books, concentrating on active living and the outdoors. Patricia Highsmith, author of *The Talented Mr. Ripley*, had a large part of her backlist sold posthumously to Norton in a six-figure deal finalized in August 2000. Norton gained the rights to publish 14 Highsmith titles, including 10 novels and four short-story collections. In 2003, Berkshire House Press was added to the Vermont operation. In addition, since 1984, Norton has added a number of agencies worldwide in London, Canada, Australia, New Zealand, Taiwan, Hong Kong, Japan, Korea and Latin America.

Dealing with the 9/11 commission

Norton scored a huge deal in May 2004, when the commission investigating the September 11 terrorist attacks named W.W. Norton as the publisher of a private edition of the panel's report before it was released to the public. Norton was chosen over a number of other leading publishing companies. Norton's initial plan was to sell 600,000 copies of the book in soft-cover format at bookstores nationwide. The chairman of the commission, Thomas H. Kean, a former Republican governor of New Jersey, said the group chose Norton because it submitted the best proposal for the book, which ended up being 568 pages long. A strong selling point in the proposal was a retail price of $10 for the book, the lowest price put forth by any of the companies that submitted proposals. Kean and his colleagues admitted to being "concerned that the report receive the widest possible circulation … available at a price that's affordable." Within a week of its initial release that July, the book sold over 350,000 copies, and Norton began gearing up for a second printing of 200,000, with a third possibly on the way. Drake McFeely, president of Norton, said it was questionable whether the book would bring a profit to his company, which incurred unusually high production and shipping expenses to get the book out on time. But, in the event that the commission's report did generate windfall profits, Norton said it had "every intention of contributing them to an appropriate charity."

Going graphic

R. Crumb, a renowned comic book artist, signed with Norton in August 2004 to produce a nonfiction graphic work, rumored in the industry to be a "literal" interpretation of *Genesis*, the first book in the *Bible*. Bob Weil, an executive editor at Norton, called the Crumb deal "major" and acknowledged that graphic novels were essential components of a "well-balanced" publisher's list of offerings. In January 2005, Norton continued with its graphic trend, announced it acquired 14 of Will Eisner's literary graphic novels posthumously from DC Comics, to be re-released in hardcover and paperback over the course of three years. Eisner was widely considered to be one of the first serious American literary graphic novelists.

GETTING HIRED

Hiring overview

The company posts available positions on its web site. In addition, interested applicants may submit a resume to:

Lisa Gaeth
Personnel Manager
W.W. Norton & Company, Inc.
500 Fifth Avenue
New York, NY 10110

About the Editor

Laurie Pasiuk graduated from Fordham University with a degree in English Literature. She started and edited the fiction section for Elsevier Science's HMS Beagle before joining Vault as a staff editor.

Visit Vault at **www.vault.com** for insider company profiles, expert advice, career message boards, expert resume reviews, the Vault Job Board and more.

VAULT CAREER LIBRARY   309